Central Asia in Historical Perspective

The John M. Olin Critical Issues Series

Published in cooperation with
the Harvard University Russian Research Center

Central Asia in Historical Perspective, edited by Beatrice F. Manz

In Search of Pluralism: Soviet and Post-Soviet Politics, edited by Carol R. Saivetz and Anthony Jones

Soviet Social Problems, edited by Anthony Jones, Walter D. Connor, and David E. Powell

The Nationalities Factor in Soviet Politics and Society, edited by Lubomyr Hajda and Mark Beissinger

The Soviet Union in the Third World, edited by Carol R. Saivetz

Central Asia in Historical Perspective

EDITED BY

Beatrice F. Manz

Westview Press

Boulder • San Francisco • Oxford

The John M. Olin Critical Issues Series

Published in 1998 in the United States of America by Westview Press, 5500 Central Avenue, Boulder, Colorado 80301-2877, and in the United Kingdom by Westview Press, 12 Hid's Copse Road, Cumnor Hill, Oxford OX2 9JJ

Library of Congress Cataloging-in-Publication Data
Central Asia in historical perspective / edited by Beatrice F. Manz.
p. cm.—(The John M. Olin critical issues series)
Includes bibliographical references and index.
ISBN 0-8133-3638-4
1. Asia, Central—History. 2. Asia, Central—Ethnic relations.
I. Manz, Beatrice Forbes. II. Series.
DK856.C46 1994
958—dc20 94-15159
CIP

The paper used in this publication meets the requirements of the American National Standard for Permanence of Paper for Printed Library Materials Z39.48-1984.

10 9 8 7 6 5 4 3 2 1

Contents

PART THREE
CENTRAL ASIA AND RUSSIA

Preface

The chapters in this book were originally presented in 1990–91 at the seminar "Soviet Central Asia in Historical Perspective," part of the John M. Olin Critical Issues Seminar Series at the Harvard University Russian Research Center, made possible by a generous grant from the John M. Olin Foundation, which has further supported the preparation of the manuscript for publication. The chapters were written by scholars representing a variety of fields and disciplines.

Many people have helped in the preparation of this work. In planning and executing the seminar, I worked together with James Critchlow; Alexandra Vacroux shared in both the organization of the seminar and the editing of the manuscript until her departure for Moscow at the end of 1991. Colleagues both at the Russian Research Center and elsewhere have been generous with their help. I want to thank particularly Carol Saivetz and Lubomyr Hajda for their advice, and Boris Rumer, Joseph Berliner, and Daniel Mulholland for useful criticisms and suggestions. Mary Towle facilitated this project as she did all projects connected with the Russian Research Center during her long tenure there. Finally I want to thank three very able typists/formatters who have worked on the manuscript at different stages in its preparation: Amy Randall, Kim Thomas, and most particularly Alan Fortescue, who has presided with unflagging good humor over the difficulties of the final preparation.

Systems of Transcription

No work on Central Asia is complete without some discussion of transcription. For Russian we have used a slightly modified form of the Library of Congress system. The same is true of Central Asian languages written in the Cyrillic alphabet. For terms and names of Arabic, Persian, Turkic, or Mongolian origin a system both consistent and easily comprehensible is more difficult to achieve.

For terms that have entered the English language, we have used spellings found in *Webster's* dictionary, such as "ulema" and "mufti." Arabic terms not found in the dictionary are given in classical Arabic transcription, minus diacritics, without regard to modern pronunciation, which varies from place to place. For other names and terms, the aim has been to use the most common form and that which best represents the current pronunciation. We have chosen not to retain the Cyrillic rendering of Persian and Turkic words, which sometimes obscures the actual pronunciation or the original spelling: thus we write Muhammad instead of Mukhamad, Leninabad instead of Leninobod, and so on. Where possible we have tried to retain a consistent rendition of names and terms throughout the book; the exception to this is cases where post-independence republics have decreed changes, as in the change from Kirgizia to Kyrgyzstan; we use the new form only for the post-independence period.

Beatrice F. Manz

Contemporary Central Asia

Introduction

Beatrice F. Manz

The break-up of the Soviet Union has brought the world to look again at Central Asia, with new perspectives and new questions. For many years it had seemed unnecessary to inquire about Central Asia's place in the world. Whether willingly or not, this region made up part of two great multinational empires—the USSR in the west and the PRC in the east. The question addressed was its place in these states. For many years Soviet Central Asia was seen as a backward colonized territory, then as the 1980s progressed, it appeared as the soft underbelly of the Soviet beast.

The issue of Central Asia's relation to the former Soviet Union is not dead, but it is no longer the most important question before us. For the independent republics other relationships matter equally—those to the outside world, and those within the region itself. We must now free ourselves from the Soviet tendency to view Central Asia primarily in relation to the Russian center. Likewise, in dealing with historical processes, we must avoid the image of a revolutionary present viewed against a static past—whether it be the golden age of Central Asian achievements, or the dark night of Central Asian absolutism. To understand what is happening now in Central Asia, we must take a new look at its historical development, at the forces which have shaped its relations to the regions around it and the cultural identities of the many peoples within it. The articles in this book address these questions, covering a long historical period, from the Mongol Empire up to the present.

Events in Central Asia since the demise of the Soviet Union pose questions which are difficult to answer within the confines of Soviet studies. We need to understand for instance why the region perhaps most different from the Russian center has been one of the slowest to separate from it. Neither a continued adherence to the Islamic world nor the well-documented anti-Russian sentiments of the region have been sufficient to create a nationalism as strong as that found in more western republics. When we look at relations among the various nationalities of Central Asia, now once again of crucial importance, we see a picture far from simple, and a matter for continuing controversy. Some scholars and politicians emphasise the importance of overarching loyalties to religion or language family, while others adhere to republican or even more local identities.

To make recent events and controversies comprehensible we must turn to earlier historical developments. Many of the actions and claims we see today are a reflection of older ideas, partially suppressed during the period of Soviet rule. We must consider how much Central Asia was transformed by Soviet control, and how much still remains of earlier systems. The different levels of identity now discussed—Turkic, Islamic, republican and local, should be analyzed in the light of historical development, and in relation to movements in other parts of the Middle East and Inner Asia. This book offers a number of different perspectives on the development of Central Asia over a long period, both within the broader world of the Middle East and the Eurasian steppe, and within the Russian and Soviet empires.

The book begins with a brief historical introduction covering the creation of structures and identities from the Middle Ages through the Soviet period. The subsequent chapters in the first section examine historical developments in Central Asia and analyze some of the influences important in shaping its society and politics. One of the most crucial events in the history of Central Asia was the creation of the Mongol Empire; this is discussed in the first chapter of the collection, by Morris Rossabi. Rossabi describes the impact of Mongol rule on Central Asia, and traces several social and political patterns which can be connected to the influence of the Mongols and of subsequent nomad empires. The importance of nomadism in the history of Central Asia is further explored in the chapter by Maria Subtelny, which shows the centrality of nomad-sedentary relations in the development of the major ethnic groups in Central Asia, particularly the Iranian Tajiks and the Turkic Uzbeks. Subtelny also shows the later effect of Soviet policies in continuing the separation of groups whose original nomad-sedentary opposition had disappeared.

Central Asia's position on the frontier between nomad and sedentary worlds was one decisive factor in its development; another was its inclusion in the Islamic realm. John Voll has addressed Central Asia's place within Islam, arguing, in contradiction to many commonly held interpretations, that Central Asia remained firmly within the central Islamic world until at least the nineteenth century, and that Russian and Soviet rule never truly severed this relation. From the nineteenth century on, the central Asians belonged also to another defined sphere, as Muslims within the Russian Empire. This is the subject of Edward Lazzerini's article. He examines particularly the dominant political force among these Muslims, namely the Tatars, using them to describe the evolution of Russian attitudes towards Turkic Muslims, and examining the role that the Tatars played in shaping Central Asia's experience of Russian rule. Both Voll and Lazzerini discuss two important intellectual movements of the Islamic world in the late nineteenth and early twentieth centuries, pan-Islam and pan-Turkism, which have now again become topics of discussion within the former Soviet Union.

The second section of the book describes the further development of ethnic relationships within the Soviet period. Donald Carlisle has analyzed the national delimitation of 1924 in relation to local and central politics, and has suggested that the outcome was determined less by ethnographic considerations than by political processes, in which Central Asian politicians played a significant part. The Uzbek state, he argues, was created along the lines of earlier political structures, while the Uzbek nation is something still in the process of formation.

Muriel Atkin examines the continued evolution of Tajik identity under Soviet rule, particularly the Tajiks' view of themselves as part of the Iranian world and their connections with Iran, showing both the importance of Iranian influence and its limitations. In his chapter, A. Khazanov explores the impact that Soviet policies and continuing underdevelopment have had on ethnic identities and relationships in Central Asia. He argues for the importance of ethnic and national loyalties during the earlier Soviet period and more recently, but also shows the continued influence of narrower tribal or local allegiances. The last chapter of this section assesses the political role of Islamic identity in contemporary Kazakhstan. Reef Altoma concludes that despite widespread interest in Islam and frequent references to it in political discussions, leaders and other political actors follow a primarily secular agenda.

The final issue addressed in this collection is the influence of Russian rule on Central Asians. Edward Allworth's chapter approaches this question from a cultural standpoint, analyzing the effect of unequal social relationships, Russian feelings of superiority and the imposition of Russian language and cultural attitudes. Bakhtior Islamov examines the relationship from an economic perspective, giving an analysis of Soviet tax and development policies from the Central Asian point of view. He argues that the close interconnections created during the Soviet period and the interchange of taxes and grants were less favorable to Central Asia than usually believed. Both Allworth and Islamov assert that Russian/Soviet influence was, on balance, harmful to Central Asia, and brought forth resentment. Both however conclude that immediate and total separation is impracticable, whether from psychological or from economic motives.

This book therefore addresses many of the issues crucial to Central Asia today. The authors represented here do not agree in all their interpretations, and there has been no editorial attempt to bring views into harmony. The contributors present different approaches—historical, political, ethnological and economic—which can be used to further our understanding of a complex region at an uncertain time.

Historical Background

Beatrice F. Manz

For the last century Central Asia has formed the border between the Russian/Soviet empire, the Islamic world, and the Chinese sphere. It has been a plural society, with a Russian or Russianized elite ruling over Turks and Iranians, a population of Christians, Socialists and Muslims. Recent events have brought into relief the variety of peoples and loyalties which belong to this region and influence its policies inside and its choice of alliances outside.

None of these characteristics is new. To an historian watching current events, what is often striking is the familiarity of many of the ideas, conflicts and structures now apparent. One can view this last century of Russian rule not as a revolutionary transformation but as yet another stage in a continuing process, under a regime which adapted to conditions already present and permitted the survival of many of the earlier structures of Central Asian society. In this essay I shall trace the history of Central Asia up to the present, showing what has been continuous in its development, and following the emergence of structures and identities which now affect its politics.

Land and Population of Central Asia

Before approaching the history of Central Asia, we must consider a central factor in its development, its geography.* Just as Central Asia is now the border between two spheres, so it was earlier a boundary between the two great worlds of pre-modern history—the settled agricultural civilizations and the pastoral nomads of the steppe. Although a frontier, it was not a peripheral region, but an important urban and agricultural center and a nexus for long-distance trade. The main east-west trade route, the Silk Road, here intersected the northern and southern routes connecting the Middle East to India and to the northern forest-steppe region. In this way Central Asia became heir to both the Perso-Islamic tradition of the Middle East and the Mongol heritage of the steppe, and was open to influences from the major cultural regions of the pre-modern world—China, India, and the Islamic world.

*I have included in this section the history of the regions of Kazakhstan and Kyrgyzstan, whose history is related to that of Transoxiana.

Within this frontier region lies a wide range of geographical terrain, which has affected the lifestyles practiced within it. Marginal lands best used for pastoral nomadism combine with rich agricultural land and cities fostering a high sedentary culture, while high mountain ranges have harbored yet a third distinct lifestyle and population. What has given Central Asia its unique configuration is the closeness of different landscapes, and the intimate contact of its different populations. The Aral Sea is adjoined south and west by two deserts—the Kara Kum (Black Sands) and Kyzyl Kum (Red Sands), most suitable for a sparse nomadic population. In contrast to these, three oases are strung across the region, the Khivan oasis near the mouth of the Amu Darya, the Zarafshan (Zeravshan) Valley linking Samarkand and Bukhara, and finally the Ferghana Valley north of the Pamirs. These regions, supporting intensive irrigated agriculture, are surrounded by pockets of mountain and steppe marginal for agriculture but providing good pasture for nomadic populations.

To the north of these oases lies the Kipchak Steppe, part of the vast steppe region of Eurasia, which for most of history was dominated by pastoral nomads. To the east and southeast lie the great mountain ranges of Central Asia—the T'ien Shan, Pamirs and Hindu Kush. The foothills of these ranges provided summer pastures for nomads, while the upper elevations were a refuge area for innumerable different populations—remnants of migrations and defeated indigenous survivors of foreign invasions. The close symbiosis of the various populations was particularly striking in the Ferghana valley and in Transoxiana, the region between the Amu Darya and Syr Darya Rivers, in which mountain, steppe and oasis form a continuous patchwork.

At the beginning of documented history the population of Central Asia and the steppe was Iranian. In the sixth century a new force arose in the steppe: the Turks. The Turks originated in Mongolia as the leading stratum of a nomad confederation which for three centuries ruled almost the whole Eurasian steppe. From this period up to that of the Mongol Empire it was the splinter groups from this empire who populated and controlled the steppes of Inner Asia and the Black Sea region. From the ninth century the Turks also began to enter Transoxiana and to acquire power even within the sedentary societies of the Middle East. The interaction between the two lifestyles and populations—nomad and sedentary, Turkic and Iranian—dominated the history of Central Asia well into the nineteenth century.

The Impact of Mongol Rule

If we are to name one decisive moment in the formation of modern Central Asian society our choice must fall on the period of Mongol rule in the thirteenth and fourteenth centuries, discussed by Morris Rossabi. To a striking extent we see in Mongol times the evolution of systems of government, society and legitimation which remained in force until the nineteenth century. The Mongol

Empire was the high point of nomad power—a time when Mongolian and Turkic nomads ruled almost all of the known world. For subsequent Turkic and Mongolian societies, descended from these conquerors, this period remained the golden age. With the conquests of Chinggis Khan in 1210–27 and the rule of his descendants the agricultural centers of Asia and eastern Europe became provinces of a world empire ruled from Mongolia. The new rulers of the world were people of a distinctly lower literary culture, but of great military prowess and political acumen. The legendary stature of Chinggis Khan and the spectacular success of Mongol armies gave a lasting prestige to the dynasty and its followers. Through the eighteenth century Chinggisid rulers continued to hold power in the Crimea and parts of Central Asia.

In the late thirteenth century the Mongol ruling class in the western regions of the empire—from Central Asia and the Middle East to the Volga—began to adapt to local conditions and traditions. The tribes which made up the Mongol armies were partly Mongolian and partly Turkic speaking; this last language gradually became the spoken language of the ruling class. At the same time, the unity of the Mongol Empire facilitated the spread of Islam throughout Central Asia and the steppe. By the mid-fourteenth century a large part of Eurasia from the Volga to the T'ien Shan, and much of the Middle East, was governed by a Muslim, Turkic-speaking elite which honored the traditions of the Mongol Empire. It is hard to think of any time in history when so vast a territory shared so much in language, tradition and culture.

The Turks who had been part of the Mongol enterprise—often called Turco-Mongolian—differentiated themselves sharply from the Oghuz (western or southern Turks) already living in the Middle East and unassociated with the Mongol Empire. The Turco-Mongolians called the Oghuz "Turkmen," and regarded them as distinctly inferior in character and achievement. It is these western Turks who founded the Ottoman Empire, and who are the ancestors of the present-day Azerbaijanis and the Turkmen of Central Asia. Almost all of the other Turks who were within the USSR are descended from the Turco-Mongolian nomads.

Within Central Asia and Iran the nomads controlled a sedentary Iranian population, and the society which developed in this period was a dual one, both Turco-Mongolian and Iranian. Although the ruling class spoke Turkic the high culture it patronized was almost exclusively Persian, produced by the elite of the subject population, mostly Iranians, called "Tajik" by the Turks. The administration was also divided, with military and court offices held by Turco-Mongolian nomads, while civil and financial administration remained in the hands of the Persian-speaking bureaucracy.

The Mongol Empire thus left behind a society with dual cultural loyalty, and along with this went a double set of ideologies. In the Islamic world, to which Central Asia and the steppe belonged, legitimacy was based on religion. A ruler might seize power by military means, but he had to justify his rule through the protection of religion and particularly of the Islamic law, the shariah. Mongol legitimation on the other hand rested on a strong dynastic tradition—only the descendants of Chinggis Khan could legitimately wield sovereign power, and to rule justly they must safeguard the traditions which Chinggis Khan himself had laid down. These two ideologies conflicted on many points and caused open friction, but nonetheless continued to coexist for centuries in Central Asia and to define ideas of legitimacy. When the Russians conquered the region, both were still alive. Descent from Chinggis Khan remained an important political factor, as was Central Asia's identity as an Islamic society.

The Development of New Identities

The Mongols had united the steppe and the settled lands into one political unit and had created a uniform ruling class over both. However as economic systems pastoralism and agriculture remained separate, and after some time the boundary between the steppe and settled worlds reappeared in Central Asia. In 1370 a new Turco-Mongolian conqueror, Temür (Tamerlane) rose to power near Samarkand and reconquered the western Mongol Empire, but although he subjugated most of the steppe he and his successors consolidated their power only over settled regions, which were easier to control and provided greater income. Once again the region of Transoxiana formed a mixed zone between the Middle East and the steppe.

With the reemergence of the frontier came sharper and more lasting divisions among the Turco-Mongolian ruling classes of the former Mongol Empire. It was at this period that more specific identities began to develop, many bearing ethnic names we know today. The process of differentiation was a largely political one, centered around the creation of tribal confederations and loyalty to individual leaders, most of them descended from Chinggis Khan. It was also intimately bound to the issue of nomad-sedentary relations. Some Turco-Mongolian groups moved nearer to settled regions to exploit the wealth of agricultural populations, while others chose to remain in the steppe and retain full mobility.

A crucial event in the development of new group identities was the Uzbek conquest of Transoxiana in 1501. The Uzbeks originated as a tribal confederation in the eastern regions of the Golden Horde, north of the Aral Sea. In the 1440s they began to organize under a descendant of Chinggis Khan, Abu'l-Khayr Khan, and to interfere in the affairs of Temür's descendants, the Timurid dynasty in Transoxiana. This undertaking required a higher degree of central power and closer relations to settled populations than some of the khan's followers liked. Two members of the Chinggisid line, Karay and Jani Beg, deserted with their followers and moved to the northeast where they mixed with other splinter groups of the Golden Horde. The new khans and their subjects acquired the appellation "Qazaq" (Kazakh), meaning renegade or outlaw. In 1501-1507 the Uzbek confederation, led by Abu'l-Khayr's grandson Shibani (Shaybani) Khan, conquered Transoxiana. Now the Kazakhs took over the former Uzbek territories, and from this time the Kazakh khans controlled a good part of the region which is now Kazakhstan, disputing the lower Syr Darya region and Tashkent with the Uzbeks. They soon split into three hordes (*zhuz*), ruled by khans of the Chinggisid line.

The Uzbek khans strengthened the Chinggisid tradition in Central Asia, but as Muslims and new arrivals eager for cultural prestige, they soon became promoters of Perso-Islamic culture. The dual cultural system of the Mongol period continued under a new ruling class defined by its descent from the Uzbek tribes which had participated in the conquest. Thus by the mid-sixteenth century one can discern several of the major peoples of Central Asia and the Kipchak Steppe—the Uzbeks as the Turco-Mongolian ruling class of Transoxiana, the Tajiks as the much larger Persian speaking sedentary subject class, keepers of high culture and religious tradition, and the Kazakhs leading a more fully nomad life on the steppes under their own Chinggisid khans.

As time went on, ethnic groupings in Central Asia became more numerous and more complex. Among both nomad and sedentary populations identities crystalized around lifestyle, political organization and function within society. In Transoxiana the greatest prestige lay with the Uzbeks. Although many Uzbeks eventually became sedentary, the politically active class had an interest in preserving a separate identity and in maintaining the tribal affiliation which secured them a place within the ruling stratum. Many high military and court offices were special to the Uzbek elite.[1]

In language and background the more nomadic segment of the Uzbeks were closely related to groups among the Kazakhs and to another nomad population, the Karakalpaks. What differentiated these peoples from each other was their recent history and their level of attachment to nomad life. The Karakalpaks, like the Uzbeks and Kazakhs, emerged from the territory of the Golden Horde. They are first mentioned in the early seventeenth century living along the middle and lower Syr Darya; in the eighteenth century some were pushed into the Aral Sea region. There they occupied lands suitable for nomadism and served in the armies of the Uzbek khans.[2]

The Turkmen were the most distinct of the Turkic groups of Central Asia. These were western Turks, related to the Ottoman Turks and Azerbaijanis, who had not been part of the Mongol ruling class. They were separate from the other Turks therefore in language, history and material culture. Most migrated into the region from the Mangyshlak area east of the Caspian Sea between the early sixteenth and the eighteenth centuries, joined in the latter part of this period by Turkmens migrating out of eastern Iran.[3]

In the steppe the Kazakhs continued a largely nomad life, distant from the centers of Islamic learning. Most lived in the Kipchak Steppe, but some inhabited the northern regions of Transoxiana. Within the region north of the Syr Darya one other group should be mentioned, namely the Kirghiz, a nomad population of mixed provenance living largely in the Ili region and in the foothills of the T'ien Shan. Unlike the Kazakhs, the Kirghiz lacked a royal dynasty and paramount supra-tribal organization. They were usually divided and their segments under the sway of neighboring people—the Chinese, the Kazakhs, or the Uzbek Khanate of Kokand. Kirghiz soldiers and tribal chiefs were eager for adventure, and were often recruited for military expeditions both in western Asia and in Xinjiang[4]. (One should note here that up to the early Soviet period the Russians used the name "Kirgiz" for both the Kazakhs and the group we now call Kirghiz, differentiating them when necessary by calling the Kirghiz "Kara-kirgiz." This was to avoid confusion between the Kazakhs and the Russian or Ukrainian Cossacks, the same word in Russian.)

Within the fully sedentary population of Central Asia, identities were somewhat less numerous; here the major distinction was that between the inhabitants of the mountains and those of the plain. The urban and agricultural population of settled Iranians, known variously as Tajiks or Sarts, formed the bulk of the city population of artisans, merchants and religious functionaries, and of the peasants. By the nineteenth century large numbers of sedentarized Turks had joined this group, and most had become either Turkic-speaking or bilingual. They were separate in function and lifestyle from the tribal Uzbeks who formed the military and ruling classes.

Within the indigenous Iranian population we must mention one other group, usually referred to as "Ghalcha," and differing strongly from Sarts and Tajiks in lifestyle and often in language.[5] Mountain populations played a distinct role in the history of Central Asia. The difficulty with which the governing power could penetrate into their regions gave them considerable autonomy and cultural independence from both Turco-Mongolian rulers and Persian scholars. Many, looking for a wider field of operations, served in the armies of the Uzbek khans, where they were prized for their hardiness and their skill in martial arts.

In considering the relationships of different groups in Central Asia, one should keep in mind that the boundaries between them were often shifting and imprecisely defined. Within nomad territories, clans and splinter groups could switch from one tribe or confederation to another, taking on the name of their new overlords. In Transoxiana Sarts, Karakalpaks, Ghalcha and other groups were identified as separate entities to differentiate them from other populations of different lifestyle and function, and to place them in relation to the ruling Uzbek dynasty. For those who served the dynasty, as bureaucrats, soldiers, or religious functionaries, this was an important distinction, as it was for historians chronicling the politics of the times. For those outside of politics, it was probably much less active.

Ethnic Identities and Regional Divisions in Central Asia

Debates inside and outside Central Asia have called into question the legitimacy of existing republic boundaries. Some maintain that the current borders define legitimate groups but should have been drawn in different places, others that the Muslim populations of Central Asia and Kazakhstan cannot be subdivided in any meaningful way. This is not the place to enter into the debate, but a discussion of the regional and ethnic dynamics of Central Asia may help to explain the terms and origins of the controversy. Two distinct issues are important here, and they should be discussed separately. The first is the question of territory: where political boundaries have existed in the past, and what regions emerge through history as centers for separate political power. The second issue is the relation of these boundaries to group identities and loyalties: what connection political structures and regional divisions had to ethnic divisions.

Within Central Asia there are a number of areas with a distinctive history and character. The Uzbek realm was decentralized, and the chiefs of Uzbek tribes used the frequent dynastic struggles to enhance their power, sometimes becoming virtual kingmakers. Tribal leaders or junior members of the dynasty acted as local rulers whose level of autonomy depended on the personality and power of the reigning khan. Certain areas provided a good base for independence, and developed as separate power centers.

One region with a particularly long and distinctive history was Khorezm, south of the Aral Sea, which became the center of the Khanate of Khiva and later of Turkmenistan. This was an ancient nexus of trade between the Middle East and the Volga region. In the Mongol period it remained largely separate from Transoxiana and closely attached to the Golden Horde. The sedentary people of Khorezm, originally Iranian, had become largely Turkic speaking by the end of the fourteenth century, considerably earlier than those in the eastern regions.[6] From the beginning of the Uzbek period Khorezm formed a separate state ruled from Khiva by a distinct Uzbek dynasty which was often at odds with the line ruling in Bukhara and Samarkand.

Differences in terrain and population separated the Khivan Khanate into several distinct regions. The rich oasis along the Amu Darya around Khiva was the only area which could support a large agricultural and urban population. This was the seat of the Uzbek dynasty, and supported the sedentary Sarts. The northern region, east of the Aral Sea, was desert inhabited by nomads—Uzbeks, Kazakhs and Karakalpaks, often independent of the center.[7] To the south lay the Kara Kum desert, also dominated by nomads. In the eighteenth century turmoil in Iran brought an eastern migration of Turkmen tribes into this region, centering around Merv (Mary), where they enjoyed virtual independence.

Eastern Transoxiana was ruled by other Uzbek dynasties, first by khans descended from Chinggis Khan, and after about 1750 by members of the Uzbek Manghit tribe. Since the Manghits were not descended from Chinggis Khan and could not formally claim the title of khan, these rulers were properly called emirs (commanders), and their state is often referred to as the Emirate of Bukhara.

When the Uzbeks first conquered Transoxiana, coming from the north, they added to it many of the neighboring northern and eastern regions. As time went on however it became increasingly difficult for the reigning khan to maintain effective authority over the outlying regions. Tashkent, just north of the Jaxartes, had almost always been disputed between the rulers of Transoxiana and those of the northern steppe, and was now contested with the Kazakhs. The Ferghana valley likewise formed a distinct territory, desired for its agricultural wealth by the rulers of Transoxiana, but close to the centers of steppe power, and often under their control. Up to the eighteenth century it remained intermittently part of the the Bukharan Emirate, then gained virtual independence and in 1798 became the Khanate of Kokand, under the Uzbek Ming tribe, who manufactured a Chinggisid and Timurid genealogy. The khans of Kokand soon expanded into the Pamir regions to the south, northwest to Tashkent and the northern Syr Darya region, and east into the Kirghiz territories of the T'ien Shan.

The western Pamirs in the southeastern corner of Transoxiana—northern Badakhshan, Kulab, Karategin and Darvaz—were largely within the Uzbek khanates, but were inhabited by mountain populations, Ghalcha, and were controlled by local rulers of Iranian descent, with little real connection to the khanates. The rulers of this area were almost the only Iranians to govern as dynasts in Central Asia. They alone in Central Asia formulated their legitimacy independent of Turco-Mongolian tradition, sometimes tracing a mythical lineage back to Alexander the Great.[8]

Even within the smaller regions of Central Asia, power was not highly centralized, nor was it wielded entirely by the dynasty. Uzbek rule was a superstructure, laid on top of a subject population with its own organization. Among the settled population the elite classes of the cities held a position of considerable strength. Much of city governance lay in the hands of religious men, major landowners, and merchants who wielded power through family and patronage networks and acted as a link between the local population and the Turco-Mongolian ruling class. In both city and countryside Sufi shaykhs controlled large holdings including charitable endowments and commanded considerable followings among the population, to whom they offered protection and important social services.

When we look at the regional configuration of Central Asia before the Russian conquest then, we see a number of separate areas whose politics and history remained distinct, though closely interconnected. While Uzbek dynasties ruled over most of these regions, for at least part of their history these were separate lineages with divergent policies and goals.

The next question to address is the relation that regional boundaries bore to the location of ethnic groups in Central Asia. Some of the peoples we have mentioned were concentrated primarily in one or two regions, most notably Kazakhs and Kirghiz, whose lifestyle depended on the exploitation of steppe and mountain. Most populations however were intermixed, particularly in Transoxiana. This was due in part to the patchwork geography of the region mentioned earlier. The primary cause for the ethnic variety within each khanate however was political. Unlike the modern European nation states, most of which attempted to represent a homogeneous population, the Central Asian khanates were organized as multi-ethnic states. The Uzbek khans retained their power neither through their bureaucratic structures, nor through the monopoly of force, but by their ability to balance the groups beneath them, and it was in their interest to have a heterogeneous population.

We have discussed above the Turco-Mongolian tradition of dual administration, combining a court staffed by Turco-Mongolian nomads with a financial administration made up of Persian bureaucrats; this system continued in Khiva well into the nineteenth century, and in modified form in Bukhara. Within the military the highest offices were usually held by Uzbeks, but the khans had an interest in bringing in other people as well. A multi-ethnic army and administration had a number of advantages. First of all, it provided the khans with a variety of expertise, that of mountain populations and the more fully nomad and mobile Kazakhs and Turkmens, as well as the Uzbeks. What was even more important was that such outside groups gave the khan protection against the tribal chiefs of his own group, who often held sufficient wealth and power to threaten the khan's authority. It was thus in the khans' interest to expand their territories to include new populations, and to attract outside peoples into their realms. This system was particularly strong in Khiva and Kokand, which had a greater variety of population than the Emirate of Bukhara. Here the khans enhanced their power by playing off the different groups of their population and their armies.[9]

At the time that the Russians conquered Central Asia then it was a heterogeneous society, divided into several different states, each including numerous politically active populations. The different groups making up the population had separate names and group identities, connected only marginally with language and territory, and used not to promote separatism, but to determine and maintain a place within a larger society.

Central Asia Within the Russian Empire

The Russian advance into Central Asia began with the acceptance of Russian overlordship by Abu'l-Khayr, khan of the lesser Kazakh horde, in 1730. This did not bring the Russian government much real control of the Kazakh steppe, but it brought the expectation of such control and served as a justification for further advance to defend Russian settlers and punish Kazakh incursions. Russian movement accelerated in the middle of the nineteenth century, with the construction of new forts in the southern Kazakh territories and the beginning of direct attacks on the Central Asian khanates. By 1876 the subjugation of Central Asia was complete. The steppe regions, Semirechie, Tashkent, Ferghana, the southern part of the Khivan khanate, and the northern part of Transoxiana with

Samarkand, were incorporated directly into the Russian Empire. The Kazakh hordes and the Khanate of Kokand ceased to exist. The Khanate of Khiva and the Emirate of Bukhara however remained in existence as Russian protectorates, though with much diminished territories. Russian possessions were administered as two Governor-Generalships, that of the Steppe, north of the Aral Sea and Lake Balkhash, which included most Kazakh and Kirghiz territories, and the Governorship of Turkestan, which contained the regions to the south.[10]

Russian rule had a very different impact on each of these two regions. The nomad areas to the north contained land potentially useful for agriculture, which the Kazakh and Kirghiz tribes owned in common and used as pasture. This was highly attractive to Russian colonists. Russian settlements began to develop in the Ili region in the 1840s. As the century advanced, colonization, both legal and illegal, increased throughout the steppe until by 1911 40% of the population in the steppe oblasts was Russian, and 17% in Semirechie. This influx of settlers brought a major change in the lifestyle and economy of the Kazakhs, who could not profitably continue as nomads with sharply reduced lands. By 1900, much of the Kazakh population was at least partially settled.[11]

In Transoxiana Russian administration had less impact on social structures. Here colonization remained minimal, since most land useful for agriculture was already exploited, and in private hands. Where possible the Russian administration ruled through local personnel and maintained previous structures of administration, education, and justice on the lower levels. Although many Russian administrators distrusted Islam, they were in general wary of interfering with religious leaders and institutions.[12] While land reforms and the introduction of cotton as a major cash crop brought forth a new class of middlemen and landowners, Russian policies did not transform agricultural and urban populations as they had the nomads of the steppe. In education also, Russian influence was greater in the north, where at least a small Kazakh intelligentsia received its training. In Transoxiana the few Russian schools opened had little impact on the Central Asian population.[13]

Islamic Intellectual Movements

In the nineteenth century new concepts of nationalism and nation-state arose in Europe, radically different from the understanding of political identity in Central Asia. These ideas reached the region slowly, and for the most part not through contact with Russia, but rather through the broader Islamic community. In the second half of the nineteenth century new movements arose in the Muslim world, most notably pan-Islam, pan-Turkism, and the beginnings of narrower ethnic or linguistic nationalism. These centered in the Ottoman Empire, most open to European pressure and ideas. They had their strongest influence on regions close to the Ottomans or strongly influenced by Europeans and among groups educated either in Istanbul or in Europe, and reached Central Asia itself relatively late.

Pan-Islamists called on the Muslims to sink their sectarian and political differences and reform society and religion in order to stand against the encroachments of European states. This platform was enthusiastically adopted by the Ottoman Sultan Abdul-Hamid (1876–1909) who now recalled the Sultan's right to the title of Caliph, ruler of all Muslims, and claimed the duty to protect Muslims outside Ottoman territory. Emissaries to foreign lands, including Central Asia, preached this doctrine, and students coming to Istanbul to study religious sciences were also affected.[14]

New concepts of identity and organization soon gained influence with the reformist intelligentsia developing among the Tatars and later the Azerbaijanis. These men, many educated in Russian schools, in Istanbul, or even in France, were open both to new currents of reform in the Islamic world, and to the increasing nationalism of the Ottoman and Russian empires. This was the era of pan-Slavism, of "orthodoxy and nationalism," and one in which the Tatars of the Volga and the Crimea were suffering considerable discrimination.[15] The pan-Turkic movement began among the Tatars of the Russian Empire, and gained wider publicity in 1905, with the publication in Cairo of an article by a Tatar reformer, Yusuf Akchura, proposing the unification of the Turks of Ottoman and Russian lands.[16]

One major concern of the new reformists of the Russian Empire was education, and their introduction of a new system, known as the *usul-i jadid,* won them the appellation of "Jadids." While the Jadids often promoted ideas of unity among Turks and Muslims of the Russian Empire, their work also led in a different direction, towards the development of separate written vernacular languages. Up to almost the middle of the nineteenth century, four written languages in the Arabic script had served the Muslims of the Russian realms and the central Islamic lands. These were Arabic and Persian and two forms of Turkic, both distant from everyday speech and strongly influenced by Persian and Arabic. One written Turkic language was Ottoman, used outside the Ottoman Empire primarily in Azerbaijan and the Crimea, and the other was eastern literary Turkic—Turki or Chaghatay—used by most other regions of the Russian Empire, Central Asia and Eastern Turkestan. Any well educated person was expected to know two of these four languages, and many knew three. In attempting to educate a broader public, many Jadids sought a simpler medium closer to the everyday speech of the local population. In Azerbaijan a vernacular language developed in the second half of the nineteenth century, with written grammar and school texts. In the later nineteenth century the Tatar Jadid, Abdul Qayyum Nasiri, promoted written Tatar, while the famous Crimean Tatar pan-Islamist Isma'il Bey Gasprinskiy advocated a simplified version of Ottoman as a common literary language.[17]

As Edward Lazzerini has written in his chapter, it was largely through the agency of the Tatars that the Jadid movement spread to the east. Here it received mixed reactions. The most receptive to nationalistic ideas were the Kazakh intellectuals. Some of these men were Russian educated; they lived under direct Russian rule, and saw their lands disappearing to Russian colonization. The resentment this caused was a spur to nationalistic feelings.[18] In Transoxiana the spread of the reformist movement was slow, even though early pan-Islamic ideas had achieved some acceptance. In the areas which the Russians controlled directly officials left religious educational institutions intact. Throughout all this area the conservative ulema remained the preponderant force in education up to the Russian revolution. In Khiva and Bukhara, rulers and ulema maintained a hostile attitude to Jadid activities.

The Formation of the National Republics

In Central Asia new ideas of identity and political organization flourished only within a very small Jadid intelligentsia, in general less politically successful than their counterparts in western Islamic regions.[19] Through the whole of the Muslim world, modernizing reformers remained a small minority, but in many places these men, due to positions of control over the press and in government, had an impact disproportionate to their numbers. In the Russian Empire this was true only of the Tatars and Azerbaijanis. In eastern Muslim regions, particularly Transoxiana, local power remained in the hands of politicians, with officials and ulema little influenced by recent trends, practicing the factional, ethnic and regional politics customary in the area.

Let us consider in this light what the early Soviet government faced when it decided to create national republics in Central Asia. The Bolshevik platform on nationality had been developed in debates with socialists of Central and Eastern Europe and to a large extent reflected the aspirations of peoples freeing themselves from the Austro-Hungarian or Ottoman Empires, wishing to become nation-states on the Western European model. The definition of a nation which Stalin formulated and later applied clearly mirrored these concerns. A nation was to be characterized by a common language, territory, psychological makeup and historical experience.[20]

This formula was now applied to a society in which ethnic identity was understood quite differently. Only the very small Jadid intelligentsia saw ethnicity in terms of common language or territory. For most of the population, identity, if they thought about it, was connected peripherally if at all to language, and much more directly to a specific function within a plural society. Theoretically, the Soviet government was committed to the right of self-determination for national groups, and in practice it was prepared to grant them a limited cultural autonomy. These groups however had first to be defined, and in Central Asia this was no easy task.

The pan-Islamic movement promoted by the Tatars presented a possible solution—the union of all Muslims in the Empire. In the earliest years of Soviet power the revolution was expected to spread to the colonial east, and the eastern Soviet peoples were assigned a role in attracting their brethren abroad. In this atmosphere the Tatar Mir Said Sultangaliev proposed a new ideology, Muslim National Communism. He suggested that socialism and a socially oriented Islam could forge the Muslims of the Soviet lands into a potent force for the liberation of the Muslim world from its reactionary rulers and the oppression of Western powers. This movement posed a clear threat to the hegemony of the Soviet government and would have required a form of extra-territorial autonomy which the Bolshevik leadership had decisively rejected. With the failure of socialist revolution outside the former Russian Empire, Sultangaliev and his ideas quickly lost the support of the government, and in 1923 he was expelled from the Party.[21]

The unity of all Muslims within the empire was clearly rejected, but alternative levels of organization remained elusive. There was no way to divide the region of Central Asia and Kazakhstan neatly into separate ethnically homogeneous units, even more so when ethnicity was defined in the new terms of territory and language. The problem was not only the intermixing of ethnic groups, but the fact that the various criteria used to define ethnicity pointed in different ways—common historical experience did not correspond with common language or lifestyle, nor "psychological make-up" with territory. To put together the entire Turco-Iranian eastern region, the Steppe and Turkestan Guberniias, would have united the speakers of eastern Turkic languages and dialects, but would also have joined together populations and regions diverse in economy and development, and territories which had only rarely and briefly formed part of one political entity. It would also have created a dangerously large republic.

What the Soviets finally did, as Donald Carlisle has shown in his chapter, was to reinstate many political borders of the past, while providing them with new names.[22] The republic of Uzbekistan centered on the former Bukharan Emirate, but now also possessed territories—Tashkent, Kokand, Khiva—which had been part of different states but had been populated or ruled by an Uzbek elite. The mountainous eastern sections of Bukhara, long semi-independent under local Iranian dynasties, were formed in 1924 into the Tajik Autonomous Republic, and in 1929 gained Union Republic status, also winning the region of Khojand, whose partially Tajik population and more importantly, economic strength, gave greater weight to the republic of Tajikistan. In 1936 Kazakhstan and the mountainous region of Kirgizia also became Union Republics.

If one looks at the formation of the Soviet republics from an historical standpoint, then, one can say that many of the borders drawn and distinctions made among peoples followed historical precedents. What was new with the Soviets was the meaning of these borders, and of the identities which they now enclosed and sought to represent.

Central Asia Within the USSR

The creation of national republics in Central Asia raised a host of issues which have remained alive to the present day. What had been a plural society with a bilingual elite using two highly evolved literary languages—Persian and Chaghatay Turkic—was now to become a set of national societies bilingual in Russian and either Turkic or Tajik. Because of the need to develop mass education the Soviet authorities, like the Jadids before them, created simplified literary languages closer to colloquial speech. This required a choice among numerous dialects and the creation of formal boundaries defining languages, a matter of no little controversy.[23] While in an Islamic society the Arabic alphabet had been the most appropriate to use, for a secular society based on Western ideology, first the Latin and later the Cyrillic were preferred. Since these alphabets have a more precise phonetic system than the Arabic, they served further to fix and separate the character of the various Central Asian languages.

Both the substance of Soviet nationalities policies and their frequent shifts resulted in the furtherance of loyalty to ethnic and regional identities, and in continued concern about the status of the new nations within the USSR. Above all, one question remained crucial and unresolved—the question dealt with in this volume—where does Central Asia belong in the world of the past and the present? The official policies of the Soviet government aimed to produce a new "homo sovieticus" who would owe primary loyalty to the Soviet Union itself, while maintaining a second identity as a member of a constituent nationality. Once national republics and languages existed and work had begun to create a modern educational system, the trappings of modern national ideologies had to be provided. Identities formerly based on political roles within a plural state were now to be anchored to a specific language, territory and history. With the decline in government tolerance of Islam in the late 1920s, the center increasingly promoted secular traditions for Central Asians; each republic required a set of national characteristics, a literature, a defined historical experience, and a vision of itself in the world. The members of the national intelligentsia set out to create these, writing a spate of national histories. Many of the problems inherent in this process are examined in the chapters by Subtelny and Atkin.

The historians of the Soviet Central Asian and steppe republics had to define their origins in acceptable terms and to evaluate subsequent stages in their history in relation first to Marxist theory and then to the history of Russia and neighboring republics. The condemnation of nomadism as retrogressive posed major problems for formerly nomadic groups—a category which includes essentially all Turkic peoples of the Soviet Union. Since moreover the dictates of the central government changed more than once, the writing of history proved both an arduous and unsettling task. It was one which kept national identities and relations with Russia and with the rest of the world constantly in view, and never settled for long.

In Central Asia as elsewhere, the mid-thirties marked a watershed in the imposition of Soviet control. Purges destroyed the generation of intellectuals and politicians which had assisted at the birth of Soviet power. These years also brought the final introduction of the Cyrillic alphabet, cutting the bridge to the writings of the outside Muslim world. The issue of Central Asia's identity might then have been considered as settled.

Nonetheless, as the chapters in this collection show, we find national traditions a continuing matter of concern and controversy in both Moscow and Central Asia. The Second World War, bringing a renewal of Russian patriotism and the rehabilitation of great Russian royal and military figures, brought again to the fore the question of Caucasian and Central Asian history, graced with a wealth of kings and conquerors. It was necessary for Moscow to indicate the inferiority of such leaders and to enforce its convictions.

Although Stalin's death ended the major purges, the post-Stalin years brought a new set of issues and problems. While Khrushchev dismantled some of the Stalinist apparatus, he proposed a doubtful future for national cultures. At the Twenty-second Party Congress in 1961, he stated that the national policy charted by Lenin had led to the flowering of national cultures, and that economic and cultural progress during the Soviet years was leading to their rapprochement. The supreme stage in this advancement was to be the fusion of these separate cultures. Along with this theory came the full development of the historical myth which L. Tillett has dubbed "the great friendship"—namely that all the peoples making up the USSR had in the past as well as the present benefitted from a cordial relationship to the Russian people and had been growing gradually closer to them through natural attraction.[24] Such a view of course required that history be yet again rewritten. From the point of view of the center, cultural figures of the past seemed less threatening than military ones, as long as they were not too clearly identified with Islam. Thus with official approval Central Asians continued to honor—if not to read—the great writers of their past, to preserve and glorify the buildings and manuscripts remaining from earlier centuries. Academies of Sciences, organized on the Soviet model, served in each republic as keepers of the flame.

Yet issues connected with such cultural legacies inevitably raised questions of Central Asia's identity and kept these issues unresolved. First of all, both in content and in form, medieval literature serves to remind Central Asians of their place within the Islamic world. It was Islamic norms which formed the literary culture of Central Asia, and many of the region's scholars and writers were central figures in the development of Islamic civilization. Furthermore, the Soviet decision to delineate national identity through both language and land led to a competitive scramble for cultural heroes. If the Tajiks had to limit themselves to figures active in their current territory, a mountainous region far from major cultural centers, they would have little to lay claim to. What they define as Tajik therefore, are either Central Asian figures known to have been of Iranian birth, or those who wrote Persian in any region. Writing the history of one after another poet or historian, they are constantly reminded that the great centers of their historic culture are not their present towns of Khojand and Dushanbe, but the cities of Samarkand and Bukhara, in Uzbekistan.

The Uzbeks suffer from the fact that while their region was the scene of great literary flowering, patronized by Turkic rulers, most of the works produced there were written in Persian or Arabic. Furthermore the greatest of their own literary figures, the star of Chaghatay (now "old Uzbek") literature, was Ali-Shir Nava'i, who lived neither in Samarkand nor in Bukhara, but in Herat, in Afghanistan. In this way the creation and codification of separate national heritages in Central Asia has continued to link the Central Asian past to that of the wider Islamic world, and also has strengthened separate and competing Central Asian identities.

Just as the search for an historical identity based on language and culture attached the Central Asian republics to a wider cultural area, so in their way did the modernizing and secularizing policies of the Soviet government. As John Voll has pointed out in his chapter, the strains of modernization have been felt throughout the Islamic world in the twentieth century, and the reaction of Central Asian Muslims to this trauma has many similarities to that of other Muslim peoples. It is possible indeed that some aspects of Soviet indoctrination have served to strengthen Central Asia's Islamic identity. Soviet authorities and the Soviet press habitually attacked practices which were identified with Islam. Visits to local shrines and consultation with their Sufi keepers, continued attachment to Islamic weddings and funerals, and the practice of marking circumcision with a large celebration were all repeatedly criticized as holdovers of an obscurantist religion. In this way the Soviet regime provided a formal Islamic identity even for peoples whose observation of much of religious practice such as daily prayers, fasting, and mosque attendance had lapsed, and many of whom may now know little of Islamic dogma.[25] The widespread indentification with Islam in contemporary Kazakhstan, described by Reef Altoma, illustrates this phenomenon.

In many ways then, Central Asia throughout the Soviet period preserved its earlier traditions, both religious and cultural. Other aspects of earlier social structure and political culture have also survived under Soviet rule. Indeed, the dual society created by Russian overlordship in some ways mirrored that of Turco-Mongolian rule. Indigenous identity was defined against an outside ruling class, and local structures and loyalties continued to give protection against outside interference, and to provide for needs which the center did not sufficiently serve. For this reason, many of the earlier loyalties to city, clan and family, and the political culture based on these, have continued to the present.

At the same time, as Edward Allworth and Bakhtior Islamov show in their chapters, Central Asia was strongly tied to the Russian center, and strongly influenced by it. The depth of Russian influence on language, culture and patterns of thought has been profound. The impact of the center on Central Asia's economic and political structures has also been decisive and in the ecological sphere highly destructive. The Russian government's insistence on cotton monoculture and on the production of a crop too large for the region to support without damage brought with it both material harm and political corruption, as politicians protected themselves and their followers by presenting the center with an acceptable set of lies. This was accompanied by a tolerance of the practices of local leadership by the center. In the era of Brezhnev in particular the center overlooked widespread corruption and interfered relatively little in Central Asian affairs below the highest level.[26] As A. M. Khazanov indicates in his chapter, the policies of the center actually encouraged the continuance of the local, patronage and kinship ties which had defined much of the region's political activity in the pre-Russian period.

The Brezhnev years then allowed considerable scope to Central Asian leadership. Along with this, the central government quietly dropped Khrushchev's prediction of international fusion. The relative comfort of these years (for the leadership at least) was shattered by the anti-corruption campaign initiated in 1983 by Andropov and continued under Gorbachev, causing havoc in republican leadership. As under Khrushchev, liberalization in the center did not bring with it greater tolerance for republican independence.

In examining Central Asia's response to Gorbachev's challenge and to the disintegration of the USSR one is struck by the relative slowness of the Central Asian republics to declare independence. Here it is useful to look back at the last period of confusion, at the beginning of the century. Then, as now, Western concepts of political separatism proved weaker in Central Asia than among the western Muslims of the USSR. Neither the conciousness of a separate identity and culture nor distaste for Russian rule led immediately to a desire for full separation.

The history of Central Asia and its place in the world shows the wealth of influences which have gone into its formation, from pre-Islamic Iranian civilization, through the coming of Islam, then the Turks and the Mongols, to its incorporation into the Russian Empire. All of these have left their mark, in the variety of populations and lifestyles, in the shape of society and the conduct of politics. The seventy years of Soviet rule added another layer of influence, changing but not obliterating the legacies of the past. In today's world Central Asia retains its former place, on the boundary of different regions and cultures, combining but not amalgamating influences from the civilizations surrounding it.

Notes

1. Y. Bregel, "The Sarts in the Khanate of Khiva," *Journal of Asian History,* vol. 12, #2 (1978), pp. 130–31, 134, 142, *Istoriia Narodov Uzbekistana* (Tashkent, 1947), vol. II, p. 79.

2. M.K. Nurmukhamedov, *Karakalpaky* (Tashkent, 1971), pp. 21–27, *Istoriia Narodov Uzbekistana,* vol. I, pp. 105–6, V.V. Bartol'd, R. Wixman, "Karakalpaks," *Encyclopedia of Islam,* N.E., vol. IV, pp. 610–11.

3. Y. Bregel, "Nomad and Sedentary Elements among the Turkmens," *Central Asiatic Journal,* XXV (1981), pp. 29–37, "Sarts," pp. 134–5, 150, *Istoriia Narodov Uzbekistana,* p. 79.

4. V.V. Bartol'd and G. Hazai, "Kirghiz," *Encyclopedia of Islam,* N.E., vol. V, pp. 134–6, C.M. Abramzon, *Kirgizy, ikh etnogeneticheskie i istoriko-kul'turnye sviazi* (Leningrad, 1971), pp. 27–42, Joseph Fletcher, "Ch'ing Inner Asia," pp. 87–90, and "The Heyday of the Ch'ing Order," pp. 385–95, in Denis Twitchett and J.K. Fairbank, eds., *Cambridge History of China,* vol. 10 (Cambridge, 1978).

5. I.M. Steblin-Kamenskij, "Central Asia: Languages," *Encyclopaedia Iranica,* vol. V, pp. 223–6.

6. Y. Bregel, "Turko-Mongol Influences in Central Asia," in Robert Canfield, ed., *Turko-Persia in Historical Perspective* (Cambridge, 1991), pp. 59–60.

7. Y. Bregel, "The Sarts," p. 144, "Central Asia," Encyclopaedia Iranica, vol. V, fas. 2, pp. 194, 196, *Istoriia Narodov Uzbekistana,* vol. II, p. 134.

8. Jan-Heeren Grevemeyer, *Herrschaft, Raub und Gegenseitigkeit: Die politische Geschichte Badakhshans 1500–1883* (Wiesbaden, 1982), pp. 31, 47–41, 74.

9. Bregel, "Central Asia,", pp. 193, 196–7, Mulla Niyaz Muhammad Khawqandi, *Tarikh-i Shahrukhi,* ed., N.N. Pantusov (Kazan, 1885), pp. 42–44, B.F. Manz, "Central Asian Uprisings in the Nineteenth Century: Ferghana under the Russians," *The Russian Review,* vol. 46 (1987), pp. 268–70.

10. Geoffrey Wheeler, *The Modern History of Soviet Central Asia* (New York, 1964), Chapts. III, IV, Appendix, Richard Pierce, *Russian Central Asia* (Berkeley, 1960), pp. 51–58.

11. Pierce, pp. 108–137.

12. Pierce, pp. 113–14.

13. K.E. Bendrikov, *Ocherki po istorii narodnogo obrazovaniia v Turkestane (1865–1924 gody)* (Moscow, 1960), pp. 66–83, 190–91.

14. Jacob M. Landau, *The Politics of Pan-Islam* (Oxford, 1990), pp. 13–65.

15. Zenkovsky, *Pan-Turkism and Islam in Russia* (Cambridge, Mass., 1960), pp. 27, 37, Landau, pp. 144–5.

16. S.A. Zenkovsky, pp. 38–9.

17. Zenkovsky, pp. 25, 32.

18. Zenkovsky, pp. 59–69, Martha Brill Olcott, *The Kazakhs* (Stanford, 1987), pp. 101–9.

19. Landau, pp. 152–63.

20. Richard Pipes, *The Formation of the Soviet Union,* revised edition (Cambridge, Mass., 1964), pp. 21–41.

21. See A. Bennigsen and S. Enders Wimbush, *Muslim National Communism in the Soviet Union* (Chicago, 1979).

22. For another discussion of this process see Bert Fragner, "Probleme der Nationswerdung der Usbeken und Tadschiken," in A. Kappeler, G. Simon and G. Brunner, eds., *Die Muslime in der Sowjetunion und in Jugoslawien* (Cologne, 1989), pp. 19–34.

23. William Fierman, *Language Planning and Development: The Uzbek Experience* (Berlin, 1991), pp. 61–74.

24. L. Tillett, *The Great Friendship: Soviet Historians on the Non-Russian Nationalities* (Chapel Hill, 1969).

See for example B.G. Gafurov, *Istoriia tadzhiksogo naroda* (Moscow, 1949), vol. I, pp. 240–6, 263–71, 292–9.

25. Uli Schamiloglu, "Religious and National Identity and their Invention," and Nazif Shahrani, "Muslim Central Asia: Soviet Development Strategies and Future Challenges," at the conference: "Islam and Democratization in Post-Soviet Central Asia," University of Massachusetts-Amherst, 26 September 1992.

26. L. Hajda and M. Beissinger, *The Nationalities Factor in Soviet Politics and Society* (Boulder, 1990), p. 309; Boris Rumer, *Soviet Central Asia "A Tragic Experiment"* (London, 1989), pp. 144–59.

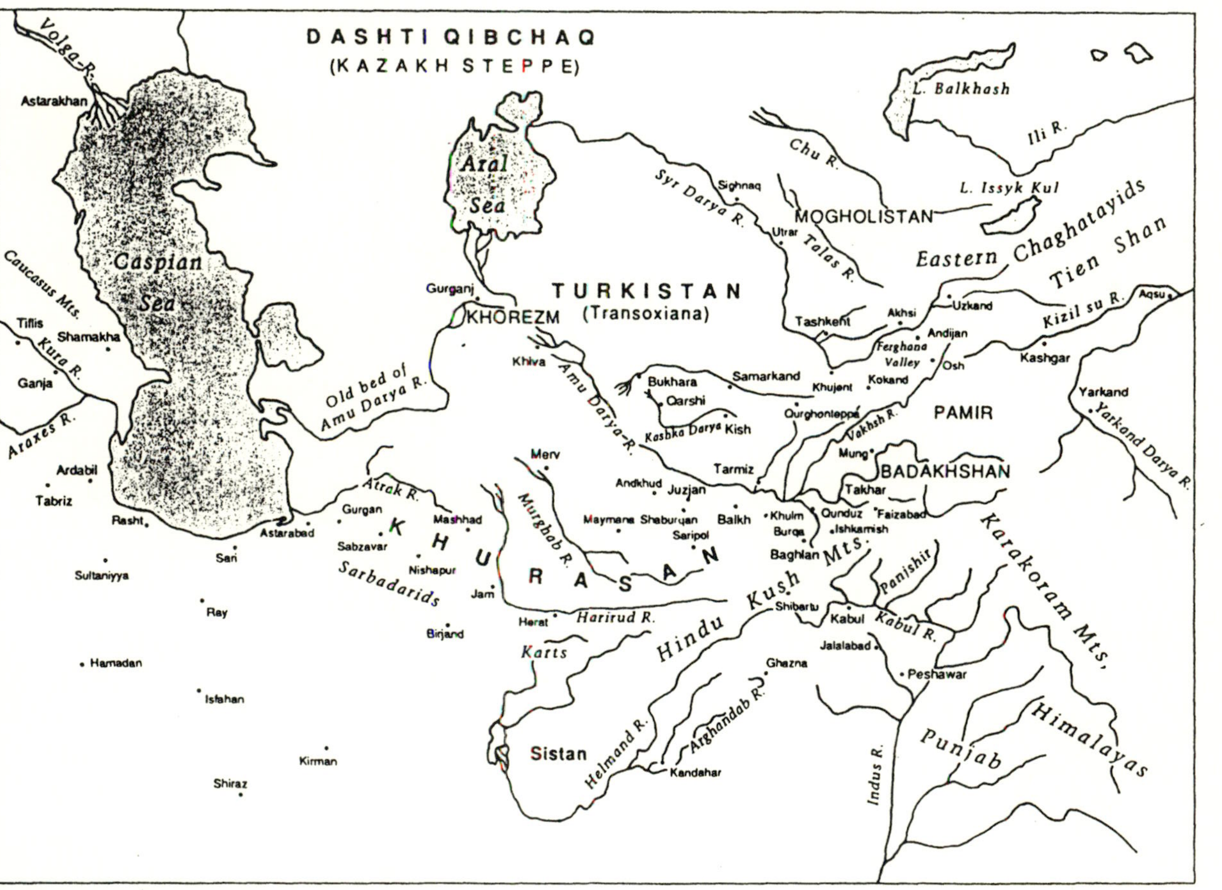

Central Asia in the Late Middle Ages
Source: Gross, Jo-Ann, *Muslims in Central Asia: Expressions of Identity and Change* (Duke University Press, 1992). Used by permission.

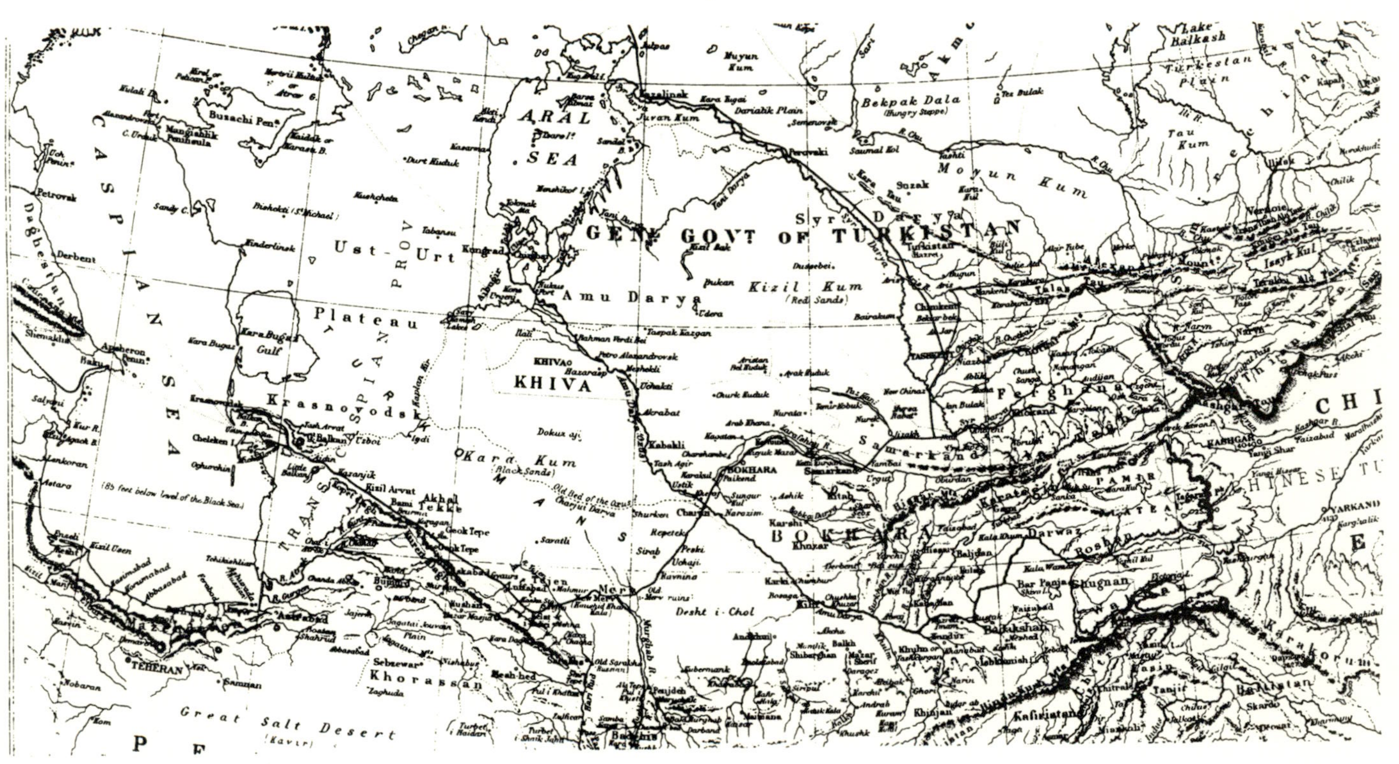

Russian Central Asia

PART ONE

THE SHAPING OF CENTRAL ASIAN IDENTITIES AND POLITICS

CHAPTER 1

The Legacy of the Mongols

Morris Rossabi

The Mongol eruption in the thirteenth century was without question the most significant impact of the nomadic peoples of Inner Asia on the sedentary world. Mongol troops reached west all the way to Hungary and Poland and south all the way to Southeast Asia and the Middle East. China and Central Asia, as the Mongols' two nearest neighbors, had greater and longer exposure than other regions to the descendants of Chinggis Khan. Most works on the Mongol impact on China and Central Asia have stressed the destruction and dislocation generated by the initial conquests. Setting aside such a one-sided view, a study of the Mongol legacy in Central Asia needs to consider two different perspectives. First, the immediate consequences of the conquest and occupation of Central Asia require investigation. The Mongols governed much of Central Asia for about a century, and their Turkic-speaking descendants dominated the region for at least another century and a half. Later still, in the seventeenth and eighteenth centuries, a powerful new Mongol confederation influenced the peoples and lands of Central Asia. Second, certain patterns of Mongol culture and society appear to have influenced the societies of Central Asia. Such shared patterns are the enduring legacies of Mongol relations with Central Asian peoples and societies.

The Mongol Conquest and Its Aftermath

The Mongols' initial encounter with Eastern Turkestan, their closest neighbor in Central Asia, was peaceful.[1] The Uighurs, the principal inhabitants of the region, submitted voluntarily and as a result were accorded a special status in the Mongol domains. Having the most literate and sophisticated population among the Turks, the Uighurs were eagerly recruited into government service.[2] A Turkic group from Central Asia had, in this case, a dramatic impact on its Mongol overlords. Uighurs adapted their vertical script to provide the first written language for Mongolian and served as tutors, secretaries, translators, interpreters, and government officials. Other Turkish groups, including Önggüd and Kipchaks, were granted positions in the Mongol military, central government, or local administration.[3]

During the century or so in which they controlled Uighuristan, the Mongols conducted censuses, devised a regular system of taxation, and organized postal stations to facilitate the speedy conveyance of official mail and incidentally to promote travel and trade.[4] The immediate Mongol legacy in eastern Central Asia was thus not destructive. By surrendering without a struggle, the Uighurs escaped the possibility of a devastating assault. Indeed, they benefited from Mongol policies. The caravan trade that had lain relatively dormant after the tenth century revived as a result of Mongol control of much of Eurasia and Mongol encouragement of commerce.[5] The flow of merchants and goods traversing Eurasia increased appreciably during the Mongol era, and caravans coming to or from China naturally traveled via the oases of Central Asia, offering numerous economic opportunities for the inhabitants. Judging from the adverse reaction to efforts made by the early Ming dynasty, the Chinese successors to the Mongols, to limit trade and so-called tribute, the Uighurs had made striking gains as a result of Mongol promotion of trade.[6]

This relatively rosy assessment of the meaning of Mongol rule in East Turkestan does not apply to the western regions of Central Asia. The Khorezm-Shah, who ruled much of this area, was much less docile than the Uighur *iduq-qut*.[7] In 1218 he even condoned the killing of an envoy dispatched by Chinggis Khan—a direct challenge to the Mongols to whom "the person of an ambassador . . . was sacrosanct."[8] Chinggis Khan now needed to avenge himself against the Khorezm-Shah and thus had a pretext to launch an invasion. The Khorezm-Shah, in any case, had a precarious hold on his domain. His army was wracked with strife; many of his subjects, particularly those in Iran who had been subjugated during his campaigns in the early 1200s, were not loyal to him, and he could not count upon support from the religious leadership.[9]

Capitalizing on the Khorezm-Shah's weaknesses, Chinggis Khan initiated an attack against Transoxiana in Central Asia in 1219. Encountering resistance, the Mongol armies responded violently and brutally. Persian historians acknowledge that the Mongol campaigns in Transoxiana were not as destructive as the ones in Eastern Persia and Iraq. Even so, they describe deliberate massacres and destruction. Juvayni, one of the greatest Persian historians, writes about one Turkish group in Bukhara that "no male was spared who stood higher than the butt of a whip and more than thirty thousand were counted amongst the slain." He quotes one refugee from Bukhara that the Mongols "came, they sapped, they burnt, they slew, they plundered and they departed."[10] According to these Islamic sources, Bukhara and Samarkand, the twin centers of culture in Transoxiana, were savaged, many of their inhabitants were killed, and thirty thousand craftsmen from Samarkand were forced, virtually as slaves, to go eastward to Northern China and Mongolia to serve the Mongols.[11]

Yet a Chinese Taoist invited by Chinggis Khan to accompany him on his Central Asian campaigns offered a somewhat different assessment than the Persian sources. Arriving in Samarkand a year and a half after its conquest by the Mongols, he reported that the occupiers were repairing bridges and boats and that "wherever we went we came to terraces, lakes, pagodas, and towers . . . ." His escorts told him that the population had fallen from 100,000 to 25,000 which no doubt overstates the casualties, but nonetheless indicates that he did not ignore the results of warfare. He also found that farm land had either not been damaged or that there had been a remarkable recovery within a brief time span, for as he noted, "fruit and vegetables were very abundant."[12] A leading historian of Central Asia also subscribes to this view when he notes that:

> the opinion that the Mongols did not appreciate culture and would have turned all the land into grazing grounds is contradicted by the facts. The Mongol rulers, at least, were bound to realize that from town-dwellers and land-owners they could obtain better revenue than from nomads.[13]

Additional confirmation derives from Mongol attempts to govern Bukhara and the surrounding Central Asian regions. The Mongols recruited reliable Chinese and Khitan advisers to help them develop a stable administration. Eventually Khorezmians joined in devising the fiscal and defense structures of the region. One of the Khorezmians, in fact, persuaded his Mongol overlords not to raze Bukhara after a rebellion against Mongol rule.[14] Still another indication that the Mongols did not aspire simply to wipe out Central Asians was their recruitment of Muslims from the region for administrative responsibilities in China.[15] Numerous Central Asians served the Mongol rulers of the Middle Kingdom.[16] The Central Asian Ahmad became a leading official, with responsibility for financial administration, in Khubilai Khan's government in Peking. The Mongols encouraged Muslims from Central Asia to form merchant associations (known as ortogh) to promote trade and to revive the caravan trade to the West.[17] The caravan trade, in turn, traversed Central Asia and no doubt contributed to the prosperity of the region.

Mongol domination thus left an ambiguous rather than purely negative legacy. The revival of trade was certainly a boon, and the Mongols' support of merchants contributed to the commercial prosperity of Central Asia. After the initial attacks and conquest, the Mongols wanted to achieve order, not merely to exploit the region. Their motive was to generate stability so that the local economy could recover and the Mongols could secure more revenue.[18] Yet a more alarming legacy was military encroachment on civilian authority. The military dominated Central Asia, and the government reflected the preponderance of military influence, a situation which inevitably generated conflicts. The Chaghatay Khans, descended from Chinggis Khan's second son, fought with local leaders as well as with the Mongol khanates in Persia and China. The conflicts occasionally had damaging effects. Bukhara, for example, was severely devastated in 1273 as a result of an attack by the Mongol khanate of Persia.[19]

Internal strife weakened the descendants of Chinggis Khan and eventually permitted the rise of new powers. The most important of these in the region of

Central Asia was the Turkic leader Tamerlane (Temür), who rose to power near Samarkand in 1370. Tamerlane inherited practices and ideas belonging to what has been called the "Turco-Mongolian tradition."[20] The principal characteristic of this tradition was adaptation of the steppe culture and institutions to those of the Mongols' sedentary subjects.

Tamerlane proved to be adroit in using this Turco-Mongolian tradition to buttress his rule. Though he derived from a nomadic background, he "based his strength on the exploitation of settled populations."[21] He was, for example, a fervent Muslim rather than a shamanist (a religion based on a shaman's direct links to ancestral spirits or gods) of nomadic heritage. On the other hand, he persisted in identifying with nomadic history by seeking to associate himself with Chinggis Khan and the Chinggisid dynasty.[22] In his effort to gain control, he followed traditional Mongol organization and strategy. Like Chinggis, he started his campaigns based on tribes, but also like the great Mongol conqueror, his objective was to place his own sons and loyal retainers in positions of power and to remove tribal leaders from such positions. He attempted to acquire control over and to elicit support from both the sedentary and the nomadic populations of Central Asia, and, following the example of Chinggis Khan, he recruited foreign troops for his army once he had subjugated their lands. Then he used them to continue his expansionist policies. Finally, he incorporated foreign systems of administration in his attempt to govern, a policy similar to the one pioneered by the early Mongols. He attempted to balance an Arabo-Persian system with its emphasis on bureaucracy and regular administration with a Turco-Mongolian system relying on military organization. Internal strife, once again, weakened the empire of his descendants, permitting the nomadic Chinggisid Uzbek Turks to conquer them in 1505–1507. The Uzbeks would then become the dominant force in the formation of modern Central Asia.

Another group that influenced Central Asia was the Zunghars. Residing in Western Mongolia and in what is now northern Xinjiang, the Zunghars were the last in a long line of Mongols to seek to unite their people to recreate the glorious past represented by Chinggis Khan and his thirteenth-century empire. Their leaders repeatedly invoked the legends and history of Chinggis Khan's exploits and made explicit comparisons with their illustrious forebears. Their ruler Galdan suffered severe setbacks in his efforts to unite the Mongols. He aimed to gain support from the Khalkha or Eastern Mongols, but they lacked allegiance to a single leader. At least three khans competed for control among the Khalkha, and the presence of the Living Buddha (Jebtsundamba Khutughtu) and his effort to seek power contributed to the turmoil in Eastern Mongolia, further impeding Galdan's grandiose plan for a unified Mongol world under his command. Without a strong base among the Mongols, he was vulnerable in his war with Ch'ing China, particularly after the Manchu dynasty in the Middle Kingdom made an accommodation with Tsarist Russia, robbing Galdan of this potential European ally. No longer fearful of a joint Zunghar alliance with the Russians, the Ch'ing could focus on dispatching Galdan's troops. By 1696 Galdan had been defeated, and the following year he died. With his death, Mongol influence in Central Asia declined considerably, though the Zunghars, under different leadership, continued in combat with China until the 1750s when a Ch'ing military leader wiped out the remnants of the enemy.[23]

Shared Patterns Among Mongols and Central Asians

The direct historical links between the Mongols and Central Asia were without question significant, but perhaps the shared patterns of organization, structure, and ideology are as vital in identifying the Mongol legacy in Central Asia. The clearest impression derived from the study of the history of the Mongol Empire and its successor states is the difficulties encountered by the Mongols in achieving unity. The pastoral nomadic lifestyle did not lend itself to groups larger than tribes, since "any would-be supratribal ruler had to bring to heel a highly mobile population, who could simply decamp and ignore his claims to authority."[24] Unity that transcended the tribal group was rare and fleeting. Mongols and the pastoral nomads who preceded them in Mongolia owed loyalty to a tribal chief. When they emerged from the steppes to challenge the sedentary peoples, in particular the Chinese, they required a larger unit than the tribe. Disputes with the sedentary states over trade or land or property necessitated the development of unions of tribes. Individual tribes could engage in hit-and-run raids against their more settled neighbors, but they had to forge alliances composed of numerous tribes to make permanent and substantial gains. Under these circumstances, tribal leaders needed to turn over some of their responsibilities to a supreme ruler who tried to empower some of his own closest associates and retainers so that he would not be as dependent on these tribal chiefs. Such unity and centralization would foster the development of a much more powerful confederation.

Yet centralization of this kind encountered resistance. Tribal chiefs developed a personal allegiance to a specific supreme ruler. They were not necessarily loyal to the office embodied by the ruler. If a ruler was ineffective or did not provide booty for the tribal chiefs or was considered to have betrayed them, they had no compunction about ending their support for him. Once he died, they were not obligated to remain in the confederation, since they had no abstract concept of loyalty to a permanent office or to a vision of a Mongol nation or ethnic group.[25]

This lack of cohesion, together with a relatively weak identity as a distinct group, repeatedly hampered the Mongols. The Mongol empire of the thirteenth century was particularly debilitated by such disunity. Chinggis Khan had been able to overcome parochial tribal loyalties and, in fact, to disperse tribal units within his larger confederation. A major element in his success was the loyalty he elicited from various Mongol tribes and peoples. His death, however, resulted in the weakening of the bonds that he had forged. Although his son

Ögödei, with some difficulty, preserved some of these links, the Mongol domains soon began to fragment. By the time Ögödei died, Mongol unity had been lost. Within a short time, four virtually autonomous domains developed within the so-called Mongol empire. The Golden Horde dominated Russia; the Il-khans governed Iran; the Chaghatay khans controlled Central Asia and Eastern Turkestan; and the Yüan dynasty ruled China and the traditional homeland of the Mongols.

The most dramatic evidence of this fragmentation was the wars between various Mongol khanates. The major conflict erupted in the Middle East when the Golden Horde cooperated with the Muslim Mamluk rulers of Egypt against their fellow Mongols in Il-khanid Persia. The Mongol governors of Persia, in turn, sought allies in Christian Europe to oppose the Mamluks and the Golden Horde. By this time, the Mongols seem to have lost their sense of kinship with one another. They cooperated with their earlier enemies against their own ethnic brothers, and they had no hesitations about doing so because they felt no special bond with peoples who in modern times would be considered part of the same group. This strife among the Mongols naturally weakened them and compelled their eventual withdrawal from the lands they had subjugated. Within each of these khanates, unity proved difficult to maintain. The Chaghatay Khanate of Central Asia in particular was frequently divided.

One reason for the recurrent internal strife within the Mongol realm was the lack of a regular and orderly system of succession. The transfer of power proved to be an Achilles' heel. Since the Mongols owed personal loyalty to a specific Khan, not to the office he represented, leaders encountered difficulties in passing on their title and their power. Traditions of lateral succession and lineal succession clashed. Even more troublesome was a system whereby an assemblage (*khuriltai*) of the Mongol elite met to select the new ruler, initially the member of the Chinggisid line whom they considered the fittest.[26] This means of selection naturally bred conflict, as there were frequent disagreements about the merits of the different candidates. The resulting disputes weakened and, on occasion, undermined the Mongol confederation. Examples of succession struggles in Mongol history are legion.

The states which developed in Central Asia and the steppe after the dissolution of the Mongol Empire looked to Chinggis Khan and his house for legitimacy; many indeed were ruled by Chinggisid khans. The Mongol system of succession was likewise largely maintained, with its attendant discord. Central Asia has repeatedly suffered from the political malady of uncertain succession. The century or so of Mongol rule under the descendants of Chinggis' son Chaghatay witnessed countless succession disputes. Tamerlane, who overwhelmed the Chaghatay but still kept a khan as a figurehead, could not guarantee stability for his successors. His son only took power after a clear-cut military victory over his rivals; his grandson was assassinated; and the last half-century of Timurid rule was beset by warfare and regicide.

The Uzbeks, who had overwhelmed and destroyed the Timurid empire by 1506, were themselves beset by continuous desertions and insurrections. The later khanates of Khiva, Bukhara, and Kokand, which had a sizable, settled population based in oases and engaged in farming and trade rather than nomads engaged in pastoralism, still failed to create a single Central Asian khanate that could have provided more successful resistance to the expansionism of the Tsarist and Ch'ing courts.[27] Despite their more sedentary lifestyle and thus their greater opportunity to achieve unity, these khanates failed to join together and were vulnerable to attacks by Russia and Manchu-governed China in the eighteenth and nineteenth centuries. By 1880, Tsarist forces overwhelmed the khanates of Khiva, Bukhara, and Kokand and began to incorporate them into the Russian empire.[28]

Eastern Central Asia in the seventeenth and eighteenth centuries was also plagued by incessant dynastic struggles among the Moghul (Chaghatay) secular rulers and the Khojas (Khwajas), Sufi religious leaders, facilitating the Manchu conquest of the region. By 1760, China completed its occupation of Zunghar-ruled territories in Northern Xinjiang as well as Southern Xinjiang oases and lands earlier dominated by the Moghuls and the Sufi Khojas. Revolts against Ch'ing rule in the nineteenth century foundered as a result of dynastic squabbling either among either the secular or Islamic leadership.[29]

The nomadic peoples to the north were even less unified and more hard pressed to retain their independence in the face of growing Russian and Chinese territorial designs. The Kazakhs, for example, were divided into a Great Horde, a Middle Horde, and a Small Horde, and even when threatened with foreign conquest and rule they could not forge an alliance, thus facilitating their adversaries' efforts to subjugate them.[30] Disunity similarly paralyzed the Kazakh, Kirghiz, and other nomadic groups in modern Xinjiang and made them relatively easy prey for the Ch'ing armies.

The early twentieth century witnessed the same recurring difficulties for Central Asia. Though a major revolt against Russian and Soviet rule erupted in the early 1920s, the inability of the largely Muslim peoples of Central Asia to rally around a single leader dissipated their strength and led, in part, to their defeat. The Soviets professed eagerness to help preserve the distinctive cultures of these ethnic minorities and established a republic for each of the principal Central Asian groups, the Uzbeks, the Kazakhs, the Turkmens, the Kirghiz, and the Tajik.

Neither the Chinese Revolution of 1911 nor the Russian Revolution of 1917 permitted Central Asia to surmount this critical and debilitating problem. The volatility of Soviet history in the twentieth century inevitably led to instability and irregularity in Central Asian leadership. The purges of the 1930s resulted in the liquidation of many in the elite of Central Asia who were branded as anti-Soviet. The excesses of the last years of Joseph Stalin, the rise and subsequent fall of Khrushchev, and the continual shifts in leadership since then had Central

Asian reverberations in the unpredictable removal and replacement of both Russian and native officials. A stable system of succession to power remained elusive.

The liberalization of the mid-1980s did not bring about unity in Central Asia nor has it lessened tensions among the various ethnic groups in the region. Reports of conflict and in some cases battles amoung these groups persist and undermine confidence in their ability to overcome differences and unite. Their common Turkic cultural heritage (save for the Persian orientation of the Tajiks), their closely related languages, and their common belief in Islam offer some hope for more concerted goals and actions. However, their historical inability to unite should be borne in mind.

The Central Asian peoples of Xinjiang have met with a similar fate. From 1911, the year of the overthrow of the Ch'ing dynasty, to 1949, when the People's Republic of China was proclaimed, they were ruled by a Chinese warlord with some economic ties to the USSR; then by a warlord with strong economic and political links with the USSR, who severed these links when Nazi Germany attacked the Soviet Union; and finally they made an abortive attempt to establish their own independent East Turkestani Republic.[31] When the Chinese Communists gained power, they too repeatedly declared their desire to ensure and guarantee the rights of the national minorities and organized the Xinjiang Uighur Autonomous Region and Ili Kazakh Autonomous *Chou,* with pledges of autonomy, as symbols of their determination. Yet their policies often diverged from their expressed objectives. During the years 1958 to 1962 and 1966 to 1976 in particular they restricted the practice of Islam, encouraged Chinese colonization of the so-called national minority territories, compelled the nomadic Kazakh and Kirghiz pastoralists to abandon their migrations, de-emphasized Turkic languages, mandated the use of Chinese in the schools and in the media, and selected the vast majority of the political, Communist Party, educational, and economic leadership in the Central Asian regime from the Chinese, not the indigenous, mostly Turkic, peoples. These policies are remarkably reminiscent of Soviet policies in the Central Asian republics.[32]

Steady though not continuous liberalization in China since 1976 has afforded minorities the opportunity to assert their historical and cultural legacies and to carry out the obligations of the Islamic religion (including, for a limited few, the opportunity to undertake a pilgrimage to Mecca). Some of the Turkic inhabitants have crossed into Soviet Central Asia to meet with friends and relatives, and each of the various Turkic groups is experiencing a renewed sense of ethnic identity. Evidence for an extended period of unity among all these groups is still lacking, and again the patterns of their history argue for difficulties in achieving this.

This same scenario of internal disunion and conflict has recurred throughout the modern history of the Mongols themselves. The twentieth century has witnessed a continuation of disunity, though the nationalism sweeping across Asia seems to be affecting the Mongols as well. Mongols have been dispersed under different political authorities and although they come under centralized governments, they themselves have not served as the leaders of these governments. The Mongols of Inner Mongolia have generally remained under Chinese jurisdiction, and at present the Mongols are a decided minority within the Inner Mongolian Autonomous Region, because Chinese governments throughout the twentieth century have encouraged Chinese colonization of the area. The influx of Chinese has on occasion resulted in conflict, though intermarriage and accommodation are proceeding apace. Tensions subsided around 1976 with the onset of less repressive Chinese policies and greater toleration of the Mongols. Yet the prevailing patterns appear to indicate growing sinicization and less identification with the Mongol heritage.[33]

The Mongols in the Mongolian People's Republic, who still constitute the vast majority in the country, have progressed toward unity in the twentieth century, but only under an authoritarian regime. The Mongol government, under pressure from the Soviet Union, reviled part of the traditional Mongol heritage, including the Lama Buddhism that had played such a prominent religious, political, and economic role since the seventeenth century, and in particular portrayed the national hero Chinggis Khan in a negative light. It also sought to curtail the migrations of nomadic pastoralists and to compel the Mongols to convert from their Uighur script to Cyrillic for their written language. The Mongol economy was integrated into and made dependent on the Soviet economy, and political policies in the USSR were, in short order, also implemented in Mongolia.[34]

The changes initiated in the mid-1980s in the USSR have influenced the Mongolian People's Republic and may invigorate the traditionally faltering Mongol nationalism. First increased liberalization and then the demise of the Soviet Union has resulted in the reduction of Russian/Soviet dominance and presence. In the late 1980s, Soviet troops started to withdraw, and the Mongols have begun to seek trading partners outside of the Soviet bloc. Decades of Soviet influence have, moreover, inspired much anti-Russian feeling and have stirred Mongol nationalism which may in part be based on hostility toward Russians. The Mongols have thus set about reversing Soviet policies, encouraging a cult of Chinggis Khan, thus rehabilitating that heroic figure, and reverting to the older and more revered Uighur script. Mongols with a more pragmatic bent and less beholden to Marxist-Leninist doctrine have taken charge of the government, and preliminary indications are that nationalism is overcoming the traditional, fragmenting loyalties of tribal, regional, and on occasion, dialect affiliations. Stirrings of interest in unity with Mongols living in other regions (e.g. Inner Mongolia, Xinjiang, Buriat SSR) have also been observed. It remains to be seen, however, whether nationalism and centralization, which have most often eluded the Mongols in the past, will prevail and be sustained.

Mongols in other lands have generally been outnumbered by the native peoples, and expressions of nationalism in the twentieth century have been frowned upon, if not repressed or made impracticable. The Mongols in Xinjiang and other northern Chinese provinces, who amounted to about half a million people as of June 1982, are decidedly a minority.[35] Similarly, the Buriat Mongols, who had their own so-called autonomous republic in the USSR, were, until recently, not generally permitted overt expressions of nationalist feelings. It is too soon to tell whether recent events will encourage the Buriats to more explicit affirmations of Mongol nationalism.

Use of Religion

Another characteristic of traditional Mongol history is the tendency to use religion to foster unity. Shamanism, which was ideally suited to the tribal stage of Mongol development, was inadequate when the thirteenth-century Mongols tried to govern the sedentary domains they had recently subjugated. This traditional religion could not be discarded but rather needed to be integrated into a wider world view and system of values. Khubilai Khan (1215–1294) was one of the first of the Mongols consciously to use religion for political purposes.[36] He cultivated and patronized dignitaries representing a great variety of religions and conveyed the impression to each of these men that he favored their specific belief and values. The Altan Khan (1507–82), however, was the first Mongol leader with the explicit objective of using religion to unify the various Mongol peoples under his jurisdiction. He converted to Tibetan Buddhism and initiated efforts to convert all the Mongols. Nonetheless, the eventual conversion of the Mongols did not translate into political unity. Indeed some scholars have asserted that the growing economic and political power and the attendant corruption of the Buddhist monasteries weakened the secular political leadership in the eighteenth and nineteenth centuries.[37] Nor did monasteries serve to rally the Mongols to resist the encroachment of China and Russia during the same time. It was only in the twentieth century that the Buddhists organized against outside influence, and ardently if ineffectually tried to stave off the profoundly secular and anti-religious doctrines espoused by the Communists. Their corruption and exploitation had alienated much of the Mongol populace, and their efforts to mount a campaign of resistance were thus futile.

If Marxism-Leninism is perceived as a secular religion, the Communists may be described as continuing the practice of employing a "religion," to bind the diverse Mongol and Turkic peoples. The recent disillusionment with Communist doctrine and policy, expressed by some Mongols as well as Central Asians, indicates that the effort has not been crowned with success. Thus Communism has failed to provide a unifying and generally accepted world view for both the Mongols and Turks living in Inner Mongolia under Chinese Communist jurisdiction, and those who live in the Mongolian People's Republic.

As a crossroads, Central Asia has harbored a variety of religions over the ages. Even during the Mongol occupation, it was inhabited by Buddhists, Muslims, Zoroastrians, and Nestorian Christians among others. Its Mongol rulers converted to Islam in the 13th century. Tamerlane tried to use Islam as a political force; his devotion to Islam may have served to justify his conquests[38] but it did not serve to preserve the unity of his domains after his death. Once he died, Muslim fought against Muslim in the later Timurid period, and such conflict within the Islamic world persisted in the seventeenth and eighteenth centuries in Eastern Central Asia with the struggles between different Sufi factions, the Black Mountain Khojas and the White Mountain Khojas. In Western Central Asia, Islam often divided rather than unified the three principal khanates of the seventeenth to nineteenth centuries.

After Central Asia fell under Chinese and Russian occupation in the nineteenth century, Islam, on occasion, did offer an ideology for resistance. Muslim religious figures were often the leaders of revolts against the Ch'ing dynasty, and the Khojas played a significant role in such anti-government activities. It is unclear whether these rebellions signified positive affirmation of Islam or simply reactions to foreign rule. Since 1949, there have been sporadic assertions of Islam (worship at mosques, abstention from pork, observance of Ramadan, etc.), but the anti-religious message has probably made some inroads. Even the limited practice of Islam, however, does not appear to have forged unity. The Russian-governed territories in Central Asia had remarkably similar experiences. Anti-Tsarist disturbances often were motivated or inspired by Islamic leaders, but these incidents principally represented anti-Russian sentiments—not necessarily a resurgence of Muslim religious identity. The anti-religious propaganda and policies of the USSR, on occasion, provoked unrest in the Central Asian republics, but the Islamic religion has not brought about unity or concerted action among the diverse Central Asian Muslims. It is difficult to tell whether Islam will serve in the future as an ideology that will link and promote joint action by the Muslims in the USSR, but the historical record suggests that there will be obstacles to such efforts.

Commerce

Commerce was crucial for the Mongols and Central Asians and often shaped their relations with their neighbors. The Mongols in traditional times needed trade with nearby sedentary peoples, as they were not economically self-sufficient. Their constant migrations did not permit maintenance of a surplus of goods as insurance against the numerous natural disasters which threatened their economy. A drought, severe winter, or a disease that killed many of their animals would endanger a tribe or confederation. In addition, nomadism prevented them from producing the manufactured articles they required, and they needed to obtain these from the sedentary civilization. Their fragile economy made them dependent on the more settled populations.

The Mongols' desire for trade repeatedly provoked tensions and hostilities with their closest sedentary neighbors, the Chinese. Restrictions on commerce imposed by the dynasty that ruled North China in the twelfth century may have been a factor leading to Chinggis Khan's initial assaults to the south, and later nomad attacks had similar motivation.

Once the Mongols had lost their power and mobility, their dependence on trade became a serious liability and what had been a danger to the Chinese now threatened the Mongols. When the Ch'ing dynasty occupied Mongolia in the late seventeenth and early eighteenth centuries, Chinese merchants capitalized on the Mongols' need for outside products in order to exploit them. The Mongols were forced to buy on credit, a practice that placed them in the hands of unscrupulous Chinese moneylenders. The Ch'ing government "limited" the interest on loans to three percent a month, but the Chinese illegally charged even higher rates. Since the Mongols were often unable to repay the interest, they found themselves perpetually in debt. To add insult to injury, the Chinese merchants brought the cheapest and worst goods from China and sold them in Mongolia at prices normally reserved for higher-quality merchandise.[39] In short, the Chinese impoverished the Mongols and retarded the development of the Mongol economy.

The onset of the twentieth century has witnessed similar exploitation of the Mongols' lack of self-sufficiency. After 1947, the Chinese Communists mandated the economic integration of Inner Mongolia to the rest of China. One of the rationales for encouraging Chinese colonization was that Chinese expertise was needed to promote the economy, though the Chinese government naturally gained greater leverage and control over this region. With the introduction of outside techniques of pastoralism and of greater sophistication in veterinary medicine, the Mongols became ever more dependent on Chinese technology and expertise. Extraction of mineral resources and industrial development linked Inner Mongolia ever more closely to China. Economic liberalization since the late 1970s has not halted the growing economic and commercial links between Inner Mongolia and the rest of China.

Similarly, the Mongolian People's Republic's need for imported products has created a dependent economy. The Russians ensured that the Mongols secured most of their foods from the USSR, thus guaranteeing that the Mongolian People's Republic virtually would become an economic colony. With growing urbanization and industrialization, the Mongols became ever more dependent on goods from the Soviet Union and Eastern Europe and thus had an unfavorable balance of trade.

Central Asia has not had the same pressing need for trade in order to survive. In traditional times, a self-sufficient agriculture and trade with pastoral nomads who lived in the neighboring valleys and mountains enabled the oases and the surrounding lands to sustain an adequate existence. Yet long-distance commerce contributed enormously to the prosperity of Central Asian towns. Kashgar,

Samarkand, and Bukhara, for example, flourished due to their vital locations along the major trade routes. Many of the residents—owners of hostelries, local merchants, and camel and horse grooms—depended upon revenue from the caravan trade across Eurasia.

The relatively peaceful conditions resulting from Mongol domination of much of Eurasia fostered a revival of commerce and led to the first direct contacts between Europe and East Asia as merchants and caravans crisscrossed Eurasia. Tamerlane and his descendants persisted in the policy of encouraging trade, and as a result envoys and merchants from as far away as western Europe and China reached the Timurid capitals of Samarkand and Herat. The prosperity of many Central Asian oases and towns continued unabated until the middle and late sixteenth century when political turbulence in China, Persia, and Eastern Central Asia, the discovery of the sea route from Europe to East Asia, and conflicts between the new peoples of Persia and the Sunnis of Turkey and Central Asia combined to reduce Eurasian land trade.[40] Commerce between Russia, China, and Central Asia continued through the eighteenth and nineteenth centuries, but as the Tsarist and Ch'ing courts began to encroach on the region, profits accrued more and more to Russian and Chinese merchants, who took advantage of these regions in the same way that Chinese merchants were exploiting the Mongols.

Russian and Chinese incorporation of Central Asia in the nineteenth and twentieth centuries initiated policies designed to make the predominantly Muslim population in these regions economically more dependent. The Russians compelled parts of Central Asia to convert from self-sufficient agriculture to widespread cultivation of cotton, which was meant for consumption in other regions in Russia and in foreign lands.[41] As a result, Central Asia's economy and commerce became inextricably linked with Russia, and policy decisions in St. Petersburg and Moscow have shaped the development of Central Asia ever since.[42]

Since 1949, China has made dramatic efforts to link Xinjiang to its core territories. The region has been made dependent for necessities on the rest of China, and Chinese colonists have moved there and have been accorded dominant positions in the economy.[43] Growing economic flexibility in the 1980s, however, has permitted trade with Soviet Central Asia, somewhat reducing dependence on China. Nevertheless, the region's most significant trading partner remains China, and as in traditional times, this part of Central Asia requires trade for its survival.

Foreign Assistance

A need for assistance from foreigners has characterized the Mongols in both medieval and modern times. Having no experience in administering a sedentary civilization, the thirteenth-century Mongols lacked the skills to govern China,

Persia, Russia, and the other territories they had subjugated. They turned first for assistance to the Uighurs and other Turks whose language and societies most closely resembled their own. These Turks served as interpreters, tutors, and officials in local and central governments.[44] Later the Mongols employed defectors from the major civilizations as officials in the governments they established. Central Asian Muslims, Chinese Confucians, Tibetan Buddhists and European Christians, for example, assumed official positions in China under the Mongol Yüan dynasty. Chinese defectors were also vital in later Mongol attempts at unification and expansion.[45] Some Mongol traditionalists opposed such cooperation with representatives of the sedentary civilizations because of fears of the strong influence and growing power of these subjects, which could be a step in the sinicization of the Mongols. This opposition on occasion led to internecine conflicts among the Mongols, which weakened them considerably. Manchus, Chinese, and Russians have often either dominated or played vital roles in Mongolia since the late seventeenth century. Manchu officials, often with Chinese assistance and officials, supervised, guided, or ruled the various Mongol khanates through much of the Ch'ing dynasty. In the Mongolian People's Republic, the Russians have been the principal foreign experts and advisers in the twentieth century. Russian troops have been stationed there throughout much of the history of the second Communist state ever to be established. Russian political, economic, and technical experts often shaped policies, programs, and development over the past seventy years. The sudden recall of these specialists in the late 1980s deprived the Mongolian People's Republic of certain invaluable skills, and its economy will surely face severe problems in this period of transition. Moreover, as in traditional times, the Mongols will need foreign assistance in the training of political, economic, and technical experts to foster economic development and political change.

Traditional Central Asia also required and made use of foreign expertise. After Tamerlane conquered Persia, for example, he used Persian bureaucrats to help him rule their land.[46] The Timurid and Uzbek dynasties also patronized Persian art, literature, and historical writing.

There is, however, a critical difference between pre-modern and modern times in the need for foreign expertise. Up to the late seventeenth century, the Mongols and Central Asian peoples recruited foreigners with specific administrative, literary, technical, and economic skills, and some of these recruits were natives of the regions that they had subjugated. They themselves sought to attract or compel foreigners to work for them. However, as was the case with trade, Mongol dependence on outsiders proved a liability later. Once the Russians and the Chinese became dominant in Mongolia and Central Asia after the seventeenth century, foreigners imposed themselves on the Mongols and Central Asians who had no choice but to accept them.

When the Tsarist and Manchu courts occupied Central Asia in the eighteenth and nineteenth centuries, Russian, Chinese, and Manchu governors, merchants, and entrepreneurs began to dominate the native inhabitants and to introduce changes in the economy. Such changes were naturally designed to benefit Russia and China, but a few of these new techniques or institutions also profited the region. New towns were constructed, old ones grew, and trade increased.

Russia and China have continued to dominate Central Asia in the twentieth century, and the Russians and Chinese have tried to make themselves indispensable to the region. Russian soldiers, engineers, Communist Party leaders, and laborers have moved into Central Asia and have served in key positions in the economy. The arrival of the Russians did contribute to economic and technological advances, but the Russians also achieved a commanding position in the republics. The Soviet pledge of and the Central Asian demand for greater autonomy in the late 1980s generated replacements of some Russians by local peoples, but non-indigenous expertise will still be required for the region's economic development in the foreseeable future.

In Xinjiang, Chinese military men, government officials, and specialists in science and technology have also assumed vital positions. Their political and economic dominance in Xinjiang since the founding of the People's Republic of China has given rise to resentment. Although Chinese expertise also has contributed to economic advances in the region,[47] at the same time it has limited the opportunities for the native, mostly Muslim, inhabitants. At the conclusion of the Cultural Revolution, the government pledged to provide more opportunities for the Turkic residents. As in Soviet Central Asia, however, it seems likely that the services of non-Turkic peoples will still be needed to promote economic development and modernization for the foreseeable future.

Conclusion

It is too soon to tell whether the patterns that have characterized the policies and practices of the Mongols and Central Asians will, perhaps in a modified form, continue to prevail in a future that appears to offer the prospects of remarkable, perhaps revolutionary, changes. Will the unity that has proved elusive in the past be within their grasp? Will orderly and regular transitions of leadership be possible? Will the inhabitants be able to withstand outside pressure for assimilation? Will an appreciation of and a stronger link to their history, culture, and religions provide the unity that they have found difficult to forge?

The future of the Mongols and the Central Asians may differ. This essay has emphasized the many characteristics they share, but there are significant distinctions, one of which is numerical. The Central Asians constitute a much larger percentage of population in the former USSR and China than the Mongols do, and their birth rates are strikingly high. The principal religion in Central Asia is Islam while Buddhism has dominated among the Mongols. At present Islam has stronger links with politics than Buddhism does, and Islam plays a more important role in Central Asia than Buddhism does in Mongolia.

Since Islam is the fastest growing religion in the world, China will need to take it into account in formulating policies toward Xinjiang. Another difference that will surely affect perceptions and policies is that Central Asia has traditionally had a much larger sedentary population than does Mongolia. China may face greater difficulties in dealing with larger concentrations of minorities who traditionally had more developed administrations and thus had more expertise than the Mongol, mostly scattered, pastoralists.

Notes

1. V. V. Barthold, *Four Studies on the History of Central Asia* (trans. by V. and T. Minorsky; Leiden, 1962), 1:110–113; Thomas Allsen, "The Yüan Dynasty and the Uighurs of Turfan in the 13th Century" in Morris Rossabi, ed. *China Among Equals* (Berkeley, 1983), 246–248.

2. Igor de Rachewiltz, "Turks in China under the Mongols: A Preliminary Investigation of Turco-Mongol Relations in the 13th and 14th Centuries," in Rossabi, ed., 282–287; on the Uighurs, see also A. von Gabain, *Das Leben im uigurischen Königreich von Qoco (850–1250)*, 2 vols. (Wiesbaden, 1973); Abe Takeo, *Nishi Uiguru kokushi no kenkyū* (Kyoto, 1955); James Hamilton, *Les Ouighours à l'époque des Cinq Dynasties d'aprés les documents chinois* (Paris, 1955); and Paul Pelliot, *Notes on Marco Polo* (Paris, 1959), 1:161–165.

3. On the Önggöds, see Paul Pelliot, *Recherches sur les Chrétiens d'Asie centrale et d'êxtreme orient* (ed. by Jean Dauvillier and Louis Hambis, Paris, 1973), 261–267; Jean Dauvillier, "Les provinces chaldéennes de l'extérieur' au moyen age"' in Mélanges F. Cavallera (Toulouse, 1948), 303–305; and Morris Rossabi, *Voyager from Xanadu* (New York, 1992).

4. On the Mongols' postal service, see Peter Olbricht, *Das Postwesen in China unter der Mongolenherrschaft im 13. und 14. Jahrhundert* (Wiesbaden, 1954); Haneda Tōru, *Genchō ekiden zakko* (Tokyo, 1930); A.C. Moule and Paul Pelliot, *Marco Polo: The Description of the World* (London, 1938) 1:242–247.

5. Some trade with the Uighurs persisted through the northern Sung era, but it certainly did not approach the number and size of caravans of the Mongol era. For the Uighur trade with the Sung, see Shiba Yoshinobu, "Sung Foreign Trade: Its Scope and Organization" in Rossabi, ed., 94–97.

6. See Morris Rossabi, "Ming China and Turfan, 1406–1517" *Central Asiatic Journal* 16:206–225; Matsumara Jun, "Minshi Saiiki-den Uten-ko," *Tōyō gakuhō* 37:4 (March, 1955), 78–103; Japanese scholars have made invaluable contributions to the study of Central Asia in Yüan and Ming times. A recent valuable listing of these studies is in *Bibliography of Central Asian Studies in Japan, 1879–March 1987* (Tokyo, 1989) and *Bibliography of Central Asian Studies in Japan, 1879–March 1987: Index and Errata* (Toyko, 1989).

7. W. Barthhold, *Turkestan down to the Mongol Invasion* (trans., T. Minorsky; London, 1968), 394–399.

8. David Morgan, *The Mongols* (London, 1986), 68.

9. John A. Boyle, trans., ('Ata malik Juvaini) *The History of the World Conqueror*, 2 vols. (Manchester, 1958), 1:95–128.

10. *Ibid.,* 106–107.

11. On a group of Central Asians who were moved eastward, see Paul Pelliot, "Une ville musulmane dans la Chine du nord sous les mongols," *Journal asiatique* 211 (1927), 261–279.

12. Arthur Waley, trans., *The Travels of an Alchemist* (London, 1931), 97, 106; a similar perception is found in Igor de Rachewiltz.

13. Barthold, *Four Studies . . . ,* 1:43.

14. Paul Buell. "Sino-Khitan Administration in Mongol Bukhara," *Journal of Asian history* 13:2 (1979), 134–139.

15. See Hsiao Ch'i-ch'ing, *Hsi-yü-jen yü Yüan-ch'u cheng-chih* (Taipei, 1966).

16. Sayyid Ajall Shams al-Din was appointed governor of the newly-conquered state of Ta-li and was largely responsible for sinicizing it and facilitating its entrance into China as the province of Yunnan. He "promoted the use of Chinese marital and funeral ceremonies, built Confucian schools, and made available copies of the Confucian classics." Morris Rossabi, "The Muslims in the Early Yüan Dynasty" in John Langlois, ed., *China under Mongol Rule* (Princeton, 1981), 290; see also Jacqueline Armijo-Hussein, "The Sinicization and Confucianization of a Muslim from Bukhara Serving under the Mongols in China" in *The Legacy of Islam in China* (Cambridge, 1989), 33–61 for a slightly different (though perhaps only semantically so) interpretation of the Sayyid's work in Yunnan.

17. See Elizabeth Endicott-West, "The Merchant Associations in Yüan China: The Ortogh," *Asia Major,* 3rd ser. 2:2 (1989); 127–154 for one view of these *ortogh.*

18. See Igor de Rachewiltz, "Yeh-lü Ch'u-ts'ai (1189–1243): Buddhist Idealist and Confucian Statesman," in Arthur Wright and Denis Twitchett, eds., *Confucian Personalities* (Stanford, 1962), 201–207 for the efforts of one Khitanese official to persuade the Mongols to adopt such a policy.

19. Barthold 1:50.

20. Beatrice Forbes Manz, *The Rise and Rule of Tamerlane* (Cambridge, 1989), 2–9.

21. Manz, p. 14.

22. Manz, p. 15.

23. This section is based on Morris Rossabi, "Ch'ing Conquest of Inner Asia" in D. Twitchett, ed., *Cambridge History of China: Early Ch'ing* (Cambridge, forthcoming). A listing of East Asian and Western sources on Galdan may be found in that work.

24. Joseph Fletcher, "The Mongols: Ecological and Social Perspectives," *Harvard Journal of Asiatic Studies* 46:1 (June, 1986), 14.

25. For the difficulties involved in maintaining unity, see Beatrice F. Manz, "Administration and the Delegation of Authority in Temür's Dominions," *Central Asiatic Journal* 20:3 (1976), 206–207 and Maria Eva Subtelny, "Centralizing Reform and its Opponents in the Late Timurid Period," *Iranian Studies* 21;1–2 (1988), 123–151.

26. Thomas J. Barfield, *The Perilous Frontier: Nomadic Empires and China* (Cambridge, Mass., 1989), 206–210, discusses the question of succession in greater detail.

27. On the Uzbeks, see the recently published work by Edward Allworth, *The Modern Uzbeks* (Stanford, 1990).

28. See Richard Pierce, *Russian Central Asia: A Study in Colonial Rule* (Berkeley, 1960) and Seymour Becker, *Russia's Protectorates in Central Asia: Bukhara and Khiva, 1865–1924* (Cambridge, Mass., 1968).

29. Joseph Fletcher, "The heyday of the Ch'ing order in Mongolia, Xinjiang and Tibet" in John K. Fairbank, ed., *The Cambridge History of China: Late Ch'ing, 1800–1911, Part I* (Cambridge, 1978), 361–375.

30. Martha Brill Olcott, *The Kazakhs* (Stanford, 1987), 28–53.

31. Andrew Forbes, *Warlords and Muslims in Chinese Central Asia* (Cambridge, 1986), pp. 11–37; 116–121; Linda Benson, *The Ili Rebellion: The Moslem Challenge to Chinese Authority in Xinjiang, 1944–1949* (Armonk, 1990), 42–66.

32. Morris Rossabi, "Islam in China" in M. Eliade, ed., *The Encyclopedia of Religion* (New York, 1987), 7:387–390.

33. Ma Rong, "Han-Mongolian intermarriage patterns in Rural Chifeng, Inner Mongolia," Paper prepared for Columbia University Seminar on Modern China (December, 1990).

34. The literature on twentieth-century Mongolia includes Charles Bawden, *The Modern History of Mongolia* (London, 1968); George G.S. Murphy, *Soviet Mongolia* (Berkeley, 1966); William A. Brown and Urgunge Onon, trans., *History of the Mongolian People's Republic* (Cambridge, MA, 1976), an official Mongol version of twentieth-century Mongol history; Robert A. Rupen, *Mongols of the Twentieth Century* (Bloomington, 1966); A.J.K. Sanders, *The People's Republic of Mongolia: A General Reference Guide* (London, 1968 and later editions); Academy of Sciences, MPR, *Information Mongolia* (Oxford, 1990); and the reportorial book by Owen Lattimore, *Nomads and Commissars: Mongolia Revisited* (New York, 1962). On the most recent event, see Alicia Campi, "The Rise of Nationalism in the Mongolian Peoples Republic as Reflected in Language Reform, Religion, and the Cult of Chinggis Khan," *Central and Inner Asian Studies* 6 (1992), 46–58.

35. Henry G. Schwarz, *The Minorities of Northern China: A Survey* (Bellingham, 1984), v.

36. Morris Rossabi, *Khubilai Khan: His Life and Times* (Berkeley, 1988), 141–147.

37. Larry Moses, *The Political Role of Mongol Buddhism* (Bloomington, 1977), 121.

38. Manz, *Tamerlane*, p. 17.

39. Sanjdorj, *Manchu Chinese Colonial Rule in Northern Mongolia* (Translation by Ungunge Onon), (New York: St. Martin's Press, 1980) p. 89.

40. Other reasons are given in Morris Rossabi, "The 'decline' of the Central Asian caravan trade" in James D. Tracy, *The Rise of Merchant Empires* (Cambridge, 1990), 351–370.

41. Becker, 183.

42. Bill Keller, "Developers Turn Aral Sea into a Catastrophe," *New York Times* (December 20, 1988), C1, C6.

43. June T. Dreyer, "The Xinjiang Uighur Autonomous Region at Thirty: A Report Card," *Asian Survey* 26:7 (July, 1986), 721–744.

44. De Rachewiltz, "Turks . . . ," 281–295.

45. Henry Serruys, "Chinese in Southern Mongolia during the Sixteenth Century," *Monumenta Serica* 18 (1959), 1–95.

46. Manz, *Tamerlane,* 108–111.

47. Dreyer, *China's Forty Millions,* (Cambridge: Harvard University Press, 1976) p. 276.

CHAPTER 2

The Symbiosis of Turk and Tajik

Maria Eva Subtelny

Just as there is no cap without a head,
there is no Turk without an Iranian.

—Old Turkic proverb

One of the most hotly debated issues today in the ethnic and cultural politics of the Central Asian republics of the former Soviet Union is the thorny and sensitive problem of the historical origins of its constituent nationalities. This problem, which first became acute during the period of *glasnost'*, is at the root of various ethnic and national disputes which are expressed chiefly in terms of conflicting claims to a given territory and even to a cultural heritage. The highly publicized clashes between the Turkic Muslim Azeris and the Christian Armenians over rights to the region of Karabagh in Azerbaijan is but one example in the Caucasus region. In Central Asia proper, the most striking example of national-territorial conflicts is that between two Muslim nationalities—the Uzbeks and Tajiks, the titular nationalities of the republics of Uzbekistan and Tajikistan, who today represent the largest Turkic-speaking and Iranian-speaking groups, respectively, in Central Asia.[1]

The aim of this chapter is to describe the historical background of the ongoing Uzbek-Tajik conflict which is the product, on the one hand, of the millennium-long relationship between Turkic and Iranian peoples in Central Asia and, on the other, of Soviet nationalities policies during this century. Firstly, it will examine the nature of the historical relationship between Turkic and Iranian peoples in Central Asia in terms of the relationship between nomadic and sedentary societies, and it will discuss the impact of this relationship on the ethnolinguistic and ethnogenetic development of Uzbeks and Tajiks. Secondly, it will review the role of Soviet nationalities policies in the formation of the modern Uzbek and Tajik peoples and analyze Soviet interpretations of their ethnogenesis (*étnogenez*) and nation formation (*narodoobrazovanie*). Finally it will consider the degree to which these interpretations are still accepted by Uzbeks and Tajiks today.

The Historical Relationship Between Nomad and Sedentary

A central theme in the medieval history of Central Asia was the relationship between two diametrically opposed cultures and modes of life—the sedentary and the pastoral nomadic.[2] This relationship has been characterized most frequently as one of mutual hostility, with the sedentary agriculturalist or urban dweller bearing the brunt of periodic nomadic incursions from the steppe, that often ended in the conquest, forcible domination, and even destruction of centers of sedentary civilization by nomadic cavalry forces led by military elites. The reasons for these incursions are to be found in the ecology of pastoral nomadism and in the politics of trade with sedentary societies, and they resulted from the formation of tribal confederations and the creation of nomadic empires.[3]

There is, however, another aspect of this relationship between nomad and sedentary that, although less dramatic and more mundane than the one just described, more accurately reflects its true character over the long continuum. Inasmuch as the difference between nomad and sedentary was based not just on mode of life, but also on mode of production (which Fredrik Barth has explained as an economic regime plus its associated context of social organization),[4] the two entered into close mutual contact through the exchange of products of their respective regimes of production. The main point of exchange and mutual interaction was always the town.[5] In return for finished goods and agricultural produce, nomads provided the town with the products of the animals they herded, including meat, milk, wool, and skins. The relationship between them may thus be characterized as symbiotic, since symbiosis refers to the intimate coexistence of two dissimilar organisms (in nature), or persons or groups (in society) in a situation of ecological interdependence or mutual benefit.[6]

Because few forms of nomadism are autarkic, and because nomads have always had an aversion to specialization, it is they who were more dependent on sedentary civilizations for the exchange of the products of their regime of production, and especially for specialized services and luxury goods.[7] On account of its peculiar geography, this applied particularly to Central Asia, because the regions where pastoral nomadism predominated not only bordered settled regions (to the north and west, that is, the Kipchak Steppe), but also alternated with them, especially in the southwest, or Central Asia proper, where agriculture and pastoral nomadism were never in competition with each other.[8] In Central Asia, therefore, the economic ties between the agricultural oases and regions of pastoral nomadism were always very close, with a very well developed exchange—so close, in fact, that the pastoral nomadic and sedentary agrarian sectors became integrated into one economic complex or, as Joseph Fletcher put it, one "nomadic-sedentary continuum."[9] The Soviet archaeologist, Boris Litvinskiĭ, who argued for a "three-component system" made up of the nomadic steppes, the agrarian oases, and the urban organism, which he regarded as an independent element, demonstrated that this complex has remained in force in Central Asia for two and a half millennia, right up to the present day.[10]

From Symbiosis to Sedentarization

But the symbiosis of pastoral nomad and sedentary did not necessarily engender mutual love and respect. It was supported by an inherent tension between the two. The peasant or townsman viewed the nomad with fear and suspicion because of the nomad's military potential—he did, after all, have an excellent track record of conquest and domination. At the same time, he held the nomad in contempt on account of his lack of knowledge and appreciation for urban civilization. For his part, the nomad viewed the sedentary with the same mixture of fear and contempt, regarding him as cowardly and disloyal, but at the same time viscerally fearing the loss of independence should he get too close to him and adopt his lifestyle.[11]

Nor did the symbiotic relationship between nomad and sedentary affect both parties in the same way. Rarely did it entail a change of lifestyle for the sedentary, and it generally had little impact on his culture and social organization. The reverse was true, however, for the nomad. Nomads were inexorably drawn into the *Kulturkreis* of sedentary civilization, and despite their initial reluctance, started to participate in it. In doing so they gradually made the transition to semi-nomadic pastoralism and finally to complete sedentarization. Hand in hand with sedentarization went acculturation to the sedentary religio-cultural complex and often, although by no means always, assimilation. The progression from mutual contact to symbiosis to acculturation and even assimilation that accompanied the nomads' transition to sedentarism, was therefore not the result of a conscious choice on their part, but rather, it was the inevitable consequence of their symbiotic relationship with sedentary populations.[12] In V. V. Bartol'd's opinion, Central Asia provided an especially poignant example of the inevitability of this process:

> To a greater degree than the history of other countries, the history of Central Asia provides material for the study of one of the most interesting questions of ethnography and cultural history, namely, the question of the gradual submission of nomadic conquerors to the influence of the population of the civilized regions subjugated by them.[13]

Ethnolinguistic Implications of the Nomad-Sedentary Relationship

As far back as it is possible to research the history of Central Asia, its indigenous sedentary population was Iranian, that is, peoples speaking Iranian (more precisely, eastern Iranian) languages. From the sixth century B.C. to approximately the eleventh century A.D., they were represented chiefly by Soghdians and Khorezmians. After the Turkic peoples entered the political arena in Central Asia in the tenth century A.D., a pattern was established whereby successive waves of nomadic Turkic and Turco-Mongolian conquerors from the steppe dominated the political history of Central Asia almost without exception until the nineteenth century.[14] At the same time, successive waves of nomads entered into a symbiotic relationship with the indigenous Iranian population, gradually made the transition to sedentarism, and became acculturated to Perso-Islamic civilization, which remained the dominant religio-cultural force in Central Asia until the beginning of the twentieth century.[15]

Turk vs. Tat

The symbiotic relationship between nomad and sedentary in medieval Central Asia was epitomized by an Old Turkic proverb recorded in the eleventh century by Mahmud Kashghari in his "Compendium of the Turkic Dialects" (*Divan lughat al-turk*), a rich source for the ethnographic and cultural history of the early Turks: "Just as there is no cap without a head, there is no Turk without a Tat (Iranian)(*tatsiz türk bolmas bashsiz börk bolmas*)."[16] Essentially, the proverb meant that, for the Turkic pastoral nomad, life without the sedentary Iranian was as unthinkable as the independent existence of a *börk* cap (felt or fur headgear worn by the nomads) without a head to wear it on. It therefore not only affirmed the symbiotic relationship between the Turkic pastoral nomad and the sedentary Iranian, but also underscored the dependence of the former on the latter.[17]

At the same time, the term Tat acquired a pejorative connotation which stemmed from the traditionally contemptuous view the nomad had of the sedentary.[18] Kashghari also records a proverb illustrative of this: "(Strike) the Tat (i.e., Iranian) on the eye, (cut) the thorn at its root," which he explains as referring to the Tat's lack of loyalty.[19] Another proverb warns the Turk against the dangers of sedentary civilization: "Just as a warrior's effectiveness suffers when his sword begins to rust, so does the flesh of a Turk begin to stink when he assumes the lifestyle of the sedentary Iranian."[20]

Turk vs. Tajik

A parallel term to the Turkic word, Tat, was the Persian word, Tazik or Tajik, which displaced it by the fifteenth century.[21] Originally the name given by Iranian speakers to Arabs after the Islamic conquest of Iran and Central Asia, its etymology going back to the Arab tribe of Tayy which had settled in Central Asia, it came to denote all sedentary Muslims. But because the sedentary Muslims with whom the Turks had closest contact were Iranian-speaking, the term was used from about the eleventh century onwards primarily for Iranians. It was also used as a self-name by Iranians when they wanted to make a distinction between themselves and their Turkic overlords.[22]

Starting from the period of Mongol domination in the thirteenth century, the term Tazik was used in historical works and official documents in the formula, "Turk and Tazik," later to be replaced by the western Iranian form, Tajik, and by the fifteenth century the phrase "Turk and Tajik" (*türk u tajik*) had become standard when referring to the entire population of a realm, both sedentary and nomadic, both Turkic and Iranian.[23] But like the term Tat, Tajik also had a pejorative connotation in Turkic usage. The worst insult that could be hurled at a Turk was that his character resembled that of a Tajik (*tajik-mizaj*), the implication being that he was cowardly and disloyal,[24] and in the famous "Genealogy of the Turks," written in the seventeenth century, we come across the statement, "A dog is worth more than a Tajik."[25]

Uzbek vs. Sart

Yet another name used by the Turks for sedentary Iranians was Sart, originally a Sanskrit word meaning merchant. When Iranian merchants took over the trade with the Turkic nomads, these naturally called them Sarts. In the thirteenth century, the Mongols used the term (in the forms *sartaul/sartakty/sartaktay*) not just for Iranian merchants, but for all sedentary Iranians, in the same sense as Tajik (i.e., sedentary Iranian Muslim).[26] The fifteenth century Chaghatay Turkish author, Mir Ali-Shir Nava'i, regularly used the term Sart when referring to the Iranian people (*sart ulusi*) and to their language (*sart tili,*) the latter as a synonym for Persian (*farsi*).[27]

When the nomadic Uzbeks came into Central Asia from the Kipchak Steppe in the late fifteenth and early sixteenth centuries, the term Uzbek gained currency alongside the older nomadic self-designation "Turk," which was now reserved for the pre-Uzbek Turkic tribes, some of whom had already made the transition to semi-sedentarism and even sedentarism. The Uzbeks, who were nomads, clearly distinguished between themselves and their sedentary subject population whom they usually referred to as Sart (also Tajik).[28] Like Tat and Tajik, it too became a derogatory term, even acquiring a contemptuous popular etymology: "yellow dog" (*sari it*).

The Problem of Mutual Influences

The close symbiotic relationship between Turkic and Iranian peoples in Central Asia not only exerted a profound influence on the political and socioeconomic history of Central Asia, but it was also decisive in shaping the linguistic and ethnic makeup of its population. The problem of mutual linguistic and ethnic influences is an extremely complex one and evidence for the period before the nineteenth century is spotty at best. What is clear, however, is that bilingualism—the result of what linguists call "language contact" situations—was widespread, and the phenomenon of "mixed language" was not uncommon. Usually, it was the minority group that became bilingual, although other factors, such as prestige, function, and setting, could also determine the dominance of one language over another.

Mahmud Kashghari recorded in the eleventh century that, in Turkish towns such as Balasagun and Talas (Taraz), the Soghdians spoke both Soghdian and Turkish and had adopted Turkish dress and manners, and although there were people who spoke only Turkish, no one spoke only Soghdian.[29] On the other hand, in fifteenth century Khorasan, south of the Oxus, which had a predominantly Iranian population, Ali-Shir Nava'i wrote that while all Turks knew the Sart (Persian) language, Sarts did not speak Turkish, and if they did, everyone could recognize they were Sarts.[30] In Central Asia, at roughly the same time, a Bavarian prisoner of war, by the name of Hans Schiltberger, wrote that the inhabitants spoke a "peculiar language" that was half-Turkish and half-Persian.[31] Ethnographic data from the early twentieth century still indicated large groups of both Turks and Tajiks to be partially or fully bilingual.[32]

Ethnic assimilation also worked both ways, depending on the particular region and circumstances. Successive waves of Turkic-speaking nomads who entered into a symbiotic relationship with the sedentary Iranian population absorbed the indigenous Iranian population or assimilated to it (especially near and in urban centers). Thus, while the region of Khorezm was totally Turkicized by Oghuz and Kipchak Turks by the thirteenth century,[33] urban centers like Bukhara remained largely Persian-speaking until the twentieth century. An example of Iranized pre-Uzbek Turkic tribes are the formerly Turkic-speaking nomadic and semi-nomadic Chaghatay. By the twentieth century, they had become not only Tajik-speaking (although a small Uzbek-speaking minority remained), but also sedentary inhabitants of the oasis towns in eastern Bukhara (where they had been pushed out by the Uzbek invasions), specializing in irrigated agriculture, especially fruit growing and viticulture.[34] In the apt phrasing of the ethnographer, Bèl'kis Karmysheva, "the peculiar economic symbiosis" which existed in the intrariverine region of Central Asia caused the process of the formation of the two peoples—Tajiks and Uzbeks—to proceed "in the closest interaction."[35]

Turkicization

Ultimately, however, the general ethnolinguistic trend was in the direction of Turkicization and in roughly a millennium the population of Central Asia was transformed from predominantly Iranian-speaking to Turkic-speaking, with the attendant ethnic changes. The balance was decisively tipped by the Uzbek invasions of the late fifteenth and early sixteenth centuries. This last great nomadic wave from the Kipchak Steppe introduced a critical mass of Turkic and Turkicized Mongolian nomads into Central Asia, a portion of whom eventually settled in the oasis towns and merged with the sedentary population.[36] At the same time, the Uzbek newcomers pushed out a segment of the Iranian as well as the older pre-Uzbek Turkic population into such regions as the Pamir mountains in present-day Tajikistan.[37]

Evidence of the degree to which the process of Uzbek sedentarization and the Turkicization of Central Asia had advanced by the nineteenth century is provided by the fact that the term Sart, which had earlier been used synonymously with Tajik to designate the sedentary Iranian population, now referred to the Turkic-speaking sedentary population which had come to constitute the majority of the urban population.[38] Khanykov, an imperial Russian official who travelled through the region in the 1840s, reported that, of the Tajiks who had been the aboriginal people, "There is but a remnant left which forms the chief population of the city of Bokhara; in other towns there are none or very few indeed."[39] Voekov, who visited the area early in this century, wrote that Iranian languages were spoken only in the district of Samarkand and in the mountains of eastern Bukhara,[40] and that the great majority of the urban and rural population was represented by Sarts who he said spoke "Turco-Tatar languages."[41] Khanykov, who used the term Uzbek rather than Sart and divided the Uzbeks into nomadic, semi-nomadic and sedentary, called them the "predominating race" in the Bukharan Khanate.[42] Bartol'd's statement that only once on all his travels did he encounter someone (in the city of Bukhara) who did not know Turkish, sums up the situation in the early Soviet period.[43]

Soviet Nationalities Policies in Central Asia

The goal of Soviet nationalities policies in Central Asia in the 1920s was to create separate national republics by means of a "national territorial delimitation" (*natsional'noe razmezhevanie*) based mainly on ethnolinguistic criteria.[44] But the problems Soviet ethnographers and Orientalists faced in implementing these policies appeared intractable.

The ethnolinguistic situation was extremely confused and complex. In some areas, such as present-day southern Uzbekistan and southern Tajikistan, Uzbeks and Tajiks had become so intermixed that it was difficult to distinguish between them.[45] There was no strong sense of ethnic or national identity and inhabitants often did not know themselves who they were ethnically, identifying themselves only by their tribal name, the name of their town ("Bukharli," etc.), or simply as "Muslim." As already discussed, the term Sart was not strictly speaking an ethnic term, since it could refer to both Uzbeks and Tajiks. Nor was there any distinct territorial identity. In medieval times, Central Asia had been known by such regional designations as Mavaraannahr, or Transoxiana ("the land beyond the Oxus, or Amu Darya river"), while in the nineteenth century it had been divided among Russian Turkestan and the Khanates of Bukhara, Khiva and Kokand. In view of the difficulties involved, the "solutions" arrived at could never have been entirely satisfactory and they eventually engendered a whole new set of problems which the era of *glasnost'* brought out in full relief.

Firstly, since it was not an ethnic designation and since it had a residual pejorative connotation, the term Sart was banned from use.[46] The designation Uzbek was substituted on the grounds that there was no separate nation called Sart that was different from the Uzbeks and no separate Sart language that was different from the Uzbek language.[47] In 1924 the Uzbek SSR was created with an autonomous Tajik republic within it, which in 1929 achieved the status of union republic. Generally speaking, the territorial delimitation favored the dominant Uzbek majority, while the Tajik minority was largely pushed out.

To satisfy the criteria of nationhood, the two new literary languages of Tajik and Uzbek were created, the latter based not on the purer vowel-harmonized Kipchak-Uzbek version of Uzbek spoken in southwestern Kazakhstan and southern Uzbekistan, but on the Iranized, unharmonized Tashkent dialect (probably the so-called Sart language), thus severing, in the opinion of Edward Allworth, another connection which linked Uzbeks to their historical, tribal past.[48] Soviet linguists denied the idea of the "cultural dominance" of one language over another and supported the Stalinist notion that every language is subject only to its own "internal laws."[49] Therefore, despite their long symbiotic relationship, there was no possibility of the "Turkicization" of Tajik or of the "Iranization" of Uzbek.[50] In an effort to deny the Turkicization of Tajik, some linguists even maintained that the original language of towns like Samarkand and Bukhara was Uzbek—Samarkand Uzbek simply having more Tajik elements, and Tashkent Uzbek more Turkic ones![51]

The Uzbek and Tajik cultural and historical heritages were also redefined, chiefly on the basis of territorial and linguistic criteria. However, since Uzbeks and Tajiks had not inhabited separate territories during their long history, but had shared the same territory and the same Islamic religio-cultural background whose chief linguistic vehicles were Arabic and Persian, the compartmentalization of individual elements from this common background into "Uzbek" and "Tajik" was bound to create confusion and overlap. Thus, while the Persian poet, Rudaki, who flourished under the tenth century Iranian Samanid dynasty which ruled in Bukhara (now an "Uzbek" city), was included in the Tajik cultural heritage, and Mir Ali-Shir Nava'i, the fifteenth century poet who wrote in the heavily Persianized eastern Turkic literary language (Chaghatay), which Soviet linguists renamed "Old Uzbek," was made the cornerstone of the Uzbek heritage, *both* Uzbeks and Tajiks both laid claim to the tenth-eleventh century philosopher, Ibn Sina (Avicenna), even though the vast majority of his works were written in Arabic—the Uzbeks on the grounds that he had been born near Bukhara in present-day Uzbekistan, and the Tajiks because he was of Iranian (probably Soghdian) origin.

Interpretations of Uzbek and Tajik Ethnogenesis

Official explanations of the ethnogenesis of the Uzbek and Tajik peoples were based first and foremost on the territories of the newly created Soviet republics.[52] In his recent book on the modern Uzbeks, Allworth has called this the search for "retrospective proof" of nationality on a given territory.[53] Secondly, these explanations were based only on the sedentary populations of those territories, since they alone had a "history" and were "cultured."[54] Nomadic elements were necessarily played down because, like the Asiatic mode of production, they had no place in the Marxist model of development.[55] This posed no problem in the explanation of Tajik ethnogenesis, since Tajiks had always been a sedentary, and therefore "historical," people. It did, however, create serious complications in the case of the Uzbeks, who had a nomadic background and who, moreover, had originated outside the territory of present-day Uzbekistan. Muhammad Shibani (Shaybani) Khan, who in the early sixteenth century led the nomadic Uzbek invasions which played a key role in the formation of the modern Uzbek people, was therefore excluded from the Uzbek historical heritage.[56]

In the official interpretation, the ancestors of the modern Uzbek nation were all the sedentary peoples who had ever inhabited the territory of the modern Uzbek SSR, and not the nomadic Turco-Mongolian tribes who came into Central Asia in the late fifteenth and early sixteenth centuries under the leadership of Shibani Khan.[57] Thus the official *Istoriia Uzbekskoĭ SSR:*

> The Uzbek ethnic group (*narodnost'*) is composed not of the fairly recently arrived nomadic "Uzbeks" of the fifteenth century Kipchak Steppe, but of the ancient inhabitants of Soghdiana, Ferghana and Khorezm. From the earliest times they led a settled life and were occupied in cultivating the soil.[58]

Uzbeks were descended therefore not from the Turco-Mongolian group, but from the same "Europoid" base as the Tajiks, since both had inhabited the same territory.[59] According to the *Istoriia Tadzhikskogo naroda* (History of the Tajik People), Uzbeks and Tajiks have the same ethnogenetic background: "The history of these two peoples may be graphically compared to two great branches emerging from the trunk of a single tree."[60] The official explanation for the difference between Uzbeks and Tajiks is that, "An insignificant percentage of elements from another—Mongoloid—race, to which Turks and Mongols belonged, was deposited on the Europoid base of the Uzbek population,"[61] while Tajiks were simply that part of the earlier population which, "to a lesser degree was subject to assimilation with Turkic tribes and preserved its language."[62]

In keeping with this interpretation, the process of both Tajik and Uzbek ethnogenesis had to be completed fairly early, during culturally significant historical periods. The Tajiks completed theirs in the ninth–tenth centuries,[63] and the Uzbeks theirs in the eleventh–twelfth centuries, well before the Uzbek invasions of the late fifteenth and early sixteenth centuries.[64] Moreover, official Soviet historiography maintained that the numbers of nomads who came into Central Asia at that time were "relatively small" (*v otnositel'no nebol'shom chisle*),[65] and the only role it accorded the historical Uzbeks was that they simply gave their name to an *already formed* Uzbek ethnic group "as the last and latest ethnic stratification (*naplastovanie*)."[66] The net result of the official interpretation of Uzbek ethnogenesis was to dislocate the term "Uzbek" from historical reality and to give it a meaning different from its historical one. "The meaning [of the word Uzbek] in the fifteenth and sixteenth centuries," writes the *Istoriia Uzbekskoĭ SSR,* "should not be confused with [the meaning] it has in our time."[67]

This view has been contradicted by some Soviet historians and ethnographers who have maintained that the nomadic Uzbek invasions were a crucial event in the historical and ethnogenetic development of the Uzbek people. The first official history of Uzbekistan, the two-volume *Istoriia narodov Uzbekistana* (History of the Peoples of Uzbekistan), which subsequent histories set as their task to "correct," stated that the Uzbek invasions "could not but have had a strong influence," and that the steppe tribes which entered the territory of Central Asia, then under Timurid control, were "numerous."[68] The second volume of the history came under strong criticism for beginning with the Uzbek conquests, thus giving the impression that they marked the start of a new historical period which did not correspond to the Marxist periodization of Central Asian history.[69]

In the 1970s, Karmysheva stated explicitly that her ethnographic data contradicted statements made by earlier historians about the small number of nomadic and semi-nomadic elements in Central Asia in the fifteenth century,[70] and in the opinion of the Uzbek historian, Karim Shaniiazov, the Kipchak nomads who migrated into Central Asia from the steppe in the period from the fifteenth to the eighteenth centuries represented "a large group."[71] In the 1980s, estimating that the number of immigrant nomads who entered the Central Asian intrariverine region was "massive" and "reached a high figure" (which he calculated to be between 240,000 and 360,000), the historian Tursun Sultanov came to the conclusion that the Uzbek conquest was "an important event in the ethno-political history of the contemporary Uzbek and Kazakh peoples."[72]

Uzbek Pressures and Tajik Demands

The national delimitation of 1924, which granted Uzbekistan the lion's share of territory in Central Asia, relegating Tajiks to the eastern backwaters of the former Bukharan Khanate, only confirmed the extent to which the process of Turkicization had progressed in Central Asia by the twentieth century. Furthermore, those Tajiks who remained in the new Uzbek SSR, particularly in the Bukhara and Samarkand regions, were pressured in various ways to register themselves as Uzbeks—the majority nationality of the republic—in the 1926 Uzbek census.[73] "We are Tajiks," they told the Russian ethnographer, Zarubin, in the 1930s, "but our children will be Uzbeks."[74] The popular Uzbek saying, "Turk and Tajik are one" (*türk u tajik bir kishi*), underscored traditional Uzbek prejudice against the Tajik and his claim to a separate identity. In the Uzbek view, Tajiks were simply Persian-speaking Uzbeks.[75] Demographically dynamic, Uzbeks tended to absorb not only Tajiks, but also other Turkic peoples (e.g., Kazakhs), as they came to represent the overwhelming majority of Turkic-speakers in Central Asia. By the 1979 census, as a result of outmigration and assimilation, Tajiks had been reduced to four percent of the total population of the Uzbek republic and to about 2.9 million in Central Asia as a whole, compared with 12.4 million Uzbeks.[76]

As for the linguistic situation, Bartol'd's statement regarding the inexorable process of the Turkicization of Iranian dialects in Central Asia appears to have been confirmed by recent studies of the North Tajik dialect, for example.[77] Gerhard Doerfer has demonstrated the degree to which Persian/Tajik has "merged" with Turkish/Uzbek, and he maintains that, since Middle Persian times, Persian/Tajik has been moving toward a point of union (*Vereinigungspunkt*) with Turkish, which can be explained by "the long-standing and close symbiosis of the two peoples."[78] In his opinion, Uzbek tendencies in North Tajik are so strong that they "may one day lead to the absorption of Tajik into Uzbek," and he calls it in fact a nascent Turkic language.[79]

Compounding territorial, demographic, and linguistic pressures are the ethnic pressures which Tajiks continue to experience in their own republic. As Soviet ethnographers and historians have pointed out, the Tajiks are not yet "consolidated" as a nation, the major stumbling block being the ethnic, linguistic, and religious differences between Tajiks and the Pamiri peoples, or "Ghalchas" (sometimes also called "Mountain Tajiks"), who live in the Gorno-Badakhshan Autonomous Region of the Tajik republic. The Pamiris belong linguistically to the eastern Iranian group, which is quite different from Tajik, a western Iranian language, and they include Yazgulemis, Yaghnobis, Rushanis, Vakhanis, and Shugnanis who, unlike the Sunni Tajiks, are mainly Isma'ilis. Until very recently, Tajiks did not officially acknowledge any difference between themselves and the Pamiris, and non-Tajik Soviet ethnographers frequently criticized them for trying to "Tajikify" the Pamiris.[80]

With national revivals currently taking place in every republic from Moldova to Kazakhstan as a result of the policy of *glasnost'* and the break-up of the Soviet Union, Tajiks too are experiencing a revival of their national and cultural life. Members of the Tajik intelligentsia, who are mainly descendants of émigrés from Bukhara and Samarkand, have started calling into question the national territorial delimitation of Central Asia and have actually made demands that Bukhara and Samarkand be returned to Tajik control.[81] Needless to say, reaction among Uzbeks has not been sympathetic, some even going so far as to maintain that Tajiks are not indigenous inhabitants of Central Asia, but immigrants from Iran.[82] Tajiks have also stepped up their cultural and educational demands. They have accused the Uzbeks of "cultural imperialism" and "national arrogance" for claiming such figures as Ibn Sina for themselves,[83] and they have complained about the educational discrimination encountered by Tajiks in Uzbekistan, such as the closure of Tajik language schools and the lack of Tajik language publications, while these rights have been guaranteed the sizeable Uzbek minority (about 23 percent of the total population of the republic) in Tajikistan.[84] They also appear to have begun to recoup some of their demographic losses of the 1920s and 1930s as many newly-conscious Tajiks who had earlier registered themselves as Uzbeks, particularly in the Uzbek republic, "reclassify" themselves as Tajiks. With the highest rate of growth in Central Asia, they now represent 67% of the total population of their own republic and 4.7% of the population of Uzbekistan, improvements over the 59% and 4%, respectively, recorded in the 1979 census.[85]

Extremely sensitive to the ever present threat of Turkicization, or more precisely, Uzbekization, members of the Tajik intelligentsia have begun to stress their common linguistic, literary and cultural ties with other Persian-speaking countries, namely Iran and Afghanistan.[86] Symbolic of their desire to reestablish their link with the classical Persian literary heritage was the renaming of their language as "Tajik Persian" (*farsi-yi tajiki*), and the movement to reintroduce the Arabic script.[87] Here, however, the policy of *glasnost'* drew the line and Tajik intellectuals were sharply criticized for "pan-Iranism," "nationalism," and "elitism"—witness the famous case of the dismissal in 1988 of the editor of the republican newspaper, *Komsomoli Tochikiston,* for, among other things, his attacks against those who stressed the differences, rather than the similarities, between Tajik, Persian, and Dari (the Persian spoken in Afghanistan).[88]

Conclusion

By the end of the nineteenth century, the millennia-long symbiosis of the Turkic nomad and the sedentary Iranian in Central Asia had resulted in the almost complete Turkicization of its once predominant Iranian population and in the sedentarization and assimilation of formerly nomadic Turkic elements. During the 1920s, with ethnic and national identities weak or non-existent, Soviet nationalities policies aimed at the creation of the modern Uzbek and Tajik nations, each with its own separate territory, history and cultural heritage. As a result, the traditional symbiotic relationship between Turkic and Iranian peoples was replaced by ethnic rivalry and competition for territory and cultural symbols that had previously been the common property of both.

It will be interesting to observe how the new histories written in Uzbekistan in particular, deal with the problems of Uzbek ethnogenesis and cultural heritage. In the current nationalistic climate, it does not appear likely, judging by recent publications, that they will either recognize the cultural role played by Iranian peoples in Central Asia, or rehabilitate the nomadic Uzbek past. Ironically, in view of increasing Tajik pressure, the safest policy appears to be to reiterate the Soviet interpretations, rather than to deal objectively with the historical relationship that had once existed between Turk and Tajik.

Notes

1. For the sake of uniformity, I have adopted the spelling "Tajik" for both the medieval and Soviet periods, in the latter case instead of the Russian form, "Tadzhik."

2. In this historical discussion, I am using the term Central Asia in the narrow Soviet sense of "*Sredniaia Aziia*" (Middle Asia), which represents chiefly the intrariverine region between the Syr Darya and Amu Darya Rivers in present-day Uzbekistan and which corresponds roughly to medieval Transoxiana (Mavaraannahr). In the nineteenth century, this region was divided among Russian Turkestan, and the Khanates of Bukhara, Khiva and Kokand. The term also includes part of present-day Tajikistan, Kyrgyzstan and Turkmenistan, but not Kazakhstan (the western part of which was referred to in medieval times as the Kipchak Steppe).

3. See, for example, Thomas J. Barfield, *The Perilous Frontier: Nomadic Empires and China* (Cambridge, Mass., Oxford: Basil Blackwell, 1989).

4. Fredrik Barth, "A General Perspective on Nomad-Sedentary Relations in the Middle East," in Fredrik Barth, *Process and Form in Social Life. Selected Essays of Fredrik Barth,* vol. 1 (London: Routledge & Kegan Paul, 1981), p. 188 and p. 192.

5. Most recently on this see M. A. Olimov, "K voprosu o vzaimootnosheniiakh kochevoĭ i osedloĭ kul'tur v srednevekovykh istoricheskikh sochineniiakh na farsi (po materialam tarikhov XVI–XVII vv.)," in *Pozdnefeodal'nyĭ gorod Sredneĭ Azii* (Tashkent: Fan, 1990), pp. 106–112.

6. *Webster's Third New International Dictionary,* p. 2316.

7. On this, see A. M. Khazanov, *Nomads and the Outside World,* tr. Julia Crookenden (Cambridge: Cambridge University Press, 1984), p. 198; also Ernest Gellner's preface to Khazanov, *Nomads,* p. xii. For a recent Soviet rejection of the idea of nomad dependency, see Olimov, "K voprosu o vzaimootnosheniiakh kochevoĭ i osedloĭ kul'tur," p. 107.

8. See A. N. Rakitnikov, "Nekotorye osobennosti istoricheskoĭ geografii zemledeliia i zhivotnovodstva v Sredneĭ Azii," *Voprosy geografii,* 50 (1960), esp. pp. 79–82. See also Joseph Fletcher, "The Mongols: Ecological and Social Perspectives," *Harvard Journal of Asiatic Studies,* 46, 1 (1986), pp. 40–41.

9. Fletcher, "Mongols," p. 40; also Rakitnikov, "Nekotorye osobennosti," p. 87.

10. Boris A. Litvinskiĭ, "The Ecology of the Ancient Nomads of Soviet Central Asia and Kazakhstan," in Gary Seaman, ed., *Ecology and Empire: Nomads in the Cultural Evolution of the Old World* (Los Angeles: Ethnographics/USC, 1989), pp. 71–72.

11. Note the prescriptions of the Chinggisid *yasa* against the adoption of sedentary habits by the Mongols.

12. On the "debate" between the "nomadizers" and "cohabiters" (i.e., those who opted for sedentarization)—see Fletcher, "Mongols," pp. 49–50.

13. V. V. Bartol'd, *Sochineniia,* 10 vols. (Moscow: Izdatel'stvo vostochnoĭ literatury, 1963–1977), vol. 2(2), p. 388.

14. Bartol'd, *Sochineniia,* vol. 2(2), p. 203.

15. Bartol'd, *Sochineniia,* vol. 2(2), p. 205.

16. Mahmud al-Kašgari [Kashghari], *Compendium of the Turkic Dialects* (*Diwan Lugat at-Turk*), ed. and tr. Robert Dankoff in collaboration with James Kelly, 3 pts. (Cambridge) : Harvard University Printing Office, 1982–1985), pt. 2, p. 103 (with modi-

fications to Dankoff's English translation to accord with the Turkish—see p. 103, n. 407). Note that although Kashghari explains that "among most of the Turks," Tat meant Persian/Iranian (*farisi*), he also says that among some Turkic tribes (no doubt those of Eastern Turkestan), it referred to Uighurs. The term Tat had been used in the Old Turkic inscriptions of the eighth century for the Turks' non-Turkic-speaking subjects who were chiefly Soghdians—see Hans Heinrich Schaeder, "Türkische Namen der Iranier," in Gotthard Jäschke, ed., *Festschrift Friedrich Giese* (Leipzig: Otto Harrassowitz, 1941), p. 5. It spread west to Iran, Anatolia, the Caucasus, and Crimea with the Turkic migrations.

17. And not the other way around, as Schaeder maintained in his discussion of this proverb (contradicting Bartol'd)—see Schaeder, "Türkische Namen," p. 4.

18. Schaeder, "Türkische Namen," p. 3.

19. Kašgari, *Compendium*, pt. 2, p. 103.

20. Kašgari, *Compendium*, pt. 2, p. 103 (slightly modified English translation).

21. *Tazik/tazhik* being the earlier form, going back to Middle Persian *tachik*.

22. Bartol'd, *Sochineniia*, vol. 2(1), p. 469.

23. Schaeder, "Türkische Namen," p. 25. It was also often rhymed together with "dur u nazdik" (far and near) to mean "everyone, far and wide."

24. Reference in Bartol'd, *Sochineniia*, vol. 2(2), p. 47.

25. See [Abu 'l-Ghazi Bahadur Khan], *Histoire des mongols et des tatares par Aboul-Ghâzi Béhâdour Khân*, ed. and tr. Petr I. Desmaisons (St. Petersburg, 1871–1874; rep. ed., Amsterdam: Philo Press, 1970), p. 167 (Fr. tr.).

26. Bartol'd, *Sochineniia*, vol. 2(2), p. 527 and p. 310; Schaeder, "Türkische Namen," p. 32.

27. 'Ali Shir Nava'i, *Muhākamat al-lughatain*, tr. and ed. Robert Devereux (Leiden: E. J. Brill, 1966), p. 6 (Turk. text); see also Bartol'd, *Sochineniia*, vol. 2(2), p. 203 and p. 527 for other references to its use.

28. Bartol'd, *Sochineniia*, vol. 2(2), p. 313 and p. 528.

29. See Schaeder, "Türkische Namen," p. 4; also *Istoriia Uzbekskoĭ SSR*, vol. 1, pt. 1 (Tashkent: Izdatel'stvo AN UzSSR, 1955), p. 239.

30. 'Ali Shir Nava'i, *Muhākamat*, p. 6 (Turk. text); Alisher Navoi, *Sochineniia*, 10 vols. (Tashkent: Fan, 1968–1970), vol. 10, p. 110.

31. Johannes Schiltberger, *Als Sklave im Osmanischen Reich und bei den Tataren 1394–1427*, tr. from Middle Germ. by Ulrich Schlemmer (Stuttgart: Thienemann, Edition Erdmann, 1983), p. 132.

32. B. Kh. Karmysheva, *Ocherki ètnicheskoĭ istorii iuzhnykh raionov Tadzhikistana i Uzbekistana* (Moscow: Nauka, 1976), p. 264.

33. *Istoriia UzSSR*, vol. 1, pt. 1 (1955), p. 371.

34. Karmysheva, *Ocherki*, p. 146 and p. 259. A portion of them had also left for India with the Timurid, Babur. There are apparently still several tens of thousands around Agra and Delhi today who claim to belong to the Chaghatay and Barlas tribes—see Karmysheva, *Ocherki*, p. 123.

35. Karmysheva, *Ocherki*, p. 265.

36. Karmysheva, *Ocherki*, p. 261.

37. Karmysheva, *Ocherki*, p. 263.

38. Note that although the term Sart continued to be used for urban Persian-speakers, their language was referred to as Tajik. It is unclear precisely when the distinction be-

tween Sart and Tajik started to be made: according to official Soviet scholarship, under Russian rule; according to Bartol'd, already under the nomadic Uzbeks—see Bartol'd, *Sochineniia,* vol. 2(2), p. 313.

39. N. Khanikoff [Khanykov], *Bokhara: Its Amir and Its People,* tr. Baron Clement A. de Bode (London: James Madden, 1845), p. 71.

40. A. Woeikof [Voekov], *Le Turkestan russe* (Paris: Librairie Armand Colin, 1914), p. 328. Bartol'd himself observed that Samarkand was mainly Persian-speaking at the time of the Russian occupation in 1868—see Bartol'd, *Sochineniia,* vol. 2(1), p. 468. According to the Russian ethnographer, Ivan Zarubin, Samarkand was still mainly Persian-speaking in 1920 and Tajiks constituted 54 percent of the population—see R. R. Rakhimov, "Ivan Ivanovich Zarubin (1887–1964)," *Sovetskaia ètnografiia,* 1989, no. 1, p. 118.

41. Woeikof, *Turkestan,* pp. 125–127.

42. Khanikoff, *Bokhara,* p. 73 and p. 81.

43. Bartol'd, *Sochineniia,* vol. 2(1), p. 468.

44. For a listing of the sources they based their decisions on, see T. A. Zhdanko, "Natsional'no-gosudarstvennoe razmezhevanie i protsessy ètnicheskogo razvitiia u narodov Sredneĭ Azii," *Sovetskaia ètnografiia,* 1972, no. 5, pp. 21–23.

45. Karmysheva, *Ocherki,* p. 260 and p. 119.

46. Thus M. Vakhabov, *Formirovanie uzbekskoĭ sotsialisticheskoĭ natsii* (Tashkent, 1961), p. 21; Bartol'd, *Sochineniia,* vol. 2(2), p. 529. Sarts were no longer listed in the 1926 census—see Zhdanko, "Natsional'no-gosudarstvennoe razmezhevanie," p. 24.

47. Zhdanko, "Natsional'no-gosudarstvennoe razmezhevanie," p. 24; Vakhabov, *Formirovanie,* p. 21; Rakhimov, "Zarubin," p. 117.

48. Edward A. Allworth, *The Modern Uzbeks from the Fourteenth Century to the Present: A Cultural History* (Stanford: Hoover Institution Press, 1990), pp. 237–238.

49. See A. K. Borovkov, "Tadzhiksko-uzbekskoe dvuiazychie i vopros o vzaimovliianii tadzhikskogo i uzbekskogo iazykov," *Uchenye zapiski Instituta vostokovedeniia,* 4 (1952), pp. 191–192 and pp. 194–195.

50. Borovkov, "Tadzhiksko-uzbekskoe dvuiazychie," p. 199 (quoting V. S. Rastorgueva).

51. Borovkov, "Tadzhiksko-uzbekskoe dvuiazychie," pp. 189–190.

52. See *Istoriia UzSSR,* vol. 1, pt. 1 (1955), p. 373.

53. Allworth, *Modern Uzbeks,* p. 236.

54. Note the approbation accorded by Soviet scholarship to those formerly nomadic rulers who made the transition to sedentarism. Thus *Narody Sredneĭ Azii i Kazakhstana,* vol. 1 (Moscow: AN SSSR, 1962), p. 174 on Abu'l-Ghazi Bahadur Khan, the seventeenth century ruler of Khiva: "This enlightened ruler of Khorezm renounced the nomadic traditions of his ancestors, having adopted the culture of the town and the agrarian oasis."

55. For a discussion of the treatment of the problem of development versus the continuity of nomadic society by Soviet scholars, see Gellner's foreword to Khazanov, *Nomads,* esp. pp. xi–xxiv.

56. In an apparent contradiction, Temür (Tamerlane) and the Timurids, who also had a nomadic tribal past, were included, probably because they originated within Central Asia and left a brilliant architectural and cultural legacy.

57. Vakhabov, *Formirovanie,* pp. 19–20.

58. *Istoriia Uzbekskoĭ SSR,* vol. 1 (Tashkent: "Fan," 1967), p. 501. Thus also *Narody Sredneĭ Azii i Kazakhstana,* vol. 1, p. 167: "In the historical and ethnographical literature there has for a long time existed the incorrect notion of the direct descent of the Uzbek people from those steppe tribes who moved into Central Asia only at the beginning of the sixteenth century, having conquered it under the leadership of Shaybani Khan."

59. *Istoriia UzSSR,* vol. 1, (1967), p. 502; *Istoriia tadzhikskogo naroda,* vol. 1 (Moscow: Izdatel'stvo vostochnoĭ literatury, 1963), p. 3.

60. *Istoriia tadzhikskogo naroda,* vol. 1 (1963), p. 3.

61. *Istoriia UzSSR,* vol. 1 (1967), p. 502.

62. *Istoriia UzSSR,* vol. 1 (1967), p. 501.

63. During the period of the Samanid empire—*Istoriia UzSSR,* vol. 1, pt. 1 (1955), p. 269; *Tadzhikskaia Sovetskaia Sotsialisticheskaia Respublika* (Dushanbe: AN TadzSSR, 1974), p. 88; *Narody Sredneĭ Azii i Kazakhstana,* vol. 1, p. 534.

64. During the period of the Karakhanid empire—*Istoriia UzSSR,* vol. 1, pt. 1 (1955), p. 269; Vakhabov, *Formirovanie,* p. 23; *Istoriia UzSSR,* vol. 1 (1967), p. 501; but not *Istoriia narodov Uzbekistana,* 2 vols. (Tashkent: Izdatel'stvo AN UzSSR, 1947–1950), vol. 2, p. 49.

65. *Istoriia UzSSR,* vol. 1 (1967), p. 502.

66. *Narody Sredneĭ Azii i Kazakhstana,* vol. 1, p. 167.

67. *Istoriia UzSSR,* vol. 1 (1967), p. 502; also *Narody Sredneĭ Azii i Kazakhstana,* vol. 1, p. 167.

68. *Istoriia narodov Uzbekistana,* vol. 2, p. 42. For the full reference to this work, see n. 64 above.

69. *Istoriia UzSSR,* vol. 1, pt. 1 (1955), pp. v–vii. It "corrected" many of its own views in vol. 1, published three years later—see the preface to *Istoriia narodov Uzbekistana,* vol. 1 (1950).

70. Karmysheva, *Ocherki,* especially pp. 258–259.

71. K. Sh. Shaniiazov, *K ètnicheskoĭ istorii uzbekskogo naroda* (Tashkent: Fan, 1974), p. 80.

72. T. I. Sultanov, *Kochevye plemena Priaral'ia v XV–XVII vv. (Voprosy ètnicheskoĭ i sotsial'noĭ istorii)* (Moscow: Nauka, 1982), pp. 21–23.

73. See Rakhimov, "Zarubin," p. 119. It is interesting to note that the 1926 census was printed only in Russian and Uzbek. For the attitude of the head of the Bukharan People's Republic and chairman of the UzSSR's Council of People's Commissars, Faizulla Khojaev (1896-1938), who stated flatly that there were no Tajiks in Bukhara, only Turks and Uzbeks, and who was accused by Soviet authorities of "ethnic discrimination," see Jiří Bečka, "Literature and Men of Letters in Tajikistan" (forthcoming in *Journal of Turkish Studies*), and Allworth, *Modern Uzbeks,* p. 194.

74. See Rakhimov, "Zarubin," p. 119.

75. See Rakhimov, "Zarubin," p. 117.

76. All figures from Martha Brill Olcott, "Central Asia: The Reformers Challenge a Traditional Society," in Lubomyr Hajda and Mark Beissinger, eds., *The Nationalities Factor in Soviet Politics and Society,* John M. Olin Critical Issues Series (Boulder: Westview Press, 1990), pp. 262–263.

77. "The history of Turkestan during the Muslim period is the history of the gradual pushing out of Iranian dialects by the Turkish language"—see references in Borovkov, "Tadzhiksko-uzbekskoe dvuiazychie," p. 180.

78. Gerhard Doerfer, *Türkische Lehnwörter im Tadschikischen* (Wiesbaden: Franz Steiner, 1967), p. 7, p. 57 and p. 64.

79. Doerfer, *Türkische Lehnwörter,* p. 72.

80. See Ann Sheehy, "Tajik Party First Secretary Addresses Concerns of Local Intelligentsia," *Report on the USSR,* 1, 3 (January 20, 1989), p. 22; and S. V. Cheshko, "Vremia stirat' 'belye piatna'," *Sovetskaia ètnografiia,* 1988, no. 6, pp. 5–6.

81. See Ann Sheehy, "Tajiks Question Republican Frontiers," *Radio Liberty Research Bulletin,* 366/88 (August 11, 1988), pp. 1–2; and James Critchlow, "Tajik Scholar Describes a Source of Ethnic Discontent," *Report on the USSR,* 2, 8 (February 23, 1990), pp. 19–20.

82. See Sheehy, "Tajik Party First Secretary," p. 21.

83. Anne Bohr, "Secretary of Tajik Writers' Union Voices Resentment over Uzbek 'National Arrogance'," *Radio Liberty Research Bulletin,* 143/88 (March 17, 1988).

84. See Sheehy, "Tajiks Question Republican Frontiers," pp. 4–6; and Bess Brown, "Limits to *Glasnost'* in Tajikistan," *Radio Liberty Research Bulletin,* 163/88 (April 11, 1988), p. 2.

85. Olcott, "Central Asia," pp. 262–263.

86. See Eden Naby, "Tajiks Reemphasize Iranian Heritage as Ethnic Pressures Mount in Central Asia," *Report on the USSR,* 2, 7 (February 16, 1990), pp. 20–22. On this point, see also Becka, "Literature and Men of Letters."

87. Naby, "Tajiks Reemphasize," p. 22. See also Becka, "Literature and Men of Letters," as well as "Problèmes de écriture au Tadjikistan," in *Mélanges C.H. de Fouchécour* (Paris, in press). Similar calls for a return to the Arabic script have been made by Uzbek intellectuals—see John Soper, "Classical Central Asian Language to be Taught in Uzbek Schools?" *Radio Liberty Research Bulletin,* 259/88 (May 18, 1988).

88. See Brown, "Limits to *Glasnost',*" p. 2.

CHAPTER 3

Central Asia as a Part of the Modern Islamic World

John O. Voll

The Muslim societies of Central Asia are a visible part of the broader Islamic world. This simple statement seems obvious, but these societies are frequently viewed as isolated and distinctive rather than as part of the larger Islamic community. As a result of this more limiting perspective, interpretations of the Muslim Central Asian experiences may overemphasize their uniqueness and miss features common to the different parts of the global Islamic community. Viewing Central Asian Muslims as a part of the modern Islamic world can help to provide explanations for the continuing vitality of Islamic affiliations in the Commonwealth of Independent States and to suggest directions of future developments in Muslim societies of Central Asia.

Two basic generalizations help to highlight the place of Muslim Central Asian societies in the broader Islamic world. The first is that these societies interact actively and importantly with the rest of the Islamic world. The second is that they share the basic experiences of Muslims in other parts of the world. These generalizations are simple and would seem to be so obvious that they do not need repeating or analysis. Yet they provide a framework for understanding relatively ignored dimensions of Muslim Central Asian experiences. As the dramatic changes taking place in the former Soviet Union direct attention to the specific experiences of the different constituent peoples, these generalizations about Soviet and post-Soviet Muslims take on increasing importance.

These two generalizations involve a basic assumption that there is a common core to the human experience that is identified with Islam. When persons in Cairo or Chicago or Tashkent say that they are Muslims, there are certain things that they share. These may include recognition of Muhammad as a messenger of God and belief that the Qur'an is the message of God. For Muslims, the identification of "Muslim" has real and significant meaning and represents this shared experience and heritage.

Muslims and Muslim societies are not, however, identical. There are real and significant differences among the many communities of Muslims in the world. The diversity of interpretations, institutions, faith, and practice within the

Islamic world is very great. Scholars rightly emphasize that the world of Islam is not monolithic and when one speaks of programs or processes of Islamization, the question can legitimately be asked: "Whose Islam?"[1] The issues of "unity and variety" or "consensus and conflict" in Islamic history have long been basic issues for interpreting Islamic experiences.[2]

Central Asian Muslim communities are distinctive. They have their own special local and regional characteristics and they are not identical with any other Muslim society. In this situation, Central Asian Muslims are no different from Muslims any place in the world. Each Muslim community or group has distinctive and unique characteristics that set it apart from other Muslim groups. It is possible, for example, to speak in some meaningful way about "Moroccan Islam" or "Malaysian Islam,"[3] but this does not mean that Morocco or Malaysia are not interactive parts of the Islamic world. Similarly, the distinctiveness of Muslim communities in Central Asia does not mean that these communities are outside of the "real" Islamic world or even isolated from it.

Interaction and Isolation

The Muslim societies of Central Asia interact in effective ways with the rest of the Islamic world. This interaction is not simply episodic or of brief duration. It is a set of long-term and profound historical processes which have gone through many different phases. However, the nature of the interactions in the past five centuries has been such that it is possible to emphasize elements of separate experience at the expense of noting the continuing relations with other Muslim areas.

There is a tendency in discussions of Islamic societies since 1500 to treat post-medieval Muslim Central Asia as an isolated area and to exclude it from discussions of modern Islamic developments. Many of the well-known introductions to Islam as a worldview concentrate on developments in the Middle East and make no mention of Muslims in Central Asia in the modern era.[4] The concentration on the Middle East is apparent in more historical accounts of modern Islamic history as well, with Central Asia often being mentioned only when events there have some impact on developments in the Middle East.[5] Even areas now considered "Central Asian" which in the early days of Islam were important centers of the Abbasid Empire, like Bukhara, are sometimes mistakenly said to "have vastly less history [in Islam] behind them" than regions like India.[6]

There is an influential interpretation of the history of Muslim Central Asia which views the region as having become isolated from the rest of the Islamic world beginning in the sixteenth century. The basic arguments have been set forth in some well-known and widely-used presentations of world history, perhaps most dramatically by Arnold Toynbee. The key to this interpretation is the conclusion that the Muslim world was dangerously divided in the sixteenth century by the expansion of Russia from the north and the development of the dynamic Shi'ite Safavid state in Iran. These developments are said to have cut off Sunni Central Asia from the rest of the Sunni Islamic world. The consequences of this isolation are thought to be the end of Islamic missionary expansion in the region and the stagnation of intellectual and political life among the remaining communities. The peripheralization and then isolation of Muslim Central Asia, as described in this view, in effect removes the region from the Muslim world.[7]

The Muslim peoples and cities of Central Asia were in an increasingly weakened condition in the post-medieval era. The wealth brought to the region by overland trade, along the Silk Route and elsewhere, decreased as global trade patterns shifted. The political and military leaders did not keep up with the developments of gunpowder technology, and intellectual leaders appear to have become increasingly conservative in their approaches. A good case can be made for the conclusion that Muslim Central Asia had become a weak part of the Islamic world, but this does not mean that it ceased to be a part of that world.

The tendency to exclude Muslim Central Asia from general discussions of the modern Islamic world is more a factor of scholarly perspective than of transformation of Central Asian society. In the division of labor in Western scholarship regarding Islamic lands, there is a shift between medieval and post-medieval scholarship. In medieval times, much of the area of contemporary Turkmenistan and Uzbekistan was included in the great Islamic states whose centers were in the core area of the Middle East. Merv (Mary), and Bukhara were important cities in the eastern provinces of the Abbasid Caliphate. In this context, these regions are studied by scholars of Middle Eastern and Islamic history. However, the scholarly coverage of Central Asia tends to shift as interaction with Russia becomes an important factor. Increasingly, Central Asia becomes a part of Russian and Soviet studies rather than of Middle Eastern studies. In this way, the academic division of labor emphasizes the isolation of the region from the Islamic world.

The actual and perceived isolation of Muslim Central Asia from the rest of the Islamic world reached a climax during the era of Stalin. For that time one can speak, as Alexandre Bennigsen did, of the "iron curtain drawn by Yosif Stalin around the Muslim territories of the Soviet Union, hermetically sealing Soviet Central Asia and the Caucasus off from the Middle East."[8] This involved obvious measures like the prohibition of individual travel by scholars and pilgrims between Central Asia and the Middle East. However, other actions like the forced adoption of the Cyrillic alphabet to replace the traditional Islamic Arabic one also emphasized the intellectual isolation of Central Asian Muslims under Stalin.

The vision of Muslim Central Asia as an area set apart from the Islamic world should not, however, be overemphasized. One of the important features of the modern history of Muslims in Central Asia is that, despite the changes, they actively interact on a significant scale with the rest of the Islamic world. In post-medieval times, Central Asian Muslims develop distinctive societies and cultures but they do not withdraw from the broader world of Islam.

The world of Sunni Islam since the establishment of the Safavid state is not as divided as would appear from reading Arnold Toynbee. After 1500 Sunni Muslim scholars and travelers were not as free to travel across Iran as they had been in earlier centuries but this did not mean a cessation of travel by such people. Instead, the travel patterns tended to shift with a greater emphasis on travel by sea. The increasing trade in the Indian Ocean basin after the entry of the Portuguese into the region aided this reorientation of travel routes. New emphasis was given to movement through India and Yemen, especially in terms of pilgrimage travel to Mecca. Sunni Muslims in Central Asia were not cut off from Mecca or the rest of the Sunni world, they just could not rely on traveling on routes north of the Caspian Sea or across Iran.

By the eighteenth century these patterns of movement appear to have become relatively well-established and Muslim Central Asia played an important role in them. The scholarly and devotional travels of Ma Ming-Hsin (d. 1781) reflect these interactions. He came from western China and passed through Bukhara on his way to Mecca. The route that he took was through India and Yemen and he was able to return the same way.[9] In broader terms, it has been suggested that, although not much research has been done on the subject, Central Asian Muslim scholars were part of a broader network of scholars in the Islamic world.[10]

In this network of interactions, the movement of ideas and influences was not simply one way. It was not only a situation where people from a "peripheral" area like Central Asia came to the center to learn. Central Asian Muslims made important contributions to post-medieval Muslim scholarship and life. One of the best examples of this is the spread and influence of the Naqshbandiyya *tariqa* (Sufi brotherhood). This brotherhood was established in Central Asia during the fourteenth century. The order became and remained an exceptionally important influence in its Central Asian homeland, patronized by most major post-medieval Muslim rulers and supported by people of all classes. The brotherhood provided organization and leadership for many conflicts, including the holy wars against the Buddhist Kalmyks in the seventeenth century and against the Russians and Soviets in the nineteenth and twentieth centuries.[11]

Over the centuries, leaders coming from Central Asia established important branches in many different areas, with the Naqshbandiyya becoming a major force in India under the Mughals and in the Ottoman Empire. Murad b. Ali al-Bukhari (d. 1720) illustrates the impact of this process.[12] He was from a notable family in Samarkand, where he was born. He studied and taught in India and then the Middle East. He was specially favored by the Ottoman sultan, Mustafa II, and his family became a major force in the intellectual and religious establishment of Damascus. Similarly, the order became a major influence by the eighteenth century in Yemen at a time when the teachers there attracted students from throughout the Islamic world. The Naqshbandiyya became an important part of the life of the Sunni intellectual establishment in the Fertile Crescent and Arabian Peninsula through the activities of immigrants like Murad b. Ali.

This intellectual interaction was paralleled by significant political and diplomatic relations between Central Asian and other Muslim societies. Russian conquests and the Shi'ite state in Iran changed the general picture and conflicts existed but in the sixteenth and seventeenth centuries, in Marshall Hodgson's view, "all of the Muslim powers of the time formed a single far-flung diplomatic world. The greatest—the Ottomans, Safavîs, Özbegs, and Timurîs—maneuvered among themselves. . . . This world was a diplomatic unity because it remained, despite the tendency of each empire to develop a distinctive regional culture centered on the court, a cultural unity."[13]

There is a long-term pattern of significant interaction, with scholars, teachers, diplomats, and pilgrims moving across the political boundaries of the post-medieval Muslim societies of Asia. In this pattern, Muslim Central Asia is not distinctively isolated. In this context, even if Stalin's "Iron Curtain" had been successful in sealing off Central Asia from the rest of the Islamic world, from the perspective of the late twentieth century this isolation was only a temporary phase in a much broader, different pattern. Ties with the rest of the Islamic world would have remained a strong part of the living memory of the Muslim communities. In this way, even during the Stalinist era, Muslim communities would have identified themselves directly as a part of the Islamic world, and been identified by Muslims elsewhere as part of that world.

This is in contrast, for example, to the emerging Muslim communities among American Blacks during the 1950s. These groups only gradually came to identify themselves with the world Islamic community. When Malcolm X went on pilgrimage to Mecca in the early 1960s, he discovered a new world for which his Muslim community had not prepared him. Similarly, if you consider conditions in the 1930s and 1940s, people in Central Asia under Stalin were probably physically less isolated than most Muslims living in Oman, and less out of touch with the rest of the Muslim world than many living in the mountains of Yemen under the old imams.

When Muslims from Central Asia were able to go on pilgrimage in larger numbers after Stalin's death and were allowed to go to study in the Middle East, they were not entering a strange world. They knew, for example, of al-Azhar in Cairo as a great center of Muslim learning in a way that North American Muslims did not. As a result, an important part of the emerging Muslim leadership in the 1980s, like Tal'at Tajuddin who became a mufti in the official Soviet Muslim establishment, had a chance to study in al-Azhar in the post-Stalin era. These students and pilgrims affirmed a long-term cultural continuity which a period of political restrictions had not been able to destroy. In this way, it is possible to argue that the Muslim communities of Central Asia, whether independently as Sunni states, or under Russian imperial or Communist rule, were not so isolated from the rest of the Islamic world that they lost touch with the basic identity, and frequently they participated in significant interactions with other Muslims. In the nineteenth and twentieth centuries, these interactions are part of the shared basic experiences of Muslims throughout the world.

Shared Basic Experiences

Muslims in Central Asia share the basic experiences of other Muslims in the modern world. There are many differences among Muslim experiences, but in some fundamental ways, these differences tend to be related to the specifics of immediate contexts. The major intellectual, political, and social issues created by modernity represent challenges shared by all Muslims. At a very basic level, the experience of living under Russian and then Communist rule did not raise fundamentally different issues for Muslims in Bukhara or Tashkent than those that were faced by Muslims trying to cope with French rule in Algeria or the British occupation of Egypt, or those challenged by Kemalism in Turkey or Nasser's Arab Socialism in Egypt.

The fundamental shared experiences relate to the interaction with Western models of modernity which came to be dominant global forces in the nineteenth and twentieth centuries. From the perspectives of Mecca and Medina, and also from Cairo, Samarkand, and Bukhara, Lenin and Woodrow Wilson are equally Western; Marxist-Leninism and Liberal Capitalism are equally foreign. The domination by states committed to imposing a Western model of modernity and the rule by local people with similar commitments create conditions which force reinterpretation and possible changes within world-views and social orders.

From the broadest perspectives of world history, the issues raised by Western models of modernity and the experiences of interacting with them are not only issues for believing Muslims. They are important issues for Jews, Christians, Buddhists, Hindus and others. They represent the challenges created by the modern transformation taking place in different ways in all societies. Although there are shared challenges, for each major worldview, there are distinctive forms that the issues take.

Muslims in Central Asia share with Muslims elsewhere the special characteristics of the interaction between Islam and modernity. Frequently, this sharing goes beyond simple parallelism of experience and the continuing interaction between Muslims in Central Asia with other Muslims is visible. In terms of the Muslim experience in Central Asia, two important developments illustrate these generalizations. The emergence of Islamic modernism and the institutional evolution of state-sponsored Muslim establishments and "parallel" popular Muslim organizations each provide insight into the ways in which Muslims in Central Asia continue to be part of the broader Islamic world in the modern era.

The development of Islamic modernism is most commonly identified with the life and work of Muhammad Abduh (1849–1905), an Egyptian intellectual who defined the modernist goal as being the "presentation of the basic tenets of Islam in terms that would be acceptable to a modern mind and would allow further reformation of it on the one hand and allow the pursuit of modern knowledge on the other."[14] The primary focus was on creating syntheses rather than rejecting Western ideas and institutions. The effort was, in many ways, based on the optimistic assumption that Western scientific methods and Islam properly understood were complementary paths to understanding truth and that faith and modern definitions of rationality were not contradictory. Abduh's work was primarily in the areas of cultural and intellectual reform.

The political dimensions of Islamic modernism appear in the work of Abduh's teacher and associate, Jamal al-Din al-Afghani (1839–1897). Al-Afghani was concerned by the challenge of Western power and believed that Muslims would not be able to defend themselves successfully unless they could overcome their political divisions. While he worked with Abduh in the effort over intellectual reformulation of Islamic thought, al-Afghani is more clearly identified with the emergence of the political movement of pan-Islam. Although pan-Islam was a program for defending Muslim lands against European imperialism, it was not a rejection of Western political ideas or institutions. Instead, it represented, like intellectual modernism, an effort to create a political synthesis of Western and Islamic political institutions and concepts. In the context of continuing European victories over Muslim states, the pan-Islamic effort had less long-term impact than the ideological efforts of Abduh and his followers.

An active movement of Islamic modernism developed in the Muslim territories under Russian control at this same time. This development was parallel to and interacted with the Islamic modernism of the Middle East and was seen by observers at the time as part of the intellectual and political developments in the Islamic world as a whole. At times, experiences in Russia provided at least some basis for programs and activities in Middle Eastern Muslim societies.

One of the key figures in this process is Ismail Gasprinskiĭ (1851–1914), a Crimean Tatar who had an important influence on the development of modernist Muslim approaches both within and outside of Russia.[15] He is often identified with the development of "Jadidism," the movement to create new (*jadid*) schools and institutions in Muslim society and to provide a synthesis of modern, Islamic, and Turkish elements as a way of renewing Turkish Muslim society. He received a modern-style education and traveled in Russia, Western Europe, and Turkey. He returned to his home, Baghchesaray in the Crimea, in 1877 and became its mayor. In that city he established the first of his new style schools in 1882. His school became an influential model for schools throughout Muslim communities in Russia and helped to inspire some similar efforts in other parts of the Islamic world. His efforts at educational reform in the framework of Islamic modernist views were pioneering ones within the Muslim world as a whole and had a long-lasting impact. He published an important and long-lived newspaper, *Terjüman,* which involved a major effort to develop a common Turkish language among the various dialects and was an important source for new ideas. This newspaper was widely known and became "one of the greatest Muslim newspapers."[16]

Russian Muslim modernists sometimes faced suppression and traveled to find places where they could advocate their ideas more freely. People like Gasprinskiĭ and Ahmad Agaoglu brought with them, as they traveled, their new ideas and methods in education, journalism, and culture. In political terms, the Muslims from Russian-controlled lands were important in the articulation and development of new concepts of political identity like pan-Turkism and pan-Islam. One of the most influential articles defining and advocating the ideas of Turkish nationalism, in contrast to Ottomanism or Muslim nationalism, was written in 1904 by Yusuf Akchura, a French-educated Tatar whose article was published in a Young Turk opposition journal. In the Young Turk movement itself, some accounts of the establishment of the early Progress and Union organization by Ibrahim Temo in 1889 list a Russian exile from Baku, Huseyinzade Ali, among the founders. Ahmad Agaoglu, who was born in Russian Azerbaijan, worked closely with the people like Gasprinskiĭ and then went to Istanbul after the Young Turk revolution in 1908. He was a major advocate of Turkism and helped to organize in 1911 the Turkish Hearth, an influential nationalist association. He was a member of the Ottoman parliament and after World war I he was elected to the Grand National Assembly in the new republic as well as teaching law in the new national universities in Ankara and Istanbul. Through the careers of men like these and others, Turkish Muslims from the Russian Empire played a significant and possibly determining role in the development of pan-Turkish and Turkish nationalist ideas within the Ottoman Empire during the decades before World War I. It could even be said that the Committee on Union and Progress, which came to rule the Empire after the 1908 revolution, initially adopted a pan-Turanian type of nationalism "because of the fact that Turks from Russia were influential on the Committee."[17]

Pan-Islamic ideas were also influenced by Muslims from the Russian Empire, especially through the work of Gasprinskiĭ. As revolutionary groups grew stronger in the Russian Empire, Muslims began to organize more consciously as Muslims. The great changes at the time of the Russian defeat in the Russo-Japanese War (1904–05) and the Revolution of 1905 opened the way for a series of all-Russia conventions of Muslims in 1905–07 in which Gasprinskiĭ played a very important role. Although the actual political organizations created by these conventions were short-lived, the idea of manifesting Islamic unity through a large, inclusive conference emerged as an important organizing concept. The Russian Muslim experience soon spread to the Middle Eastern Islamic world through the actions of Gasprinskiĭ who, through his newspaper, issued a call in 1907 to Muslims throughout the world to come together in a great conference.

He viewed Cairo as a better place to hold such a congress and went to Egypt to organize the gathering. Although the congress itself never took place, "the press coverage in Turkish and Arabic, the circulation of invitations and the congress charter, and the attendant controversy, which spanned several years, gave the congress idea widespread currency. Gasprinskiĭ was not the first to suggest a Muslim congress, but he was the first to pursue the idea with vigor and give it form through organization . . . and with him, the congress idea became popular."[18] When international Muslim congresses actually took place in the period between the world wars, they reflected the heritage of Russian Muslim experience, and post-revolutionary Muslims from the Soviet Union attended them, although they did not play a major role in their organization or deliberations.

Muslims from Russia also were involved in developing Islamic policies and positions in the last decades of the Ottoman Empire. Many were active in the emerging Young Turk movement at the end of the nineteenth century, and some, like Murad Bey, who was born in Daghistan and educated in Russia, articulated an explicitly pan-Islamic perspective. Murad's journal, *Mizan,* was for many years an influential force among intellectuals within the Ottoman Empire and among the political opposition to the Sultan.[19]

Muslims from Central Asia and other parts of the Russian Empire thus played an important role in shaping and articulating both pan-Turkish nationalist ideas and pan-Islamic sentiments. In this, the emergence of Islamic awareness, both nationalist and religious, among Russian Muslims was not simply parallel to experiences of Muslims elsewhere, it represented shared experiences which illustrate the continuing involvement of Central Asian Muslims in the modern Islamic world.

Islamic modernism has become during the course of the twentieth century the standard ideological and intellectual position of the formal or official Muslim establishments throughout the Muslim world. Although the faculty of the great Islamic university in Cairo, al-Azhar, initially opposed Abduh's views, by the middle of the century al-Azhar had become a modernist bastion. As Muslim scholars throughout the world dealt with the issues of modernization, they found the modernist positions to be the most effective basis for their positions. As formal Muslim institutions were established in the Soviet Union, the leaders reflected these same tendencies.

Certain key themes of Islamic modernism can be seen reflected in the recent pronouncements of Muslim leaders in the Soviet Union. There is an emphasis on the compatibility between Islam and modern science, seeing both as a search for truth. Like Abduh before them, contemporary Central Asian Muslims cite the significance of medieval Muslims' scientific contributions, noting the special contributions of medieval Central Asian Muslim scientists, as an important proof of the compatibility of Islam and science. The clearly modernist conviction is expressed that "the Almighty and the All-Knowing is the source of all sciences and knowledge. Consequently, serving science, the development of cultural and spiritual life likewise, means serving its source, serving Allah."[20] These modernist positions have been more freely expressed after the beginning of *perestroika,* when the militant Soviet-sponsored atheist campaigns were muted, and even more now that they have ceased. This perspective has been reflected throughout the Muslim world during the twentieth century by the modernist scholars in the intellectual and religious establishments.

Other Muslim modernist themes which reflect the ideas and teachings of the early leaders like Abduh and Gasprinskiĭ are also part of the current presentations of Muslim positions in Central Asia as well as in the broader Islamic world. In addition to defining the relationships between Islam and modern science, the Islamic modernists also had to define their views regarding traditional and popular religious practices. Modernists had a major concern for "purifying" society from the superstitions of popular religion and the "dead hand" of tradition. Gasprinskiĭ's major concern in his educational reforms, for example, was to replace the rigid traditional schools and to reduce the influence of the local leaders usually associated with Sufi orders. From the Muslim modernists' attacks on the religious practices associated with the *marabouts* (Sufi "saints") in North Africa to the criticism by the Muhammadiyya modernist movement in Indonesia of the weaknesses of the traditional rural Qur'anic education, modernist opposition to the "superstitions" of the uneducated masses is a continuing theme of the twentieth century in every Muslim society. In this context, the frequent criticism by Central Asian Muslim leaders of "the various superstitions that exist among the population" and the influence of "charlatans . . . [and] self styled imams, ishans, piras and miras"[21] was not simply a reflection of Soviet governmental attitudes, it was an authentic expression of the Islamic modernist position.

The modernism of the official Soviet Muslim leadership should not be surprising. Their own educational experience emphasized the Islamic modernist perspective both in terms of the continuing tradition of Gasprinskiĭ's curriculum in the Soviet Muslim schools and in their advanced training. For example, the mufti of the European part of the Soviet Union and Siberia, Tal'at Tajuddin, was educated in Bukhara and then went to al-Azhar in Egypt in the 1970s. In Egypt he was described as having studied the works of Abduh and al-Afghani, and he believed that the ideas of the reformers "are being implemented in the daily life of Soviet Muslims."[22] In a very real sense, official Islam represented "the last vestiges of the brilliant pre-revolutionary or Islamic modernist tradition, the influence of which was felt throughout the entire Muslim world."[23]

Official and Parallel Islam

Muslims of the Soviet Union also shared an institutional experience with Muslims in other parts of the Islamic world. Most discussions of Islam in Soviet

Central Asia identify two different styles of Islamic experience and life. One is the "official" Islam of the state-regulated establishment and the other is a "parallel" Islam of popular religious practice and non-state, frequently underground, organizations. Each style has institutions and structures which are usually distinctive to that format for Islamic experience.

The center of the official establishment was a structure of Muslim Religious Boards or Directorates and state-regulated schools and mosques. There were four such boards functioning since the 1940s, with administrative authority for Muslim affairs in four major regions—Soviet Europe and Siberia, North Caucasus and Daghestan, Transcaucasia (in Baku), and Central Asia and Kazakhstan. Early in 1990, a separate board was established for Kazakhstan. The directorates were led by muftis (or the *Shaykh al-Islam* in Baku) elected by regional congresses and subject to the authority of the central government in Moscow. "Mufti" is a traditional Islamic title for a scholar who provides authoritative legal interpretations regarding the application of Islamic requirements, and this was one of the functions of official Soviet muftis as well.

The official establishment sometimes served as a vehicle for presentation of government views to the Muslim populations and also provided a means for the continued public survival of Islamic tradition and institutions. In doctrinal terms, "official Islam has sought its own ideological and existential compromise with the officially atheistic state . . . and has devoted considerable attention to expounding the possibilities of reconciling what would seem to be two inherently contradictory doctrines."[24] This situation opened the institutions and leaders of Soviet official Islam to a wide range of criticism over the years. They have been seen by some as uncritical supporters of a state hostile to religion and bureaucrats willing to compromise in order to maintain their positions, and by others as reactionary artifacts of the past.

In contrast to this official Islam, there was also the popular Islam of the life of the people. Many in Central Asia over the years continued to participate in activities which could be described, at least in some ways, as Islamic. There is the continued popularity of basic social rituals and rites of passage—birth, marriage, and death ceremonies—and for some, a continuing participation in organizations of devotional piety associated with tombs and other holy sites and with the Sufi orders. Unauthorized mosques and "unofficial clergy" also have operated in many areas, especially among rural peoples. In recent years, most of these activities have taken on increasing importance as growing numbers of people in Central Asia and other Muslim areas actively and publicly participate. This whole area of Islamic life outside of the formal structures of Soviet official Islam was aptly called by many observers, "parallel Islam."[25]

This dual structure was an important characteristic of Muslim life in the Soviet Union and continues in the independent republics. It is very important, however, to recognize that the emergence of this dichotomy is not unique to the modern Soviet context and is not simply the product of the interaction of Islam with communist rule. This pattern of "official" Muslim institutions which are separate from the organizations of "popular" or "parallel" Islam has deep roots in Islamic history. Even in the high caliphate of the medieval period, which is now regarded by some Muslims as the model for an Islamic state, this type of separation existed. In the ninth century, the Abbasid caliphate evolved as a state structure with Islamic functions but this was separate from the emerging awareness of Muslim community with its own sense of order and society.[26] Even in that early era, there was a state-supported establishment of Muslim scholars and judges and a broader parallel set of popular organizations which included learned scholars and devotional leaders. It is out of the communities of this non-official, parallel Islam that the teachings which define Islamic Law (the Shariah) emerge.

Islamic Law is not the product of government leaders or judges in an official establishment; it is created by scholars and groups outside of the official structure. Official Islam of the government establishment has, with the exception of the first few decades of Islamic history, almost always been peripheral to the main stream of developments in Islamic thought, social organization, and community experience. Often the leading figures in this communal, parallel Islam mistrusted the political and religious establishments and rejected the idea of participation in government. Partly this attitude was the result of the natural tensions between ideal pious visions and pragmatic needs of state. It was also the product of early civil wars from which the leaders of the state emerged more as imperial sovereigns than as true successors to the prophet Muhammad. The general exceptions to this division are those times of revolutionary change when inspired popular Islamic leadership has gained control over the state structures through a revivalist or messianic movement.

The existence of the two types of Muslim institutions is an important part of more recent history as well. In the Ottoman Empire, the state had a complex hierarchical structure of Muslim officials who served as judges, scholars, and official tutors, and as teachers in the government-regulated schools. Along side this was the vast array of Islamic institutions and groups that provided the structure for life for most of the Muslims living in the empire. In the twentieth century, support for "official Islam" has been an important part of the policies of most major Arab states,[27] and similar experiences are visible in virtually every independent country with a Muslim majority. "Parallel Islam" has been similarly important in such countries. The strength of popular piety continues to be reflected in the importance in daily life of shrines, like that of Sidi Ali in Cairo or the many tomb shrines of North Africa. In addition, the great strength of the Islamic resurgence of the late twentieth century is built on the popular following of non-government, and often anti-government revivalist groups like the Muslim Brotherhood in Egypt, Syria, and Sudan or smaller and more militant groups like Jihad or Hizballah in Lebanon. Much of the actual life of Islamic faith takes place not through the official institutions but in the structures of popular Islamic life.

The existence of "official" and "parallel" Islam in the Soviet Union is very important, but it does not reflect the isolation or uniqueness of Central Asian Muslim societies. Instead, this division emphasizes the similarity of the experiences of Soviet Muslims and Muslims in other parts of the world. This similarity may help to provide some added dimensions of understanding the dynamics of the contemporary changes taking place within the former Soviet Muslim communities. Viewed within the broader historical perspective of the modern Islamic world, it may be possible to see what the possible lines of development are for Muslim institutions in post-Soviet Central Asia.

Parallel Islam usually involves two different manifestations of Muslim experiences. One style is the parallel Islam of popular and often private piety. This frequently involves special acts of pilgrimage to holy places and distinctive devotional recitations. Often, the organizational framework is provided by a Sufi order with its special guide-disciple relationships and its ability to provide a sense of communal identity for people from all levels of society. This style is usually the target of charges by reformers (both religious and anti-religious) that it involves superstitions and misguiding of the masses. Hasan al-Banna, the founder of the Muslim Brotherhood in Egypt, for example, spoke of the positive aspects of Sufism but said that it had become corrupted historically and "provided vast scope of sacrilegious activities against Islam in the guise of spiritualism."[28]

The second style of parallel Islam is very different. It involves a sense of active mission to purify Muslim society of non-Islamic practices. Sometimes identified as "fundamentalist," this puritanical approach can take many different forms as it arises among the scholars and committed lay persons in society. In contemporary Central Asia, advocates of this approach are sometimes called Wahhabis, after the fundamentalist movement which laid the foundations for Saudi Arabian state and society in the eighteenth century. In the past, fundamentalist movements have often taken the organizational form of a Sufi order. In some areas, fundamentalist parallel Islam has been identified with the Naqshbandiyya.

The pietist and the fundamentalist styles of parallel Islam are not always going to be mutually supportive. In fact, some goals of the fundamentalists involve elimination of many practices which are the heart of popular piety. The eighteenth-century founder of the Wahhabi movement in Arabia, Muhammad ibn Abd al-Wahhab, was an active opponent of tomb visitation, and fundamentalists down to the present oppose the "superstitions" involved in a wide range of popular practices. Pietists and fundamentalists actually become allies only under the special conditions of great apparent challenge to the basic Islamic identity of the society and when the popular masses can be coordinated in a major effort by the fundamentalists. In the Soviet Union, these conditions appear to have existed and the pietist-fundamentalist alliance provided the foundation for much of the increasingly visible Muslim activity in the last years of the Soviet Union.

It is not clear what the future relationship will be between the two styles of parallel Islam. In a similar situation in Afghanistan among the movements of opposition to the Soviet-imposed communist government, when the Soviet forces withdrew and then the communist government in Kabul fell, the effective alliances between fundamentalist Islamic groups and more traditionalist organizations began to break up. In post-Soviet Central Asia, the fundamentalists have become more influential politically, while the representatives of more traditionalist practices have had less visibility. The latter are less effectively organized in terms of broader social and political issues, while the fundamentalists have been able to form alliances with secular democratic opposition groups or to emerge in interaction with continuing regimes. However, in the months following independence in 1991–92, there were some signs that the more fundamentalist approach could preempt the more traditionalist approaches claiming to represent Islam in the emerging order by combining puritanical reformism with nationalist and democratic impulses. In Tajikistan, for example, the demonstrations against the old communist leadership in the capital, Dushanbe, became schools for Islamic instruction as thousands of people who were camped in the main city square for extended periods of time received instruction in proper modes of prayer and standard Islamic behavior. In this type of effort, the old Muslim establishment and the Islamists can work together.

Leaders of the Muslim establishment have themselves reacted differently to the new conditions. Some, like Mufti Muhammad Sadyk Muhammad Yusuf in Uzbekistan and Mufti Ratbek Nysanbaev in Kazakhstan, remained relatively closely allied to the old party leadership that continues to lead their republics. However, in other cases, people like Hajji Akbar Turajonzoda, the *qadi* of Dushanbe, the capital of Tajikistan, have provided active support and Islamic legitimacy for democratic—and secular—opposition groups. Others from the old Muslim establishment can be found among the leadership of some of the activist Islamist parties, like Alash in Kazakhstan or the Islamic Renaissance group in Tajikistan. This diversity reflects the fluidity of conditions within Muslim societies.

The broader spectrum of activities involved in parallel Islam in general may also change significantly, if experience elsewhere is any guide. The old saint cults and faith healers of traditional popular Islam have decreasing influence in most of the Islamic world. In Soviet Central Asia, one reason that they remained significant is that they became important features of ethnic cultural identity in the struggle to maintain an authentic tradition in the face of Soviet communist rule. The tombs of Sufi teachers who led revolts against Russian and Soviet control, for example, became increasingly important pilgrimage sites in the

1970s and 1980s.[29] As the republics gain a stronger sense of political independence, other cultural elements of a more modern character, like language reform and new literatures, will make it less necessary to cling as tightly to customs that seem to many to represent a past of ignorance.

In recent years the pietist style has itself been undergoing some significant changes. The improved communications networks have brought even the rural areas into significant contacts, through radio and audio casettes, with Muslims throughout the world. In this context the local shrines and their keepers may emerge more as artifacts of cultural identity than focal points in the worldview of Central Asians. Increasing numbers of Muslims are able to travel outside of the country and growing numbers go on pilgrimage to Mecca, where they can gain knowledge of Islam and perspective on their own local institutions, both official and parallel. In this more cosmopolitan context, for example, almost 5,000 Soviet Muslims went on pilgrimage in 1991, and while in Mecca they learned that the Saudis had donated Qur'ans for free distribution but that these were being sold by the Soviet religious councils. This was an important factor in the opposition to the mufti of Tashkent in the Assembly during July 1991.[30]

The changing nature of opposition to the leaders of official Islam also reflects the changing nature of participation in parallel Islam. Throughout Islamic history, popular religious leaders have attacked the leaders of official Muslim establishments for venality and corruption, and for caring more for position than for the faith. Fundamentalist criticism of the teachers of al-Azhar University in Cairo in recent years continues this tradition. Similar criticism continues in Central Asia but in the changing context the opposition now takes political forms as well as the more traditional methods of militant opposition or simple withdrawal. The ability of opposition to challenge the position of the current mufti of Tashkent in the official congress of Central Asian Muslims reflects these changes. The willingness of establishment leaders to cooperate with popular opposition, as in Tajikistan, or to try to mobilize popular support, as in Kazakhstan, also shows the growing interaction between popular and official Islam. The increasing awareness and involvement of the general Muslim public and the greater activism of establishment leaders have strengthened the process of bringing official and parallel Islam closer together.

In many ways, the old Islam of saint cults, tomb visitations, and Sufi orders is being transformed from a traditional "popular Islam" into a more activist "populist Islam" in which the average believer feels more empowered to bring about change in the official institutions without having to engage in open revolt. In a similar way, leaders in the official establishment appear to be more sensitive to populist issues, and new political-communal perspectives may be emerging. The creation of a separate directorate for Kazakhstan in 1990 is an early example of this trend. The new Mufti was said to be a deputy in the Kazakhstan Supreme Soviet and "has created an effective power base by supporting opposition anti-nuclear and environmental movements" and he is sponsoring the translation of the Qur'an into Kazakh, starting a newspaper, and building new schools and mosques.[31] In these activities the boundaries between official and parallel Islam are less clear than in the past.

This dynamism is part of what many call the resurgence of Islam. In the former Soviet Union, it is a post-communist era where there is no longer the same pressure from an authoritarian government committed to reducing the influence of the old religions. Post-Communist Islam has less need for the sharp divisions between official and parallel Islam, and there seem to be emerging different approaches to the creation of an acceptable socio-political order. However, the current movements are not efforts to recreate Muslim society as it was before Russian and Soviet control. Rather than aim to go beyond, the goals of the Westernizers and modernists was to create a fully modern but morally committed society based on the fundamental principles of Islam. In undertaking this effort the Muslims of Central Asia continue to share the basic experiences of other Muslims throughout the world.

Conclusions

The end of the Soviet Union transformed the circumstances of the Muslim peoples and societies of Central Asia. Long-term predictions are difficult, but within a year after independence the new republics were assuming new roles in the patterns of global relationships. The fact that these peoples had been a part of the broader Islamic world, which had been obscured by Russian and Soviet control, was becoming obvious to all observers as the republics interacted more directly with their Muslim neighbors.

One significant new element which emerged as part of the politics of Central Asian independence is a higher degree of choice in terms of policy orientation and cultural identity than had been previously available. One of the conscious and unconscious processes of the current socio-historical evolution is the definition of the regions relationship with both the Islamic and the Russo-Soviet heritages. This process is particularly noticeable in Kazakhstan, where there is a significant Russian population.

In the past the primary task for Central Asian Muslims, as Muslims, had been to discover ways of preserving their Islamic heritage in the context of Russo-Soviet domination and anti-Islamic policies. In post-Soviet society, Muslims must cope with the existence of a real socio-cultural heritage resulting from the extended interaction with Russians and Communism. This is part of the distinctive situation of Central Asia, while the need to balance local and regional characteristics with the broader Islamic heritage is an experience shared with Muslims everywhere.

The definition of the relationship between post-Soviet Russia and Central Asian republics is one of the basic issues. In early 1992, informed observers in Russia were already speaking of the "the 'near foreign countries'—the newly independent states in the south of the former USSR" and stating that "today Russia has the longest border with the Moslem world of all the European countries."[32] From this perspective, the Central Asian republics are clearly a part of the Muslim world, separate from the European world of Russia. However, Central Asian leaders at that same time tended to emphasize more the nature of Central Asian societies as being syntheses of Western and Asian elements. It was said, for example, that Kazakhstan is "part of Europe and part of Asia—a unique Eurasian path. Its 'mother' is Orthodox Russia and its 'father' is the Moslem South," and that "Kyrgyzstan intends to become a kind of bridge between Western and Eastern civilizations."[33] Despite such recognition of the continuing importance of ties to others parts of the former Soviet Union, the separation of the Central Asian Muslim societies from Russia proceeds.

Parallel with this separation is a growing interaction with other states and societies in the Islamic world. Soon after independence in 1991–1992, the question ceased to be whether or not Central Asia was a part of the Muslim world. Instead, it became a question of with which part of the Muslim world would the new states be most closely associated. The United States and Russia hoped that the Muslim republics would not emerge as Islamic fundamentalist forces, and viewed the emerging political situation as a potential field of competition between a "fundamentalist" Iran and a more secularist Turkey.

Many Muslim states became active in developing relations of various kinds with the new Central Asian republics. Pakistan and Saudi Arabia had been involved for some time in the region, and in Afghanistan various ethnic groups that straddled the Soviet-Afghan border had developed ties during the Afghan war. The future relationships among Afghan and post-Soviet Tajiks and other groups are only beginning to be defined.

It is clear that the more extensive reintegration of Central Asia into the broader Islamic world is not a simple matter of deciding whether to be fundamentalist or secularist. Early in 1992, Muslim efforts to defuse potential competitions and to bring the new republics into more broadly defined international communities were reflected in the revitalized efforts of the Economic Cooperation Organization (ECO), a group formed in 1964 by Iran, Pakistan, and Turkey. At an ECO summit in February 1992, Azerbaijan, Kyrgyzstan, Tajikistan, Turkmenistan, and Uzbekistan were admitted as members and Kazakhstan was granted observer status. This made the ECO the largest regional organization of Muslim states in the world, with a population of more than one quarter billion people. At the summit there were optimistic comments about the long-term possibility of an ECO common market, but leaders did not see the organization as the basis for a more explicitly political entity.[34]

The spirit of the ECO meeting emphasized the general tone of relations in the emerging post-Soviet era. The Muslim peoples of Central Asia were reestablishing more formal connections with other Muslim peoples. Iranian President Rafsanjani commented after meeting with the president of Turkmenistan that "It is like a family reunion. We are not strangers."[35] This emphasizes the long-term realities of Central Asia as a part of the modern Islamic world. There has been a continuing, and now a strengthening, interaction between Central Asian Muslims and the rest of the Islamic world. They also share and participate in the major experiences of the emergence of a more populist political order and of the continuing effort to create modern societies which reflect the moral commitment of the Islamic tradition.

Notes

1. See for example, the comments in John L. Esposito, *Islam, the Straight Path,* expanded ed. (New York: Oxford University Press, 1991), p. 192.

2. Classic Orientalist perspectives on this issue can be found in Gustav E. von Grunebaum, ed., *Unity and Variety in Muslim Civilization* (Chicago: University of Chicago Press, 1955), while more recent approaches are discussed in Andrew C. Hess, "Consensus or Conflict: The Dilemma of Islamic Historians," *American Historical Review* Vol. 81, No. 4 (October 1976).

3. See Dale F. Eickelman, *Moroccan Islam: Tradition and Society in a Pilgrimage Center* (Austin, Texas; University of Texas Press, 1976) and J. Nagata, *The Reflowering of Malaysian Islam: Modern Religious Radicals and Their Roots* (Vancouver: University of British Columbia Press, 1985).

4. See, for example, old "standard" texts like H.A.R. Gibb, *Mohammedanism, An Historical Survey,* 2nd ed., rev. (London: Oxford University Press, 1961); and Fazlur Rahman, *Islam,* 2nd ed. (Chicago: University of Chicago Press, 1979).

5. See for example, the coverage of Russian expansion in the 19th century, which is noted only for its impact on Iranian policy in the old classic, Carl Brockelmann, *History of the Islamic Peoples,* trans. J. Carmichael & M. Perlmann (New York: Putnam's, 1939).

6. Wilfred Cantwell Smith, *Islam in Modern History* (Princeton: Princeton University Press, 1957), p. 263.

7. Arnold Toynbee, *A Study of History* (New York: Oxford University Press, 1963), 8:225–227. A presentation which emphasizes the loss of missionary zeal and the importance of the Sunni-Shi'i split is William H. McNeil, *The Rise of the West* (Chicago: University of Chicago Press, 1963), pp. 617–628.

8. Alexandre Bennigsen, "Soviet Muslims and the World of Islam," *Problems of Communism* Vol. 29, No. 2 (March–April, 1980), p. 38.

9. A.D.W. Forbes, "Ma Ming-Hsin," *Encyclopedia of Islam,* New Ed. (Leiden: E. J. Brill, 1983), 5:850–852. The research of the late Jospeh Fletcher is of great importance in understanding this figure and the development of the Naqshbandiyya *tariqas* in general.

10. E. J. Lazzerini, "The Revival of Islamic Culture in Pre-Revolutionary Russia: Or, Why a prosopography of the Tatar *Ulema*?" in *Turco-Tatar Past, Soviet Present,* ed. Ch. Lemercier-Quelquejay, G. Veinstein, S.E. Wimbush (Paris: Editions Peeters, 1986), p. 370.

11. Alexandre Bennigsen and S. Enders Wimbush, *Mystics and Commissars* (Berkeley: University of California Press, 1985), pp. 7–9.

12. His biography is presented by his descendant in *Muhammad Khalil al-Muradi,*

Silk al-durar fi a'yan al-qarn al-thani ashar (Baghdad: Maktabah al-Muthna, 1301/1883–4), 4:129–131.

13. Marshall G. S. Hodgson, *The Venture of Islam* (Chicago: University of Chicago Press, 1974), 3:81–82.

14. Fazlur Rahman, Islam, p. 217. A useful description of Islamic modernism with a good bibliography can be found in Ali E. Hillal Dessouki, "Islamic Modernism," *Encyclopedia of Religion,* ed. Mircea Eliade (New York: Macmillan, 1987), 10:14–17.

15. Helpful discussions of Gasprinskivk's life and work as related to issues in this paper can be found in Jacob M. Landau, *The Politics of pan-Islam, Ideology and Organization* (Oxford: Clarendon Press, 1990), Chapter 3, and Martin Kramer, *Islam Assembled, The Advent of the Muslim Congresses* (New York: Columbia University Press, 1986), Chapter 4.

16. Alexandre A. Bennigsen & S. Enders Wimbush, *Muslim National Communism in the Soviet Union* (Chicago: University of Chicago Press, 1979), p. 197.

17. Feroz Ahmad, *The Young Turks* (Oxford: Clarendon Press, 1969), p. 154. This discussion of pan-Turkism influences is based on Bernard Lewis, *The Emergence of Modern Turkey* (London: Oxford University Press, 1961), pp. 192–193, 320–321, 342–346; Jacob M. Landau, *Pan-Turkism in Turkey* (Hamden, CT: Archon Books, 1981), pp. 34–35; Fahir Iz, "Aghaoghlu, Ahmed," *The Encyclopedia of Islam* (New edition), Supplement (1980), p. 47.

18. Kramer, *Islam Assembled,* pp. 46–47. This discussion of Gasprinskivk's involvement in pan-Islamic conferences is based on Kramer, *Islam Assembled,* Chapter 4, and Landau, *The Politics of Islam,* Chapter 3.

19. Information about the Islamic influences of the Muslims from Russia in this period can be found in Feroz Ahmad, *The Young Turks, passim;* For Murad Bey in particular, see Lewis, *The Emergence of Modern Turkey, pp. 189–190, 211; and Ernest Edmondson Ramsaur, Jr., The Young Turks: Prelude to the Revolution of 1908* (New York: Russell and Russell, 1957), pp. 40–45, 48–51.

20. Jafar Panchayev, "Islam and Science," *Muslims of the Soviet East,* No. 2–3 (1410/1989), p. 20. See also, for example, Abdulgani Abdullah, "Muslim Scientific Contribution to the Development of World Civilization," *Muslims of the Soviet East,* No. 4 (1409/1988), pp. 3–4.

21. See, for example, Abdulgani Abdullah, "Sermon in Islam and Inter-ethnic Relations," *Muslims of the Soviet East,* No. 2 (14120/1990), pp. 1–3.

22. "Mufti Tal'at Tajuddin," *Muslims of the Soviet East,* No. 4 (1409/1988), p. 5.

23. Alexandre Bennigsen and S. Enders Wimbush, *Mystics and Commissars* (Berkeley: University of California Press, 1985), p. 45.

24. Yaacov Ro'i, "The Islamic Influence on Nationalism in Soviet Central Asia," *Problems of Communism* Vol. 39, No. 4 (July-August 1990), p. 50.

25. Bennigsen and Wimbush, *Mystics and Commissars, passim.* A good description of the increased activity by the early 1980s is Alexandre Bennigsen, "Mullahs, Mujahidin, and Soviet Muslims," *Problems of Communism* Vol. 33, No. 6 (Nov.–Dec. 1984), pp. 28–44.

26. See, for example, Ira M. Lapidus, "The Separation of State and Religion in the Development of Early Islamic Society," *International Journal of Middle East Studies* 6, No. 4 (Oct. 1975), pp. 363–385.

27. See, for example, Ali E. Hillal Dessouki, "Official Islam and Political Legitimation in the Arab Countries," in *The Islamic Impulse,* ed. Barbara Freyer Stowasser (London: Croom Helm, 1987), pp. 135–141.

28. *Memoirs of Hasan al-Banna Shaheed,* trans. M.N. Shaikh (Karachi: International Islamic Publishers, 1981), p. 76.

29. Bennigsen and Wimbush, *Mystics and Commissars,* p. 96.

30. See reports in *Foreign Broadcast Information Service: FBIS-SOV-91–131* (9 July 1991) and *FBIS-SOV-91–133* (11 July 1991).

31. Ahmed Rashid, "The Islamic Challenge," *Far Eastern Economic Review,* 12 July 1990, pp. 24–25.

32. Statements by Aleksei Vasiliev, President of the Russian Center for Arab, African and Islamic Studies, in *Izvestia* 10 March 1992. "Assessing Russia's Ties with Moslem World," *The Current Digest of the Post-Soviet Press* XLIV, No. 10 (8 April 1992), 1.

33. "Nazarbayev: A Post-Totalitarian Leader," and "Will Ethnic Strife Sink Kirgiz Experiment?" *The Current Digest of the Post-Soviet Press* XLIV, No. 10 (8 April 1992), pp. 4, 7.

34. See the various speeches and press conference reports contained in FBIS-NES-92–032 (18 February 1992), pp. 46–52.

35. Ibid., p. 48.

CHAPTER 4

Volga Tatars in Central Asia, 18th–20th Centuries: From Diaspora to Hegemony

Edward J. Lazzerini

Since the formation of the Union of Soviet Socialist Republics in 1922, Central Asia has been narrowly identified with those five republics whose titular ethnic groups are, respectively, the Kazakh, Kirghiz, Uzbek, Turkmen, and Tajik. Many scholars, however, support a broader concept of the region that includes territories extending from the confluence of the Volga and Kama Rivers south to the Caspian Sea and east across southern Siberia, and into China's Xinjiang province, which has been inhabited since medieval times mostly by Turkic-speaking peoples.

Principal among these are the Tatars, an ethnic group whose very identity has been the subject of much confusion for centuries. The seed of the problem was planted in the late twelfth century when tribes of Mongols united under one of their chieftains, Temujin (later Chinggis Khan), and embarked on an extraordinary military venture that would produce the largest empire in human history. In the process, numerous other tribes—some Mongol, some Turkic—were absorbed into the confederation, helping to swell the size of the armies sent against great centers of civilization. One of those tribes was named something akin to Tatar, and its presence in the Mongol horde from an early stage served to encourage the popular impression among outsiders, particularly in western regions, that Tatar and Mongol were one and the same. That impression survived the fragmentation of the Mongol Empire when Turkic peoples comprising successor states on the eastern frontier of medieval Russia (the so-called "Golden Horde" and its successors, the Khanates of Kazan, Astrakhan, Crimea, and Siberia) acquired the "Tatar" designation in Russian (and then European) historiography and folklore.

But the problem does not end here. Since the Mongol elements within the Empire and its successor states were always distinct minorities and were, in fact, assimilated over time by the larger Turkic pool, the original identity of the people later called "Tatar" has remained a subject of intense debate. Are they descendants of the Mongol Tatars, or are they linked to the Turkic Bulgars who had formed a state centered on the upper Volga in the ninth and tenth centuries, but who can hardly be clearly distinguished from other peoples in "Central Asia" with Turkic roots? This is the kind of question applicable to most peoples inhabiting Central Asia, but it is one that acquired sharper focus in the second half of the nineteenth century when self-identity became a major issue for "Tatars," and then reemerged in recent years under rather different circumstances. The need to represent and sustain corporate identity is strong everywhere, not least in Central Asia; for Tatars it is tied intimately to larger issues of cultural, linguistic, economic, and political relationships with other Turkic peoples from the Central Asian republics, in Siberia, the Caucasus, and even Crimea. While much research remains to be done concerning these relationships, in the following pages I will suggest their outlines and argue that they were determined in large measure by several factors:

1. that the Tatars were the first non-Russian, Turkic-speaking, and Muslim people that the Muscovite state incorporated into its confines;
2. that the Russians found immediate and long-term use for the Tatars in extending contacts with other Turkic and Muslim peoples along the shifting southern and eastern frontier of their realm;
3. that this use stimulated the dispersion of significant numbers of Tatars throughout greater Central Asia; and
4. that in the process the Tatars sought and frequently gained advantage from their diaspora circumstances against both Russian and other Central Asian interests.

The "Volga Tatars in Central Asia," then, is a theme that is not a matter just of geographical interest but of social, economic, cultural, and political import as well. Moreover, to a greater extent than for many other communities, Tatar identity became shaped by exceedingly complex relationships riddled with ambiguities. Later in my discussion we shall see something of the "problem" Tatars posed for other Turkic peoples; let me commence my excursion over several centuries of relatively uncharted terrain, however, by introducing portions of two Russian texts that suggest how and why the Volga Tatars became a "problem" for their conquerors as well. The two realities are not unconnected.

On June 27, 1891, N.I. Il'minskiĭ penned one of his many letters to K.P. Pobedonostsev, then Ober-Prokurator of the Holy Synod. Professor of Turkic languages at Kazan Theological Academy and Kazan University, and developer of a system of education that stressed basic reliance on native languages for non-Russians inhabiting the Empire's eastern borderlands, Il'minskiĭ had for decades functioned as Russia's foremost lay missionary. Dedicated to strengthening the Russian Christian orthodoxy of oriental converts, he saw himself as a bulwark against the cultural and political advances of other religions, especially Islam. He also evinced an unyielding antagonism toward one of the major ethnic groups still committed to Islam despite being under Russian rule since the middle of the sixteenth century: the Tatars of the Volga region. In this particular letter to Pobedonostsev he offered an argument for promoting minority languages that was candidly linked to fear of Tatar influence beyond the confines of Kazan Province, where it would touch the lives of many others:

> This is the dilemma: If from fear of separate nationalities we do not permit the non-Russians [of the eastern borderlands] to use their languages in schools and churches, to a degree sufficient to ensure a solid, complete, and convinced adoption of the Christian faith, then all non-Russians will be fused into a single race by language and faith—the Tatar and Muhammedan. But if we allow the non-Russian languages, then even if their separate nationalities are thus maintained, these will be diverse, small, ill-disposed to the Tatars, and united with the Russian people by the commonality of their faith. Choose![1]

Three years later, an unidentified but presumably Russian correspondent writing for *Novoe vremia* from Kazan under the *nom de plume* "Zdeshniĭ" (A Local), produced an article entitled "Sovremennaia 'tatarshchina'" (Contemporary Tatar Hegemony). Typical of much late-imperial writing, laboring under orientalist assumptions about Asian "others," this article imagined Tatars to be eternal aliens, people who "hold fast to their Asiatic distinctiveness [*samobyt-nost'*], their barbaric tastes and habits," and who, "in the depths of their souls . . . hate all Russians and everything Russian." Casting the Tatars as reprehensible and disreputable, the author proposed an explanation for their behavior that echoes classic anti-Semitic attitudes:

> In a world where commerce is critical to the struggle for survival, the Tatar prepares himself from early youth for this kind of activity. Each Tatar, the father of a family, strives to place his son in the shop of a merchant. When this does not work out, he builds "his own business" without even a second thought. With just 30–50 kopeks, the Tatar youth purchases some wares and begins to hawk them. I can say with confidence that nine out of ten Tatars in Kazan are in business.
>
> Anyone who looks closely at the business activity of the Tatars will easily see that the distinctive sign of that activity is their complete solidarity both in petty affairs and in the largest deals. Thanks to this solidarity, the Tatars play a rather appreciable role, and all their strength is directed always to the exclusive benefit of their class [*soslovie*], while, of course, to the detriment of Russian interests.[2]

From Il'minskiĭ and "Zdeshniĭ" we hear Great Russian voices speaking to different audiences—one official, the other popular, with a disturbing message about a small segment of the imperial population. The Tatars are represented as a threat disproportionate to their numbers, one resulting from a combination of demographic and cultural factors only hinted at in these sources. In truth, by the end of the nineteenth century the Tatars were a substantial diaspora group (*etno-dispersnaia gruppa*, in recent Soviet ethnographic literature), numbering about two and one-half million, but spread over twelve provinces of the Volga/Trans-Ural region, with a significant and growing presence in the Kazakh Steppe (earlier Kipchak Steppe), the lower Volga, and Central Asia proper, as well as in key urban centers of the Russian heartland, especially St. Petersburg and Moscow.[3] The numbers are most impressive not as revealed statically in, say, the census of 1897, but when placed next to those from earlier revisions or other sources. The pattern thus illuminated speaks much less of fertility than of migration and assimilation of other Turkic peoples (e.g., Mari, Chuvash, and even Bashkirs), as an ongoing historical experience since at least the mid-sixteenth century.

Pockets of Tatars over a large expanse of imperial territory would never have generated a problem in some minds were not crucial socioeconomic and cultural trends, as well as a pattern of governmental policy since the mid-eighteenth century, coincidental with these demographic ones. Together a web of factors increasingly thrust the Tatars into diplomatic, political, commercial, and religio/cultural positions of influence that, as the Empire faced its late nineteenth- and early twentieth-century demise, opened up unusual hegemonic opportunities for a statistically minor people. It would be among the diverse Turkic peoples of greater Central Asia that these opportunities would play themselves out most fully, and the Tatars would employ their diaspora circumstances to extraordinary advantage.

Diaspora Beginnings

Since the conquest of the Khanate of Kazan in the mid-sixteenth century, when Muscovy made its opening move eastward, a growing proportion of the Tatar population of the middle Volga region has been living outside its original homeland. Russian victory prompted an immediate exodus eastward and southward of at least several thousand Tatars, and episodes of intensified colonial pressure through the first third of the eighteenth century ensured that additional thousands of Tatar peasants would become refugees. Most sought to continue their agricultural pursuits, but some turned to what would increasingly become a Tatar signature: commercial activity.

The traditional Tatar elite, comprising *murzas* (nobility) as well as men from other social strata, underwent mixed experiences in the century and a half following the Khanate's defeat. Some migrated with their social inferiors, whether motivated by a desire to continue resistance to Russian incursions, establish a new base for restoring the Khanate, or merely retain their social authority under new conditions. Many more seem to have remained within the recently-conquered territory and to have accommodated themselves to the new power structure. Now classified as *sluzhilye liudi* (state servitors), these men moved relatively easily into Russian service and seem to have enjoyed advantages commensurate at times with those enjoyed by Russian elites themselves. Thus, we know that a decade or so after the conquest there were at least two hundred Tatar *pomest'ia* (fiefs in return for Russian state service) on the left bank of the Volga River alone; that several *murzas* had received large land grants from Ivan IV for participating in the suppression of peasant rebellions between 1552 and 1557; and that well into the seventeenth century special cavalry units of Tatar *sluzhilye liudi* served the Tsar's military.[4] Moreover, in a period when Muscovy, for reasons of diplomacy, economics, and simple self-defense, found it advantageous and prudent to further long-established relations with the peoples and states of the steppe and Central Asia, Tatars were drawn into the Russian diplomatic service, staffing the *Posol'skiĭ Prikaz (Ambassadorial Office)* as interpreters, guides, envoys, and clerks in Russia's dealings with Asian lands. As those relations expanded, so too did reliance on Tatars, whose language Russia adopted for international communications beyond its eastern and southern frontier. With the establishment of Muscovite control of the entire Volga river and its arterial system by the 1570s, commercial opportunities with Central Asian Khanates were enormously enhanced, reaching a level of significance by the mid-seventeenth century that exceeded trade with Europe. Again, among those in the forefront of such activities were Tatars.

While Russian policies displayed little consistency before the reign of Peter I, revealing an ambiguous attitude rooted in the different priorities of *raison d'état* and religion in Muscovite society, their preponderant effect was discriminatory against Tatar nobles who refused to convert to Christianity. Owing to cumulative attacks on their agrarian economic base, they became collectively an impoverished group with severely weakened social authority. All found themselves eventually registered in 1718 with the Kazan office of the Admiralty, under which they were required to procure supplies and cart naval timber.[5] The efforts to minimize traditional elite influence over Tatar society were complicated, however, by several realities. First, conversion from Islam to Christianity effectively transformed outsiders into insiders. The Turkic roots of quite a number of "Russian" surnames may attest the significant level of Christianization. From the available evidence, the ranks of such elite *kreshchenye tatary* (baptized Tatars) appear to have provided much of the personnel that the Russian government used in its dealings not just with Tatars but with other Turkic polities to the south and east. Secondly, frontier requirements put a premium on members of the Tatar elite who remained Islamic in faith and cultural practice. However helpful converted Tatars might prove to the Russian government, reliance on those who rejected assimilation for a more limited accommodation could not be checked. This was true in the Muscovite period and also later when official policy turned more repressive under Peter I and his immediate successors. Thus, information gathered for the Muscovite embassy to the Crimean Khanate in 1563–73 was provided by *sluzhilye* Tatars,[6] while twenty-three were hired as translators in 1723 and seventy-six more were added to the corps of interpreters in 1726.[7] Thirdly, bureaucratic ineptitude and inability consistently to enforce laws and regulations created opportunities for unassimilated Tatars to satisfy their own aspirations while effectively reducing the impact of colonial power. Ongoing construction of village mosques in the face of repeated decrees prohibiting building, and others ordering the destruction of mosques, provides testimony to the limits of practical authority;[8] so too does the growing involvement of Tatars in commerce despite the prohibition against this prior to 1686.[9]

Russian policy aimed at assimilating the Tatars by combined means of positive incentives and outright repression had achieved few intended results by the second quarter of the eighteenth century. Besides episodes of violent insurrection rooted in popular grievances, middle and upper levels of Tatar society undertook activities and voiced protests of their own—most prominently to the Legislative Commission of 1767—that contributed to a growing sense among Russian authorities that changes were needed in official policy. So too did unresolved problems along the eastern frontier of the Empire, where a series of fortifications, command posts, and the settlements around them, running from Astrakhan through Orenburg in the direction of Omsk and Siberia, served as the forward line of Russian presence among the Bashkirs and then the Kazakhs—the former more sedentary but long troublesome, the latter tribal, politically unstable, and uncooperative. Falling under Russian suzerainty between 1731 and 1740, the Kazakhs were proving an obstacle to Russian political and commercial interests further to the south and east. Disorder in their midst stemming from political rivalries and economic ruin created untenable conditions from the Russian perspective. Aside from the value of trade with the Kazakh hordes, access through their lands was crucial to expanding commerce in the Central Asian polities of Khiva and Bukhara. Moreover, security along the empire's fortified line would be compromised without pacification of the Kazakhs on its interior. To achieve these various Russian goals, the Tatars increasingly seemed useful agents. How this was so deserves a closer look.

Proposals to expel or otherwise eliminate the Kazakhs from their accustomed territory enjoyed some administrative support, first in the early 1740s, again in the 1750s, and finally in 1763. Imperial policy makers, however, rejected this option and came instead to heed the recommendations of a series of regional administrators, including A.I. Tevkelev (a Tatar), P.I. Rychkov, I.I. Nepliuev, and O.A. Igel'strom. Despite differences among them, these men were apparently imbued with the new anthropology associated with the Enlightenment. Belief in a hierarchy of peoples and cultures, the dependency of culture on climate and way of life, and the possibility of changing culture (and, hence, behavior) led them to recommend policies that would force an ethnographic turn in the lives of the Kazakhs to reshape their traditional customs and ethnic character. As nomads, the Kazakhs were believed to be inherently savage and rebellious, beyond the pale of civilization. Disabusing them of their native traits and turning them into loyal subjects of the Empire seemed more achievable by encouraging their involvement in agriculture and commerce (rather than caravan raiding) and by utilizing Islam as a civilizing force. Who better to serve as a vanguard in these efforts than the Tatars, a people deemed more civilized than the Kazakhs by virtue of their long tenure within the Russian orbit and their commitment to Islam?[10] Besides, the Tatars had already proved themselves loyal enough (most recently by not participating in Bashkir uprisings) to warrant permission to settle on Bashkir lands. The most notable enterprise of this kind occurred with the establishment of a Tatar settlement in the vicinity of Orenburg in 1744, the so-called Seitov *posad* (suburb), initiated by the migration from Kazan of some two hundred families with commercial interests.

Pacification of the steppe, fear of Ottoman influence in the region, the safety of Russian trade, and the prospects of further penetration into Central Asia combined in the mid-eighteenth century to encourage Russian authorities to adopt a more conciliatory attitude toward the Tatars and to address some of their more pressing grievances.[11] It was well into the reign of Catherine II, however, before anything resembling a coherent imperial policy could be identified, and even then its formulation was initially cautious. In the 1780s, fearful of the potential for new outbursts of popular discontent following the nearly insurmountable crisis that the Pugachev Rebellion posed, and faced with the need in far-off Crimea to seize control of a faltering Turkic and Islamic society, Catherine grew convinced that the southern and eastern frontier could not be left to the self-government of natives. Accepting an enlightened view of Islam and trusting in the faithfulness of the Tatars, she became the latter's chief patron and encouraged their merchants, mullahs, and intelligence gatherers to mingle and work among those resistant to Russian expansion. Under the Tatar aegis, Islam received government subsidies in several forms. Tatars were appointed to head the *Musul'manskoe Dukhovnoe Sobranie* (Muslim Spiritual Assembly), established at Orenburg in 1788 but shortly moved to Ufa, for the purpose of organizing and strengthening the influence of a Russophilic Islam outward into greater Central Asia. There were also payments for the construction of new mosques, *maktabs* (Islamic primary schools), and caravansarais for the use of traveling Muslims, and funds given to finance the expense of printing texts for use in Tatar-run schools. The Seitov *posad* was rewarded with its own town council in 1782, and two years later the *sluzhilye* Tatars were granted equality of rights with the Russian nobility.[12]

New Vistas

The opportunities for Tatars and their status within the Russian Empire had increased measurably by the end of the eighteenth century. They were clearly in the vanguard of Russia's "oriental" subjects, accepted for being Muslims (at least for the moment) and encouraged to pursue their own self-interest on the assumption of its compatibility with larger imperial aspirations. Tatars were now expected to spread and consolidate the Islamic religion among the nomadic

Kazakh, trade for themselves and for Russia in lands further south and east to which Russian/Christian merchants were denied access, and assist as commercial middlemen between Central Asian traders and interior Russian markets. Largely for *raisons d'état,* then, the Russian authorities extended the Tatar diaspora. During the nineteenth century these developments helped to accelerate the emergence of a Tatar middle class and fixed its domination, induced fundamental shifts in the traditional Tatar *Weltanschauung,* and spawned Tatar ethnic consciousness. The consequences were profound for Tatar society, but they also had wider repercussions. By the turn of the twentieth century the Tatar diaspora, with its modernist mentality and the economic resources to support a range of reformist activities involving publishing, education, religion, economics, language, and social relations, would shape a developmental model attractive to many Turkic brethren faced with the challenge of preserving known ways while evolving a modern society.

By the first quarter of the nineteenth century, agitation within Tatar society, in the Caucasus, and across Central Asia (as well as in the larger Islamic world encompassing the Ottoman Empire, Muslim India, and even relevant parts of China) becomes increasingly noticeable. Among the Tatars, apostasy of a large number of Christians (the so-called *starokreshchenye,* or "early converts"), the spread of Sufi brotherhoods and radicalization of some (especially the Naqshbandiyya), as well as the call by certain ulema for rejuvenation of society and the individual based on the traditional modality of reform (*tajdid*), were aspects of this ferment. The cumulative effects of contacts with Russian culture, and through its prism, that of Europe at large, coupled with contrasting experiences in Central Asia undergone by Tatar merchants and students in the great madrasas of Bukhara, Samarkand, and Tashkent, further added to the brew.[13]

Meanwhile, particularly by the reign of Nicholas I, Russian authorities began to reconsider the merits of subsidizing Tatar enterprise and Islamic expansion. Great Russia's own emerging national consciousness, and the latter's intimate association with Christian Orthodoxy, explains much of the sensitivity to these matters, as does the threat to imperial integrity arising from the discontents with colonialism epitomized by the struggle of Shamyl and his forces in Daghestan. Finally, competition for control of commodities in trade moving between Russia and its southern and eastern neighbors, as well as the developing attitude that Russia had legitimate imperialist interests in Central Asia, added a sense of urgency to the opinion favoring modification of the compromise Catherine had effected. Under these circumstances, the Tatars appeared less necessary (and even potentially dangerous) as middlemen for dealing with Central Asia. As pressure for establishing direct and permanent Russian influence in the region grew from the 1840s onward, reliance on Tatars seemed less and less justified. Moreover, fear of the kind of Islamic unity that Tatar hegemony might produce loomed ever larger in certain Russian circles.

The middle decades of the nineteenth century witnessed the eruption of a polemic between proponents of Great Russian nationalism and Tatars struggling to define their own identity and their relationship to other "others" in the Empire, in circumstances turning increasingly against them.[14] Given little attention at the time, this polemic was, I believe, fraught with more than passing import. It voiced sets of firmly held but generally untenable assumptions and bales of mistrust, all the while disguising more honest concerns and agenda. Much of the debate rattled on about the appropriate representation of Islam—its teachings, founder, and adherents—typically at a somewhat "scholarly" level. But the sticking point always seemed to be the Tatars. As one of the Russian polemicists declared with apparent exasperation: "Many write in the newspapers of the Polish question, the German question, and the Finnish question, but no one wants to recognize the birth of a *Tatar* question."[15] The author of these words was, of course, wrong, because many were bothered by the "Tatar" question, not the least of whom were N.I. Il'minskiĭ and the anonymous "Zdeshniĭ" cited at the opening of this discussion.

It was not just Great Russians, however, who railed against the extravagant and dangerous influence of this wide-ranging ethnic group, but also representatives from among some of the very "others" it most influenced. The one who perhaps epitomizes such voices was Chokan Valikhanov, the Kazakh aristocrat and enlightener who in several texts complained bitterly about Russian policy that fostered Islam among the Kazakhs and had allowed the Tatars, almost always described as "fanatical," to implement that policy. "Islam has not yet eaten into our flesh and blood," he wrote:

> It does threaten to disconnect our people from its own future . . . . In general, for the Kirghiz [pre-Soviet Russian usage for Kazakh] people, the future has in store the disastrous prospect of gaining access to European civilization only after going through a Tatar period, just as the Russians went through a Byzantine period. However repellent Byzantine hegemony was, it nevertheless introduced Christianity, an indisputably enlightening force. What can the impressionable Kirghiz expect from Tatar culture, except dead scholasticism, capable only of inhibiting the development of thought and feeling. We must at any price avoid a Tatar period, and the [Tsarist] government must help us to do so.[16]

Written at the end of 1863 or beginning of 1864, these words warned of Tatar hegemony. They were prescient, but they missed a crucial point: the Tatars Valikhanov believed to be a threat to his people were, in fact, being supplanted by a different breed less committed to the ways of the past than to the waves of the future. They were more likely to have been educated in Russian and even foreign schools, to have traveled extensively, to know Russian and perhaps a second "foreign" language, and to be accepting of cultural diversity yet committed to the aspects of modern culture that appeared universal. They were *jadidchiler* (the "new people," or modernists, hereafter Jadids), determined to bring their own societies into conjunction with the progressive world around them, but they thought in much larger terms to include in their plans all Turks and/or all Muslims. Thus they were to varying degrees pan-Turks and/or pan-Islamists, in search of the power that derives from collective action.

Their modernism explains their cultural leadership by the late nineteenth century because it pledged a resolution to the growing disparity between the world of Muslims and Turks and the world of the West. Tatars were in the forefront of educational reform, economic development, women's issues, publishing, and the basic assault on individual apathy and social stagnancy.[17] Who could resist the call to be different so as to be better? Of course, hegemony is double edged: it means preeminence and encourages imitation, but it also breeds resentment both among those whose own authority is displaced and those who object to being imitators. The reaction, for example, of the Bukharan religious establishment can only be speculated upon, but based on admittedly skimpy evidence I would contend that it was typically unfavorable to Tatar modernist influence. This was true even in the early nineteenth century, when Bukharan domination of Islamic thought and training was still unchallenged. As for secular Central Asian intellectuals, many of them voiced animosity toward Tatar influence in the manner of Ghazi Yunus Muhammad-oghli, who described Tatars "as the last generation to obstruct Turkistan's [Central Asia's] progress."[18]

Tatars offered new pedagogy and social visions not just to their own but to other Turkic peoples within the Russian orbit. Revolutionary educational ventures, both at the primary and secondary levels, led the way, attracting students from throughout greater Central Asia by the early twentieth century. Tatar publishing initiatives—books, newspapers, and periodicals included—made available an increasing array of secular information that suggested alternatives to theologically-dominated perspectives, even as they helped spread a reformist brand of Islam amenable to the demands and aspirations of modern life. The first printed books in Uzbek, Turkmen, Kumyk, Karakalpak, and other Turkic languages appeared thanks to the efforts of Tatar publishers; by 1917, the number of books in Kazakh was second only to those in Tatar itself, prompting A. Karimullin to conclude that "the appearance and development of book printing in the Kazakh language during the pre-revolutionary period was directly linked to the history of the Tatar book and book trade."[19] Likewise Martha Olcott has observed that before 1905, when the first typographer of Arabic script opened for business in the steppe, Kazan served as the Kazakh intellectual center.[20] Elsewhere in Central Asia, Tatar initiatives had similar results, although increasingly after 1905 virtually every major Turkic group was doing its own publishing, under its own auspices, and with its own equipment.

Tatarization as much as Russianization, then, appears to have functioned as a critical process in the eastern borderlands in the last decades of the *ancien régime.* It received more than passing assistance from the Tatar commercial and industrial bourgeoisie who not only defended the Jadid movement but became its most reliable patrons throughout the diaspora, particularly by subsidizing the construction and maintenance of schools, paying teachers' salaries, and establishing public libraries, reading rooms, and mutual-aid societies.[21]

The linkage between modern economic interests and the forces of cultural transformation reflected and encouraged an overriding spirit of collaboration not only across social classes but also the full range of Turkic sub-groups, a spirit epitomized in the slogan that the Crimean Tatar Jadid, Ismail Bey Gasprinskiî, used as the masthead of his newspaper, *Terjüman,* in 1905: "Dilde, fikirde, ishte birlik" (Unity in language, thought, and action). Proponents of separate Turkic paths of development based upon emerging sub-ethnic identities and aspirations increasingly voiced opposition to calls for unity, but the appeal proved strong well into the third decade of the twentieth century.

In the midst of the agitation sweeping the Empire during the years surrounding the 1905 Revolution, the rallying cry for *birlik* (unity) took an inevitable political turn. Not surprisingly, Tatars once again led the way, taking advantage of their economic and cultural preeminence to coordinate collective action first locally and then at the all-Russian level, creating an imperial-wide organization called *Rusya Müslümanlarining Ittifaki* (Union of Russian Muslims), establishing ties with the Constitutional Democrats, the Bolsheviks, and the Octobrists, and forming a Muslim Faction in the State Duma.[22] Partly from their own experience, partly from the failure of other Turkic communities to develop programs of political action, and partly from a near obsession with unity, the Tatars dominated at every turn. They needed a pan-movement to guarantee an appropriate place for themselves in an empire facing an uncertain future with the potential for extreme social, economic, and ethnic competition. The Third All-Russian Muslim Congress held in Nizhni-Novgorod in August, 1906, offers a telling illustration of Tatar aspirations and dominance: ten of the fourteen members of its presidium were Volga Tatars, as were at least eighty percent of the eight hundred participants. Likewise, of the seventy-seven deputies elected to the four Dumas between 1906 and 1912, thirty (39%) were Tatars. For the short term, unity appealed to all the Turks; but its glamour would prove short-lived in the face of burgeoning nationalism.

The collapse of the Tsarist regime in early 1917 seemed to offer an opportunity to restructure the relationship between traditionally dominant Great Russians and the multitude of typically oppressed minorities, among whom were the Turkic peoples. Of these the Tatars, because of their long subordination to Russian rule, felt a particularly strong antipathy toward the mechanisms and policies of Russification. The most popular Tatar solution called for the establishment of a centralized, democratic Russian Republic within which the principle of extraterritorial cultural autonomy would operate for non-Russian peoples; all Turks/Muslims, while pursuing the social practices and symbols that reflected their diversity, would additionally focus on developing instruments for an overarching unity. This principle surely reflected the realities of the Tatar diaspora. Federalism, the alternative posed generally by Azerbaijanis, Crimean Tatars, and Central Asians (especially Uzbeks), was appropriate for those with more clearly defined territories or homelands. Not surprisingly, a series of conferences and congresses in 1917, both provincial and national, found Tatars above all advocating the need for Turkic unity based on class, ethnic, and religious solidarity. This voice found expression through several periodicals, such as *Ulugh Türkistan,* which had the telling characteristic of being published in Tatar and Uzbek in Tashkent under the editorial auspices of various Tatar intellectual and commercial interests. The appearance of such periodicals (six from April to December, 1917 alone), reflects the political significance of the Tatar diaspora.[23]

The relative monolithism of Tatar views on state building, however, began showing clear signs of fragmentation in the throes of the Bolshevik coup. Those Tatar socialists who had already joined Bolshevik ranks were followed by others drawn to a new regime seemingly dedicated to the eradication of ethnic, social, economic, and political inequities. The humanism of the Communist ideology was clearly its most attractive aspect. With repeated promises from Lenin of the right to shape ethnic life without hindrance, and with a series of goodwill gestures designed to win Tatar support for the October Revolution, hopes were raised for the institutionalization of genuine autonomy within the emerging Soviet system. By the end of the Civil War, however, Communism in the USSR was revealing itself to have a Russian face. One by-product was the reemergence of a more typical Tatar perspective, this time under the guise of "national communism" most associated with the name of Mir Said Sultangaliev.[24]

Sultangaliev arrived at Marxism only after a long apprenticeship as a Jadid. Becoming the most prominent Muslim Communist by the early 1920s and a leading figure within Bolshevik ranks, he remained imbued with the cultural concerns of his earlier years and with a vital commitment to the preservation of Tatar identity. In the still heady climate of debate among Bolsheviks before 1923 Sultangaliev spoke boldly on issues of practical concern, but he is most remembered for articulating theoretical positions on several critical issues: the affiliation between Communism and Islam, the relationship between social and national revolution in the economically backward countries, and the role of the Tatars in spearheading the revolution's expansion beyond the Soviet Union to the south and east. In brief, he saw the future of the revolution in the East and not in the West, among peasant and semi-colonial societies and not the advanced capitalist ones. He spoke of proletarian nations and not classes, of the need to preserve the cohesion of the Turkic/Muslim world and, therefore, of delaying indefinitely the playing out of any internal class struggles. On the highly charged issue of the formation of the new Union of Soviet Socialist Republics, Sultangaliev opposed plans for a federation of ethnically-based units, small and divided vis-à-vis the large and powerful Russian Republic. Instead, he and other national communists advocated creation of a Republic of Turan, a pan-Turkic entity combining the territories of Central Asia, the North Caucasus, Azerbaijan, Daghestan, and the Middle Volga, governed by its own centralized, monolithic, and autonomous party and controlling its own army. Moreover, Sultangalievism called for the establishment of a "Colonial International" to focus attention and resources on the societies perceived to be most vulnerable to the revolutionary program. "If we want to sponsor the revolution in the East," wrote one Tatar Communist, "we must create in Soviet Russia a territory close to the Muslim East, which could become an experimental laboratory for the building of Communism, where the best revolutionary forces can be concentrated."[25]

As for the Tatars themselves, Sultangaliev insisted that they were "the pioneers of the social revolution in the East." Thanks to their more advanced cultural condition, they could inspire the development of more backward areas. "Already we witness people from all corners of the Urals, Siberia, Central Asia and Turkestan, Khiva and Bukhara, and even far-off Afghanistan arriving in Tataria with demands of its cultural leaders . . . ."[26] The implications of Sultangaliev's program are striking: Not only would Communism take on a "Muslim" face, but it would likely speak Tatar and have as its headquarters not Moscow but Kazan! The challenge to Russian dominance of the international revolutionary movement was direct and blunt; if unobstructed, Sultangalievism would likely have carried Tatar hegemonic impulses to their logical political end.

For Stalin the challenge was too profound. As the party's chief spokesman next to Lenin on nationality issues, as an adamant proponent of extreme centralization, and as one whom we know from hindsight to have possessed unlimited political ambition, he felt that the national communists would have to be defeated. The Tatars, "the worst of them all," as he is quoted[27] were chosen to be broken first, and Tatar influence within the larger Turkic world dismantled. As early as the end of 1918, the campaign against the independence of "native" organizations was well underway; over the next several years, leading up to Sultangaliev's first denunciation by Stalin himself in 1923, the pressure would continue, setting the scene for the all-out assault against national communism in the late 1920s.[28] As with the murder of Sergeĭ Kirov in 1934, the arrest and imprisonment of Sultangaliev in 1928 opened a flood-gate that trampled lives and alternatives to Stalinism far and wide.

The crusade against national communism resulted in the elimination of independent-minded ethnic leaders all across the Soviet Union; it was particularly devastating in greater Central Asia. By the eve of the Second World War, few if any such figures were left alive. As these men were the most powerful public defenders of *korenizatsiia,* the policy of the 1920s by which formation and development of native cadres were encouraged along with the flourishing of indigenous cultures, their absence made full betrayal by Stalin of the Revolution's ethnic promises largely unstoppable. Respect for diversity gave way to demands for conformity, and under the guise of "internationalism," Russification became the objective. The ambition to create a new Soviet man and woman, as the Tatar historian and activist, G. Ibragimov, underscored in his 1927 essay *Tatar Mädäniyeti nindi yul belän barajaq?* (Which Way Will Tatar Culture Go?), would toll the death knell of native cultures.[29] The threat was particularly grave to the Tatars, whose fragmentation and isolation under diaspora circumstances made them especially vulnerable. Soviet power and moral indifference shortly overwhelmed Tatar counter efforts, rendering them pitiable and tragic for their inefficacy. Obversely, Central Asians in the five established republics benefitted from this development, insofar as Tatar influence over their cultures was broken and Tatars in their midst rendered innocuous.

The fabric of deceit that clothed the USSR from the early 1930s on survived for decades after Stalin's death. It is true, taking the Tatars as a case, that from the late 1950s on the opportunities to recover bits and pieces of social memory, seemingly obliterated in earlier decades, were eked out little by little; but all such advances, important as they were, indirectly acknowledged the regime's continued viability and its unfettered control over Soviet society. Hence Mikhail Gorbachev's espousal of a new social and economic discourse in the USSR in 1985, building as he did, of course, on initiatives launched by Yuri Andropov had critical significance.

One of the barely recognized consequences for Tatars and Central Asians generally was a renewed diaspora consciousness.[30] While it is too early to assess its long-term effects, the attention given to the dispersion of the Tatar people is one reflection of the larger question of identity and sovereignty riveting so many. Deciding who the Tatars are may well be the key to resolving numerous social issues. Thus, the debate over ethnos and ethnonyms among all the Turkic peoples rages not only as an esoteric concern of withdrawn intellectuals, but as a popular theme with clear political implications.[31] Are the Volga Tatars the lineal descendants of the tenth-century Volga Bulgars? If so, then the name Tatar—a much later colonial attribution—ought to be replaced with Bulgar, as members of the social organization, *Bulgar al-jadid* (The New Bulgar), have advocated.[32] To adopt that argument, however, out of the legitimate desire to reject Russian domination, raises other questions, some of which are bluntly posed by the writer Robert Batulla:

> Let's admit that we are Bulgars. What will then happen to the Kriashens? Obviously, they are not Bulgars. What about the Penza, Siberian, Crimean, Baraba Tatars? Their ancestors did not live on the territory of the Middle-Volga Bulgar state. This will lead to confusion, discord, and a terrible division of the ancestral inheritance. And after the division, only the chips of one great culture will remain. . . . How can people not understand? We are a united multi-million Tatar people."[33]

He might have included other Turkic peoples as well in his anxiety about "a terrible division of the ancestral inheritance."

Palpable concern for the diaspora elements of the extended Tatar family has manifested itself with growing scope at least since early 1988. *Kazan Utlarï,* the monthly Kazan Tatar literary review that has played a leading institutional role of cultural defender for many years, introduced a new section entitled *"Tatar khälk'i: Törle töbäklärdä, törle illärdä"* (The Tatar People: In Various Places, in Various Lands), that carries information about Tatars abroad, whether in Finland, Japan, Turkey, or the United States. Moreover the journal has been publishing letters from individual Tatars in other countries, all designed to assist with "filling in the blanks" of history and bring the diaspora at least spiritually back to the hearth. Contributing to this task have been important articles by the Tatar literary scholar Ibrahim Nurullin and the historian A. Khalikov, both of whom have challenged the charge of treason long applied to those Tatars who had emigrated after October, 1917, and have criticized the "conspiracy of silence" surrounding émigré contributions to the Tatar heritage.[34]

One striking cultural event has been the announcement from M.Z. Zakiev, director of the Institute of Language, Literature, and History (Kazan) concerning plans for compilation of a Tatar encyclopedia as part of a larger effort to "reconstruct the history of the entire Tatar people." As Zakiev argues, this is a task "complicated even more by the fact that only one quarter of the Tatar people reside in their titular republic. Many Tatars, in fact, *though remaining on the territories they have always inhabited* [emphasis added], are found outside the borders of the TASSR. A significant number of Tatars make up a diaspora scattered throughout the Soviet Union."[35] The encyclopedia, treated as a project of immense cultural import, will apparently be international not only in content but in authorship.

On the socio-political scene, a congress of the Tatar diaspora convened from February 17–18, 1989, in Kazan, reaffirming "the sovereignty and indivisibility of the Tatar nation and the units of Tatar culture across the administrative territorial divisions of the USSR." The Congress's resolutions called also for the "consolidation of the Tatar nation," and requested of UNESCO a Tatar-language version of its publication *Courier*. The final articles in the resolutions proclaimed solidarity with the Crimean Tatars and their struggle for return to their homeland.[36] In June 1990 we learned of a project for the creation of a Volga-Ural Federation, although the geographical delimitations of that federation were left undefined. Two months later formation of a political party calling itself *Ittifaq* (Unity) again saw stress placed on the return "home" of diaspora Tatars and a call, at least temporarily, for a regional federation, presumably on the order of the Volga-Ural project. In October of that same year another party's founding was announced—*Vatan* (Fatherland)—which, appropriately all-Union, aimed at the recreation of Tatar statehood either within the USSR or outside it, on the territory of the former Astrakhan, Kazan, and Siberian Khanates![37]

In these extraordinary and unsettling times of late, the outcomes of astounding processes underway throughout the former Soviet Union defy easy prognosis. The fate of the Tatar Republic and of the millions of Tatars scattered about the former union will be subject to long, complex, and intense debate before being resolved. Creating new mechanisms for establishing close relations between the homeland and the diaspora will undoubtedly continue to consume the energies and imaginations of many; formation of a larger pan-Turkic federation (cultural and economic, if not political), involving some of the Central Asian republics, may well be part of any solution.[38] Many will probably agree with the sentiments expressed by R. Kharis in *Kommunist Tatarii* that "to hold a wake for the past is to forget an old brotherhood," or with I. Tahirov's rhetorical question: "Is it pan-Turkism, this desire of related peoples, in this case of the Turkic peoples, to live together as brothers?"[39] Still, the Tatar tendency toward what Edward Allworth terms "monoethnicity" is likely to be obstructed even by those who dream of [re]creating a Great Turkistan. The perspective from Central Asia's many parts is simply too heterogeneous to carry this particular dream very far.

Notes

1. N. I. Il'minskiĭ to K. P. Pobedonostsev, as quoted in A. A. Voskresenskiĭ, *O sisteme prosveshcheniia inorodtsev* (Kazan, 1913), p. 38. Il'minskiĭ was hardly exceptional in his attitudes, and his writings represent merely a small portion of a considerable body of anti-Tatar literature produced in the nineteenth and early twentieth centuries.

2. Zdeshniĭ, "Sovremennaia 'tatarshchina'," *Novoe vremia,* No. 6524 (April 24, 1894), p. 3.

3. In 1976, John A. Armstrong wrote a seminal article on diasporas in which he distinguished between the archetypal (complete, permanent, and unable to constitute a compact majority anywhere), and the situational (partial and temporary). Armstrong recognizes an intermediate type of diaspora, which he gives no designation, characterized by possession of a territorial base that has long been under foreign domination and "had suffered an equally long period of economic and cultural eclipse compared to the affluence and vitality of the diaspora." He cites the Armenians as typical; I would offer the Tatars as a second example. See "Mobilized and Proletarian Diasporas," *The American Political Science Review,* LXX, No. 2 (June, 1976), pp. 393–408.

4. S. Kh. Alishev, *Istoricheskie sud'by narodov Srednego Povolzh'ia XVI—nachalo XIX v.* (Moscow, 1990), pp. 180–181.

5. *Polnoe sobranie zakonov Rossiĭskoĭ imperii,* First Series, V (1713–1719), No. 3149, p. 523. Hereafter cited as PSZ.

6. *Puteshestviia russkikh poslov XVI–XVII vv.* (Moscow, 1954), p. 373.

7. S. Kh. Alishev, *Istoricheskie sud'by,* p. 195.

8. See *Akty, sobrannye v bibliotekakh i arkhivakh Rossiĭskoĭ imperii Arkheograficheskoiu ekspeditsieiu Akademii Nauk* (St. Petersburg, 1836), I, No. 358 (1593); PSZ, First Series, IV, No. 1946 (1713); PSZ, First Series, XI, No. 8664 (1742); and PSZ, First Series, XII, No. 8875 (1744).

9. S. Kh. Alishev, *Istoricheskie sud'by,* p. 158.

10. Arguments for using Tatars to settle among the unruly Bashkirs can be found in:

Materialy po istorii Bashkirskoĭ ASSR (Moscow, 1956), IV, Pt. 1, doc. 414, pp. 202–206; "Zapiski Petra Ivanovicha Rychkova," *Russkiĭ arkhiv (1905)*, pp. 289–340; "Zapiska Dmitriia Volkova ob Orenburgskoĭ gubernii 1763 g.," *Vestnik Russkago geograficheskago obshchestva (1859)*, Pt. 27, vol. II, pp. 49–61; "Zapiski Orenburgskago gubernatora Reinsdorpa v nedostatkakh vverennoĭ ego upravlenii gubernii," *Vestnik Russkago geograficheskago obshchestva (1859)*, Pt. 27, vol. II, pp. 90–104.

11. Ottoman influence on the Turkic peoples inhabiting the Russian Empire has received little attention from scholars, except the French research team originally headed by Alexandre Bennigsen and focused largely on the Crimean Khanate. Ottoman interests in the Black Sea and its surrounding territories always troubled Russia those interests were frequently projected (accurately or not) by Russians onto Turkic communities further afield, in Central Asia proper, the Kazakh steppe, and the Volga region as well. Rumors of Ottoman infiltration, particularly by mullahs functioning as some sort of subversive fifth-column fomenting mass anti-Russian sentiment and behavior, were common even as late as the early twentieth century.

12. On the creation of the Muslim Spiritual Assembly and the definition of its duties and personnel, see PSZ, First Series, Vol. XXII, Nos. 16710, 16711, 16759, 16897, and 17099 (1788); on construction subsidies, PSZ, First Series, Vol. XXII, Nos. 16255 (1785); on the printing of texts, "Arkhiv Grafa Igel'stroma," *Russkiĭ arkhiv*, No. 11 (1886), doc. 17, and PSZ, First Series, Vol. XXIV, No. 18287; and on noble status for *murzas*, PSZ, First Series, Vol. XXII, No. 15936 (1784).

13. For a fuller treatment of this analysis and particularly the difference between *tajdid* and *Jadid* modalities of reform, see my "Beyond Renewal: The Jadid Response to Pressure for Change in the Modern Age," in *Muslims in Central Asia: Expressions of Identity and Change*, ed. by Jo Ann Gross (Durham: Duke University Press, 1992), p. 151–166. That same volume also contains a very useful article on the prominent nineteenth-century Naqshbandiyya sheikh, Zaynullah Rasulev, in which the international linkages among expressions of ferment are effectively underscored. See, Hamid Algar, "Shaykh Zaynullah Rasulev: The last Great Naqshbandi Shaykh of the Volga-Urals Region," pp. 112–133.

14. For an exposition of this polemic, see my "Defining the Orient: A Nineteenth-Century Russo-Tatar Polemic," in *Muslim Communities Reemerge: Historical Perspectives on Nationality, Politics, and Opposition in the Former Soviet Union and Yugoslavia*, ed. by Andreas Kappeler (Durham: Duke University Press, 1994).

15. M. Mashanov, *Istoricheskoe i sovremennoe znachenie khristianskago missionerstva sredi musul'man* (Kazan, 1894), p. 261.

16. Ch.Ch. Valikhanov, "O musul'manstve v stepi," *Sobranie sochineniĭ v piati tomakh* (Alma-Ata, 1985), IV, p. 71.

17. The best and most comprehensive work on this subject is Azade-Ayşe Rorlich, *The Volga Tatars: A Profile in National Resilience* (Stanford: Hoover Institution Press, 1986).

18. Quoted in Edward Allworth, *The Modern Uzbeks from the Fourteenth Century to the Present: A Cultural History* (Stanford: Hoover Institution Press, 1990), p. 191. Allworth goes on to acknowledge Central Asian hostility towards Tatars as being rooted in fear of the Tatar hegemonic agenda. This led, for example, to Central Asian charges that Tatars were distorting their history. Moreover, many Central Asians seem to have distrusted Tatars for their perceived association with the region's Russian conquerors.

19. A. Karimullin, "Tatarsko-Kazakhskie knigoizdatel'skie sviazi." *Knigi i liudi.*

Issledovanie (Kazan: Tatarskoe knizhnoe izdatel'stvo, 1985), p. 171. Karimullin has published extensively and masterfully on the history of the Tatar book, his works including: *U istokov tatarskoĭ knigi (ot nachala vozniknoveniia do 60-kh godov XIX veka)* (Kazan, 1971), *Tatarskaia kniga nachala XX veka* (Kazan, 1974), and *Tatarskaia kniga poreformennoĭ Rossii* (Kazan, 1983).

20. Martha Brill Olcott, *The Kazakhs* (Stanford: Hoover Institution Press, 1987), p. 108.

21. Work is desperately needed on the relationship between the Tatar entrepreneurial spirit and wealth and the evolution of *Jadidism.* Good places to begin are: G.S. Gubaidullin, "Iz proshlogo tatar," *Materialy po izucheniiu Tatarstana, vyp. 2* (Kazan, 1925), pp. 71–111; Kh. Kh. Khasanov, *Formirovanie tatarskoĭ burzhuaznoĭ natsii* (Kazan, 1977); and Ahsen Bore (ed.), *Gani Bay* (Helsinki, 1945), a reissue of an important collection of correspondence (originally published in 1912) between Gani Bay Huseinov, a wealthy Orenburg merchant and philanthropist, and various prominent Tatars.

22. For general surveys of these developments see A. Rorlich, *The Volga Tatars,* Chapter 9; A. Arsharuni and Kh. Gabidullin, *Ocherki panislamizma i pantiurkizma v Rossii* (Moscow, 1934); and S. A. Zenkovsky, *Pan-Turkism and Islam in Russia* (Cambridge, Mass., 1960).

23. The editorial position of *Ulugh Türkistan,* as Edward Allworth notes, was "evidenced by its sponsorship, audiences, and linguistic media—Kazak, Turkistanian, and Tatar. By the newspaper's definition, then, all the subregions and Turkic peoples of Tatarstan and Central Asia, including Kazakstan and eastern (Chinese) Turkistan, . . . were partners in this Great Turkistan." Edward Allworth, *The Modern Uzbeks,* p. 180.

24. The literature on Sultangaliev is growing and will likely continue to do so. The most detailed work thus far includes: A. Bennigsen and Ch. Quelquejay, *Les Mouvements nationaux chez les musulmans de Russie* (Paris, 1960); A. Bennigsen and S. Enders Wimbush, *Muslim National Communism in the Soviet Union: A Revolutionary Strategy for the Colonial World* (Chicago, 1979); Stephen Blank, "Stalin's First Victim: The Trial of Sultangaliev," *Russian History/Histoire Russe,* XVII, No. 2 (Summer, 1990), pp. 155–178; and Azade-Ayşe Rorlich, "The Disappearance of an Old Taboo: Is Sultangaliev Becoming Persona Grata?" RFE/RL *Report on the USSR,* I, No. 39 (September 29, 1989), p. 16–19.

25. Sahib-Girey Said Galiev, cited in Bennigsen and Wimbush, *Muslim National Communism,* p. 67.

26. M. S. Sultangaliev, "Tatary i oktiabr'skaia revoliutsiia," *M. S. Sultan-Galiev. Stat'i* (Oxford: Society for Central Asian Studies, 1984), pp. 38 and 40. This article originally appeared in *Zhizn' natsional'nosteĭ,* No. 24 (November, 1921).

27. Stalin's antipathy to Muslims generally and Tatars in particular is recalled by Semen Lipkin, "Bukharin, Stalin i 'Manas'," *Ogonëk,* No. 2 (1989), pp. 22–24, and Indus Tahirov, "Kem ul Soltangaliev?," *Kazan Utlarï,* No. 4 (1989), pp. 163–174.

28. The assault would include maneuvers to replace the Arabic alphabet with the Latin (ultimately, the Cyrillic), and further reducing the opportunities for Tatarization.

29. For a detailed analysis of Ibragimov's essay, see Azade-Ayşe Rorlich, "'Which Way Will Tatar Culture Go?' A Controversial Essay by G. Ibragimov," *Cahiers du monde russe et soviétique,* Nos. 3–4 (1974), pp. 363–371.

30. See Azade-Ayşe Rorlich, "Tatars and Azerbaijanis Reach Out to the Diaspora," RFE/RFL *Report on the USSR,* I, No. 34 (August 25, 1989), pp. 27–29.

31. For a scholarly treatment of the issues, see A. Karimullin, *Tatary: etnos i etnonim* (Kazan', 1989).

32. For a survey of the early activities of this group, see Azade-Ayse Rorlich, "Tatars or Bulghars? The New Winds of Glasnost' Bring Back an Old Apple of Discord," *RFE/RL Report on the USSR,* I, No. 31 (August 4, 1989), pp. 22–24. Rorlich notes in passing that "speeches of those who addressed the participants contained remarks offensive to Russians and Crimean Tatars," providing interesting evidence of Tatar views counter to that implicit in diaspora consciousness.

33. R. Batulla, "Iabloka razdora," *Vecherniaia Kazan',* November 5, 1988, discussed in Azade-Ayşe Rorlich, "Tatars or Bulghars," pp. 23–24.

34. I. Nurullin, "Vozrashchenie Gayaza Ishaki," *Vecherniaia Kazan',* October 17, 1988, and A. Khalikov, "Galim yaktashlar," *Sotsialistik Tatarstan,* January 15, 1989, as discussed in Azade-Ayşe Rorlich, "Filling in the Blank Spots of Tatar Cultural History," *RFE/RL Report on the USSR,* I, No. 17 (April 28, 1989), pp. 20–22.

35. M.Z. Zakiev, "Tatar Encyclopedia to be Created," *Central Asia and Caucasus Chronicle,* IX, No. 4 (August, 1990), p. 1–3.

36. For a translation of the resolutions of the diaspora congress, see "The Tatar Public Centre" (TOTs), *Central Asian Survey,* IX, No. 2 (1990), pp. 155–165. A translation of the Center's platform can be found in *Central Asia and Caucasus Chronicle,* VIII, No. 2 (May, 1989), pp. 5–9. R. Batulla may have summed up most succinctly the popular attitude toward ties between Kazan and Crimean Tatars: "Until the Revolution, more exactly until the replacement of the Arabic alphabet, Crimean and Kazan Tatars had one cultural life, subscribed to the same periodicals, exchanged artists and writers. The change of the alphabet severely divided our people. An artificial barrier was created." See Batulla's "Iabloka razdora," *Vecherniaia Kazan'* (November 5, 1988), cited in Azade-Ayşe Rorlich, "Tatars or Bulghars," p. 23.

37. *RFE/RL Report on the USSR,* October 26, 1990, p. 27.

38. For expression of pan-Turkic aspirations by a prominent Central Asian, see James Critchlow, "Will Soviet Central Asia Become a Greater Uzbekistan?" RFE/RFL *Report on the USSR,* II, No. 37 (September 14, 1990), pp. 17–19.

39. R. Kharis, "Tatary. Poema-monolog," *Kommunist Tatarii,* No. 3 (1989), p. 90, cited in Azade-Ayşe Rorlich, "Tatars or Bulghars," p. 24; and I. Tahirov, "Kem ul Soltangaliev?" p. 173.

PART TWO

RELIGION AND ETHNIC RELATIONS IN 20TH-CENTURY CENTRAL ASIA

CHAPTER 5

Soviet Uzbekistan: State and Nation in Historical Perspective

Donald S. Carlisle

The use of concepts like "nation" and "state" requires that their meanings be clarified and separated. The crucial and elusive distinction was underlined by Hugh Seton-Watson when he wrote:

> States can exist without a nation, or with several nations among their subjects; and a nation can be coterminous with the population of one state, or be included together with other nations within one state, or be divided between several states. There were states long before there were nations, and there are some nations that are older than most states which exist today. The belief that every state is a nation, or that all sovereign states are national states, has done much to obfuscate human understanding of political realities. . . . The frequently heard cliché that "we live in an age of nation-states" is at most a half-truth. What is arguably true is that we live in an age of sovereign states. . . . [1]

This is an essential prologue to an attempt to provide historical perspective on Uzbekistan—once a subordinate republic of the USSR and now an independent state and member of the United Nations. It cautions against the assumption that state-making is identical with nation-building. For while the former is often clear and concrete, the latter is more likely to be murky and problematic. Success on one front does not necessarily provide victory on the other and there is no reason to assume that these are mutually reinforcing processes; indeed their relationship may be dialectical rather than unicausal.

This approach to Uzbekistan's origin is necessary in view of its relatively short life span and its inadequately explained emergence in clouded circumstances: it is essential to remember that it was only in 1924 that Uzbekistan surfaced as a separate and distinct entity within the USSR. The distinction between state and nation underlines a concern of this study; it also draws attention to the problematic character even today of an integrated Uzbek nation in contrast to the uncontested existence of a state named for it.[2] What must be underlined in probing Uzbekistan's origin and subsequent history is the priority of politics, not demographics, in its formation. The tale to be told is one of state-creation and attempted nation-building. The primary role in this endeavor was played by the Soviet state and not by an emerging Uzbek nation.

The Argument

The following pages document the decisive role of intra-elite politics and the subordinate place of national or ethnic considerations in Uzbekistan's origin and maturation. Two key episodes are discussed. First is the story of the rise and fall of the "Muslim Bureau"(*Musbyuro*) in post-Revolution Soviet Turkestan. Initially Muslim or Turkic native Communists, led by Turar Ryskulov, tried to create a supranational State based on the unity of the region's people. They sought to sublimate local differences in a larger Turkic identity and create a Communist Turkestan which they hoped would serve as a revolutionary magnet, attracting to itself other oppressed Asian peoples.

This effort was quickly rejected by Lenin and the Bolsheviks; in fact, we shall show what has not been generally recognized in Western scholarship—that as early as 1920, Moscow reacted with a proposal for dividing Turkestan into national units. However, this proposed subdivision was rejected by Lenin. Later, in 1924, the Bolsheviks—in concert with local native politicians—were to propose a revamped version of the 1920 partition plan known as the "national delimitation" of borders, which was implemented.

The second case study investigates the events from which emerged Uzbekistan and the other states into which the Central Asian region is now divided.[3] A novel interpretation of the national delimitation is presented. While recognizing the importance of figures in Moscow (Stalin in particular), emphasis is on the play of local politics and the place of native politicians whose cooperation with the Center was essential for the success of the project. Local divisions and mutual animosities, plus the power and personal ambitions of Central Asian politicans, are crucial variables, although they are often missing from the accounts of Soviet and Western historians.

This analysis thus focuses on the major cleavages among as well as the ambitions of the main Central Asian leaders. These divisions were by no means primarily ethnic in nature; the identities in conflict were essentially political and they produced patriotisms that were also regional or geopolitical, not merely "national." To focus exclusively on nationality as the key is to distort the story and to exclude the political element: indeed the long-time Soviet effort was to dress these players in purely national garb so as to disguise what was a thoroughly political drama.

The politically-oriented approach adopted in these pages emphasizes the principal instigators and main local beneficiaries of the national delimitation: they were the Bukhara Jadids—in particular Faizulla Khojaev and his followers. The argument is that "Uzbekistan," which appeared for the first time in 1925 with a capital at Samarkand, should be viewed as a product of their lobbying and a reflection of their influence. What emerged as Uzbekistan was in fact a Greater Bukhara.

Finally, in the conclusion, it will be argued that this analysis, which unearths two alternative routes rather than one inevitable national path of development, is relevant to Uzbekistan's present predicament. It suggests a possible evolution into something other than the narrow nation-state framework championed in 1925 by Faizulla Khojaev and Moscow.

The Muslim Bureau in Turkestan

We begin with a consideration of Moscow's 1919–20 experiment in Soviet Turkestan where it temporarily tolerated a "Muslim Bureau" (*Musbyuro*) as a party branch, and the hectic career of its leader, Turar Ryskulov. Moscow's policy in Turkestan reflected the central regime's attempt to tap the radical impulse among Muslim reformers for the Communist cause. The Tatar Sultangaliev represented an example of the hoped for conversion of Muslim radicals to Bolshevism. It was believed that by courting Ryskulov and his associates, the Bolsheviks could bring about a similar metamorphosis in Turkestan.[4]

Ryskulov was born in 1894 in Semirechie to a kazakh family of cattle-breeders. When his father was deported to Siberia in the wake of the 1905 Revolution, Turar moved to live with a relative in Aulie-Ata. As a horticulturist he worked during 1915–16 in the Tashkent area and became acquainted with Marxist literature. Returning to Aulie-Ata during the 1916 uprising, he played an active role in the rebellion, for which he was arrested.

Released from prison after the downfall of the Tsar, Ryskulov organized "a circle of revolutionary-oriented youth," and in September 1917 entered the ranks of the *RSDRP.* In 1918 he was named *Narkom* of Health for Turkestan—a responsibility not easily met in view of the widespread hunger and famine in native areas. By March 1918 he had risen to even loftier heights for, while continuing as head of the "Committee Combatting Hunger," Ryskulov was appointed Assistant Chairman of Turkestan's Central Executive Committee of Soviets itself.

From this point his star seemed to rise and fall simultaneously with that of another native leader, the Jadid reformer, Sagdulla Tursun Khojaev, who was an Social Revolutionary but who in March 1918 joined the Bolsheviks.[5] Both men were to play crucial roles in the rise of the Turkestan Muslim Bureau in mid-1919 and its equally sudden decline a year later.

The First Conference of Turkestan's Muslim Communist organization took place at the end of May 1919. Up to this time, the Tashkent Soviet regime—this Russian-dominated outpost of Bolshevism—had shown little interest in any liberation mission. Concern with an "Oriental Revolution" was confined to protecting proletarian power from being swamped locally by native numbers and the overriding need to suppress the native rebellion, the so-called Basmachi.[6]

However, the Muslim Bureau exhibited a preoccupation with imperialism and its members intended to oppose the enemy at home and abroad—whether in British or Russian garb.

Local Russian-native antagonisms were evident in the hostile atmosphere at the Muslim Conference. George Safarov wrote: "Even while the Conference was meeting, the Tashkent Soviet was actually promoting its campaign of suppression against the native population of Turkestan and the Conference found itself obliged to provide its members with special certificates exempting them from search and arrest without the consent of the conference presidium."[7] At the same time an historic extraordinary directive from Moscow dated July 10, 1919 ordered "proportional representation" for natives.[8] It provided the detonator for the political explosion that followed, reinforcing the confidence of Ryskulov and his colleagues and boding ill for the local Russians. The Muslim Bureau had taken on the major task of recruiting natives so as to build local support and to isolate the Basmachi. The Russian-based Party was ignored as this separate and parallel—though officially subordinate—Muslim counterweight emerged. The Directive calling for "proportional representation" demanded a radical adjustment in the local Russians' power structure and a substantial curtailment of the influence of the "Europeans" as they were euphemistically labeled.

By July, 1919 the Muslim Bureau was dealing on an almost equal footing with the local Russian proletarians. During the fall and winter—after the arrival from Moscow of Lenin's emissaries, the so-called "Turkestan Commission" (*Turk Komissia*), its Russian opponents were disgraced and some removed from high positions, as Muslims were elevated to replace them. Ryskulov, Tursun Khojaev and their Jadid associates must have been dizzy with success as they watched the Russian lords shipped out of Turkestan and some of Tashkent's railroad organizations—the first strongholds of Bolshevism in Central Asia—disbanded and sent packing. But they may have missed the key lesson implicit in all this: the Center's determination and superior power that produced this favorable outcome could orchestrate their own disgrace if deemed necessary.

Muslim Communists as Turkic Bolsheviks

In January 1920 the Communist Party of Turkestan's Fifth Regional Congress and the Third Conference of the Muslim Bureau simultaneously convened. A prior effort of the Turkestan Commission to unify the three Party branches under one leadership was approved, and S. Tursun Khojaev was chosen Secretary of the Party's united Executive Regional Committee. Since Ryskulov was then Chairman of the Turkestan Party Executive Committee this moment marked the high tide in the Muslim Communists' fortunes. They had been lifted to dazzling heights; they were soon to experience an even more precipitous fall. Ryskulov unveiled his program at these January meetings. A "Turkic Republic" had to be recognized and the Communist Party of Turkestan had to be transformed into a "Turkic Communist Party."[9] The periphery or borderlands would exercise extensive control in all realms amounting to virtual state and party independence from Moscow. His program also called for creation of a Muslim army and the rectification of the land question in the interest of the natives.

Whether Ryskulov demanded that all Russians be excluded from a "Turkic Communist Party" and all European peasant settlers evicted from Turkestan is not clear. The available outlines of his program suggest that, if these were not explicit planks, they were at least implicit in real independence based on loose ties with the Center.[10] What Ryskulov envisaged seemed to be a confederative framework with Soviet Russia. It seemed far removed from even the federal union that the Bolsheviks were reluctantly to accept as the most expedient means to recapture the Tsarist patrimony. It was profoundly incompatible with Lenin's centralized Party.

In January 1920 Moscow's trusted emissaries, the recently-arrived members of the Turkestan Commission, were in no position to provide clear direction. Initially, they were divided as to Ryskulov's proposals regarding a "Turkic" Party and state. The arrival of another Turkestan Commission member, Frunze, with his troops fresh from a victorious Transcaspian campaign, proved the turning point. Frunze reconvened the Commission and demanded that approval for a "Turkic" Party and state be revoked. Sometime in the spring, with Lenin's approval, Frunze and the Turkestan Commission imposed Bolshevik norms and implemented centralizing directives from Moscow. Henceforth, Soviet Turkestan was to enter into an even tighter embrace with the RSFSR, and the Party's local branch had to accept *oblast,* or provincial, rather than republic-level status.

In March 1920 the Russian Communist Party's (*RKP*) Central Committee dispatched guidelines for future relations between Center and periphery. Leaving some questions open for negotiation, they made clear that no real autonomy, and certainly no territorial enlargement, would be tolerated. Then in something of a coup in July, Frunze ejected Ryskulov and his associates from their posts. He was suspicious of the Muslim Communists and skeptical as to the depth of their conversion to the Bolshevik cause. A confidential appraisal he sent to Lenin states:

> As to the Muslim group which has from time to time attained an extraordinary national aggressiveness, it is essentially very weak and in fact itself recognizes its own weakness. Regarding its Communism it is possible to speak only by stretching a point; minus a few people whose politics you cannot imagine, the group consists of definitely non-Communist elements who only by force of circumstances took up the Communist banner. In my judgement their political weight is very minimal; the masses are not with them. This they feel, and therefore on the proper and honest principled line implemented by the Center, they rapidly gave up their position and came to terms with the Center. Just how sincere this is, well, that's another question.

> The most important of these Muslim Communists are the Kirghiz [i.e. Kazakh] Ryskulov and the Uzbek Tursun Khojaev, Chairman of the *Kraikom* [Regional Party Committee]. The first is a most outstanding fellow, besides intelligence possessing energy and an outstanding character. . . .
>
> I stood for and continue to stand for our taking over the local organs [of power], not hesitating about entering them ourselves, but on the contrary, adopting this as a definite practical objective. . . .[11]

Earlier, as the dispute had deepened, Ryskulov and his supporters had refused to submit meekly and appealed to Lenin, believing that Lenin might share their views if acquainted with local conditions. Therefore in May 1920 Ryskulov led a delegation to Moscow. He was to be deeply disappointed. A special Central Committee group was appointed to study the Turkestan question. It submitted a draft proposal, which—with minor adjustments made by Lenin personally—provided the framework for future Soviet policy in Central Asia. In his notes to the draft proposal, Lenin made clear that while some reforms—particularly in the agrarian sphere—would be implemented, Ryskulov's major proposals had to be rejected.

A very crucial Center-inspired project for an ethnic partition of Turkestan had surfaced in this period and proved a harbinger of Moscow's later plan for the region. It sought to subdivide Turkestan into Uzbek, Turkmen, and "Kirghiz" (actually Kazakh) units. When precisely it was unveiled and who exactly was behind it is uncertain. We do not know whether it had already surfaced during the initial deliberations of the Turkestan Commission in the winter. If so, then perhaps Ryskulov knew about it and tabled his "Turkic" proposals in reaction. We do know that the ethnic partition plan appeared not much later than January—perhaps when Frunze arrived on the scene. It is likely that Ryskulov's protest and trip to Moscow were related to it. However, it is also possible that he was kept in the dark as to this subdivision scheme. Perhaps only during his lobbying effort in Moscow was he apprised of its existence, and the threat to implement it used to silence him.

In discussion of Ryskulov's proposals, Lenin considered various options and we know that this plan for a division of Turkestan into Uzbek, Turkmen, and Kirghiz (Kazakh) parts was definitely one of them. However, Lenin rejected it while recommending that relevant data be gathered and ethnographic maps be prepared;[12] later, we were to be told by Soviet commentators after Lenin died that he was in principle for a national delimitation but had not approved it only because it was untimely and ill-prepared. This is a strained or even disingenuous argument. True, he had directed that appropriate ethnographic materials be gathered, but the important fact was that in 1920 he had definitely rejected it. He opted for the continued existence of the huge unit Soviet Turkestan—just as Ryskulov wanted—but of course he demanded it be fully dependent on Moscow. Lenin realistically recognized that ethnic principles were not relevant and a national subdivision in the region was absurd. It is tempting to see the hand of Stalin and some of his *Narkomnats* (People's Commissariat for Nationality Affairs) crew behind this 1920 delimitation plan: it was an application to Turkestan of a subdivision scenario Stalin had used to "solve" the Tatar/Bashkir dispute the year before.[13]

The Fall of Ryskulov

On July 19, 1920, Ryskulov, Tursun Khojaev and their associates were removed. The former party *kraikom's* membership was overturned and a Temporary Central Committee was established under Frunze and Kuibyshev's direction. It was virtually a political coup with only two members of the previous body finding places on the new *kraikom.*

The Muslim Bureau as an organization simply vanished when Ryskulov and his group were removed. There was no announcement that it was disbanded or that it had been superseded; it was simply erased, and all acted subsequently as if it had never existed. There is no better evidence of Moscow's fears and intentions than the way it reacted to the Muslim Bureau as an independent organization and to the possibility that it might become an attractive magnet for Muslim peoples and to provide the embryo of a pan-Turkic party and state.

Native newcomers—some would label them opportunists—climbed over the wreckage of Ryskulov's Turkic ship of state. Former Muslim Bureau Communists such as Turakukov and Rahimbaev—the first identified as a "kazakh" and the latter as a "tajik"—moved into key positions vacated by Ryskulov and Tursun Khojaev. It was not the last time, as we shall see, that personal ambition and ethnic rivalry combined with local feuds to provide the Bolsheviks with needed local collaborators.

The "Lenin of the Uzbeks": Faizulla Khojaev

The political game that Moscow played in an effort to keep its opponents off-balance and its enemies divided demanded much patience, considerable luck, and local collaborators. As early as the 1920 Muslim Bureau episode, it was clear that radical Turkic Communists could be induced to ally with the Bolsheviks, or to betray their associates for political advantage. A similar convergence of Moscow's interests with the ambitions of native politicians was demonstrated in 1924–25 during the national delimitation in Central Asia. This time Moscow's local allies were to be found in Bukhara and were grouped around the Young Bukharan radical, Faizulla Khojaev.

A Bolshevik version of conscious state construction and nation-building, the 1924–25 "national delimitation," divided the Turkestan ASSR into several ethnically-based new units. In addition, both Bukhara and Khiva—at the time quasi-independent Soviet states—were included in the pool of territory and peoples out of which new national republics were to be carved. As a result, there emerged Uzbekistan and Turkmenistan as Union republics, an enlarged Kazakhstan (augmented by territory from the defunct Soviet Turkestan), and Kirghiz and Tajik units, which were not yet given Union Republic status. Kirgizia became part of the RSFSR and Tajikistan was to be an autonomous republic within the Uzbek SSR.

It was in Soviet Bukhara—the successor state to the Bukharan Emirate—established in September 1920 with the assistance of the Red Army, that Moscow found its primary native allies and the talented politician on whom its major gamble would be made in Central Asia during the NEP (New Economic Policy). This was Faizulla Khojaev, son of one of Bukhara's wealthiest merchants and a radical figure in Bukhara's reform movement.[14] He served during 1920–24 as Chairman of the Bukharan *Sovnarkom* (Council of People's Commissars) and from 1925 until June 1937 held the comparable post in Uzbekistan.

Early in the NEP period, the Bolsheviks came to rely on Khojaev and his Jadid associates from Bukhara's reform movement; he and his followers came increasingly to depend on Moscow in order to master their local opponents and to checkmate recalcitrant traditional forces, which would have overwhelmed them without Bolshevik support.

In March 1917 Khojaev had sought the Russian Provisional Government's backing for the effort to transform the Emirate, but he failed in his endeavors. Radicalized by this failure, later in the year he persuaded Tashkent's new Soviet regime to mount a military expedition against the Emir. With its failure in March 1918, he fled Bukhara and Turkestan for Moscow and there established contact with Lenin and the Bolsheviks. Returning to Turkestan under Bolshevik auspices, in September 1920 his "Young Bukharans" with the support of the Red Army overthrew the Emir.[15] Although brought to power by Soviet arms, Khojaev and his wing of the Jadid movement set out to transform the Emirate in their own fashion. An account of Bukhara's politics by a resident Soviet diplomat describes Khojaev as "an astute and able man who thought in terms of the future," and adds:

> The Young Bokhara Party did not inspire confidence. It was divided into two groups based on political and blood affiliations—the Khojaev, led by Faycoulla Khojaev, and the Moukhedinov(sic). The Khojaev seemed to be the most modern in outlook and more inclined to us. . . .
>
> The new masters of Bokhara may have need of our assistance, but at heart they regard us as enemies. The power of the Soviets is still for them the power of Russia; and they fear it . . . If it were not for the ceaseless energy of Faycoulla Khojaev, the Turkish sympathies of the Moukhedin group would long ago have gained the day.
>
> Khojaev was so small he was sometimes nicknamed "the Lenin of the Uzbeks," and was the victim of a devouring energy in spite of the malaria which often gave his face a greenish tinge. He was in love with life, and could laugh gaily beneath an almost crushing load of work. He knew his people, was a great

> orator and a clever politician. He was much beloved. . . . He alone was capable of devising terms in which the little revolution of Bokhara and its big brother of Russia could understand one another. Later, he was instrumental in settling with the Central Committee the national frontiers of Turkestan.
>
> I several times went to see him. . . . His appearance was sickly, but there was a look of energy in his face, and his eyes were piercing. He wore a simple military tunic, though when he appeared in public he always put on a turban and draped himself in a khalat [robe].[16]

It would appear that quite early, Khojaev looked to a future revitalization of a region that extended beyond Bukhara's present borders; his projects already anticipated what finally surfaced as the national delimitation of 1924–25.[17]

Uzbekistan's Origin: Faizulla Khojaev as "Founding Father"

The 1924–25 national delimitation radically restructured local boundaries, erasing Soviet Turkestan and the ancient states of Bukhara and Khiva. The delimitation scheme appeared to dissolve the Bukharan SSR and in fact it did disappear from maps as a discernable entity. In the post-1925 State formations, most of old Bukhara was to be found in new Uzbekistan, although some of its western territory was incorporated into Turkmenistan. Its more isolated and mountainous terrain—East Bukhara and the Pamir region—were re-packaged as "Tajikistan," and, until 1929 this part of defunct Bukhara remained intact—as did virtually all of Bukhara—within Uzbekistan.

If we shift our analytical prism somewhat and refocus our attention, it becomes apparent that old Bukhara's fate was actually not as disastrous as a cursory reading of pre- and post-1925 maps might suggest. But the correct cartographic conclusion would be missed if the political machinations of the time were not introduced. Consider carefully Maps 5.1 and 5.2.[18] In the post-1925 Soviet map, Bukhara officially disappears as an independent unit, its territory supposedly incorporated in the new republics. But look again: actually what reappeared as Uzbekistan might be viewed as a Greater Bukhara. "Uzbekistan" was essentially Bukhara writ large! As Turkestan and Khiva were liquidated, the Samarkand region of Soviet Turkestan, as well as the Tashkent area and the major part of the rich Fergana valley, were merged with virtually all of the Bukhara SSR—and much of ancient Khiva/Khorezm—to constitute a new entity. What in fact emerged under Faizulla Khojaev and the Bukharan Jadids' control with its capital at Samarkand was old Bukhara now enlarged and disguised as new Uzbekistan.[19]

Faizulla Khojaev had in effect achieved the objectives which had escaped the Bukharan Emirs for centuries, for with the backing of the Russians, he presided over the absorption of territories once held by the Kokand and Khivan Khanates; he constructed a political entity that harkened back to much earlier times. Adopting this unconventional geopolitical perspective on the national

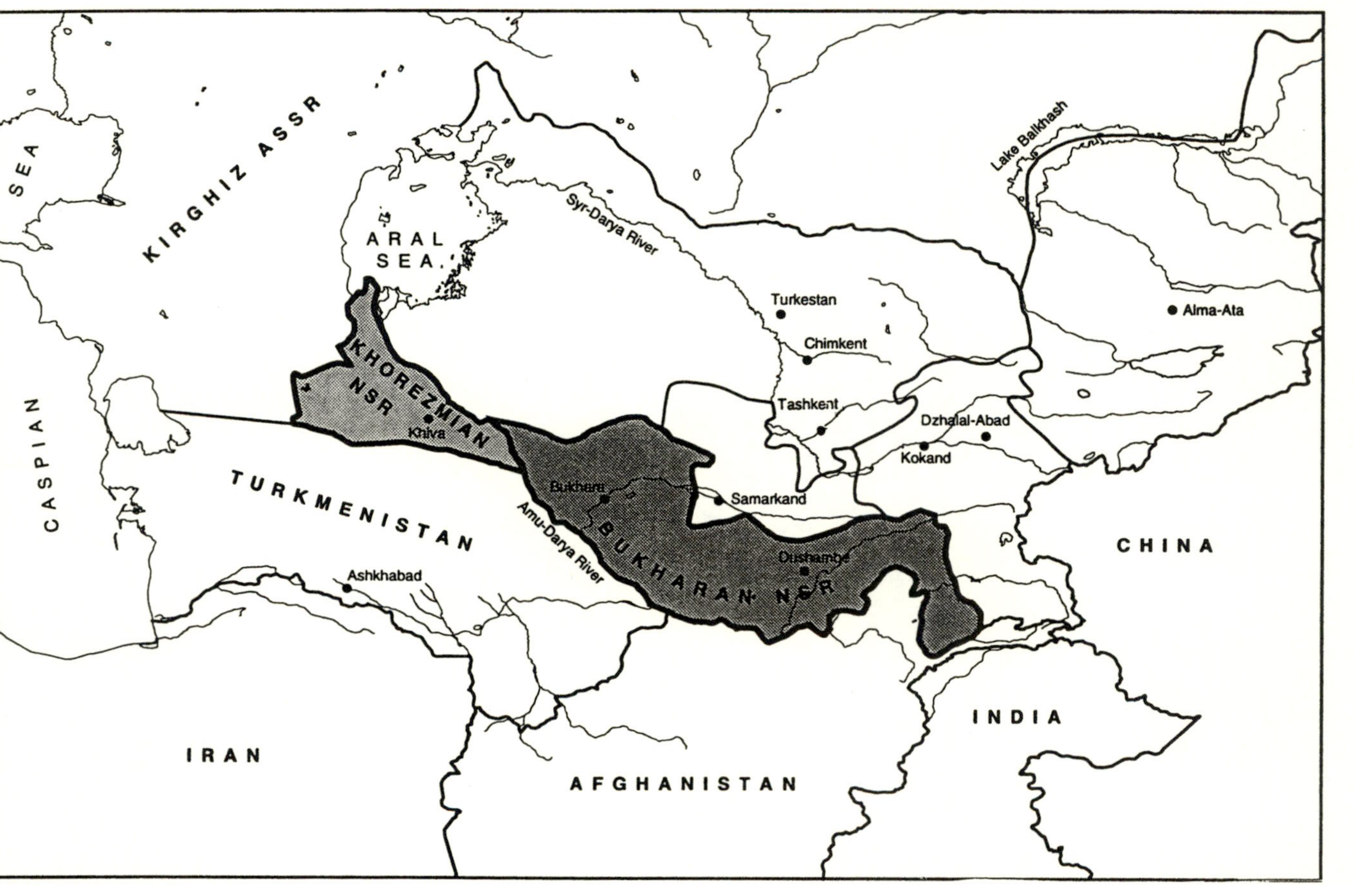
KIRGHIZ ASSR
CASPIAN SEA
ARAL SEA
Syr-Darya River
Lake Balkhash
Turkestan
Chimkent
Tashkent
Alma-Ata
Dzhalal-Abad
Kokand
KHOREZMIAN NSR
Khiva
Bukhara
Samarkand
BUKHARAN NSR
Dushambe
TURKMENISTAN
Amu-Darya River
Ashkhabad
CHINA
INDIA
IRAN
AFGHANISTAN

Map 5.1

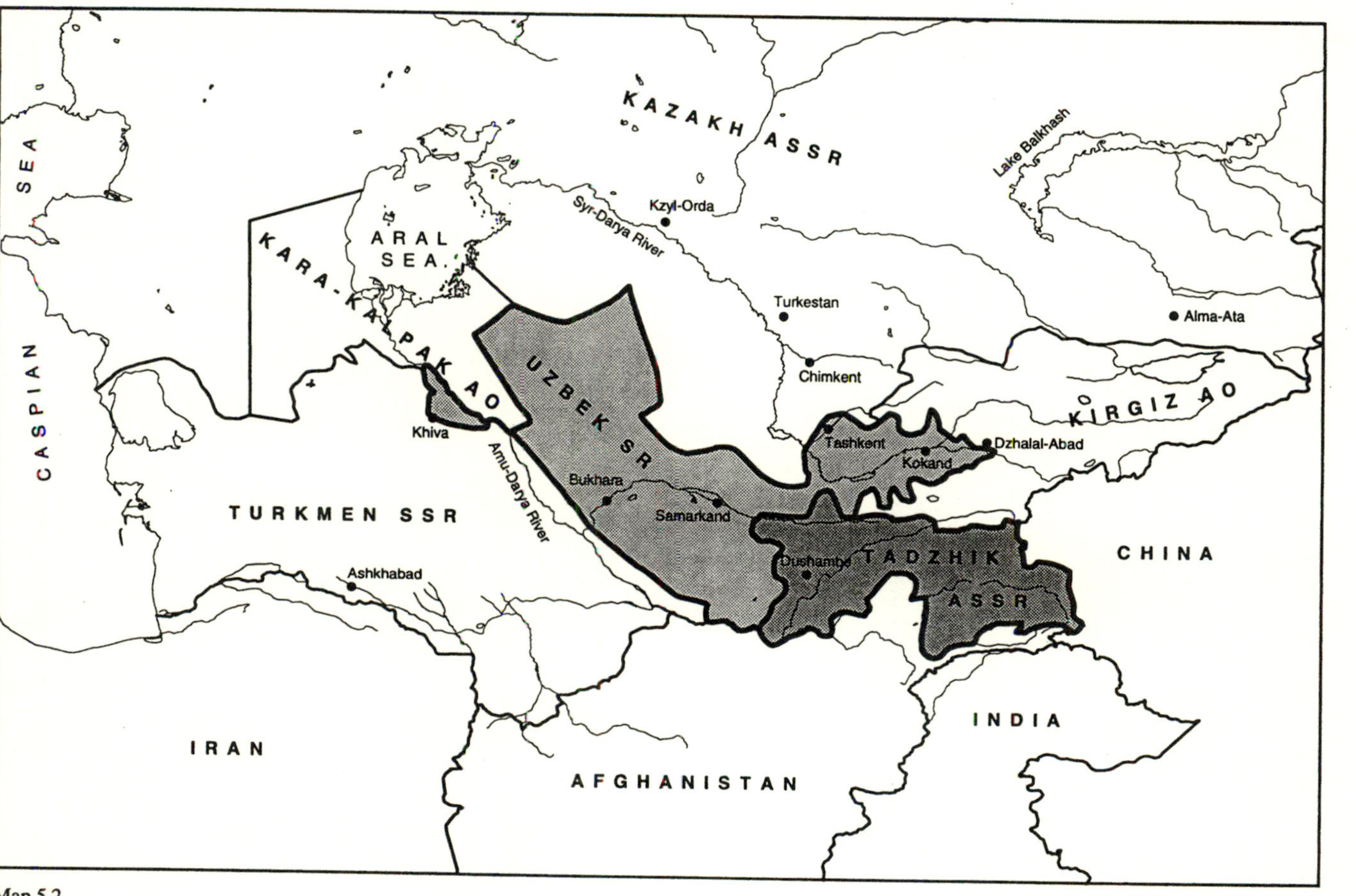
KAZAKH ASSR
Lake Balkhash
Kzyl-Orda
Syr-Darya River
ARAL SEA
KARA-KALPAK AO
SEA
CASPIAN
Turkestan
Alma-Ata
Chimkent
UZBEK SR
KIRGIZ AO
Khiva
Tashkent
Dzhalal-Abad
Kokand
Amu-Darya River
Bukhara
Samarkand
TURKMEN SSR
Dushambe
TADZHIK
ASSR
CHINA
Ashkhabad
INDIA
IRAN
AFGHANISTAN

Map 5.2

delimitation exposes a reality too long ignored yet staring us squarely in the face. The Soviet regime's preoccupation with "national" aspects of the delimitation and its emphasis on the ethnic basis of boundaries had ideological dimensions, but also served to throw sand in our eyes. However, if one sidesteps the formal rhetoric, downplays ethnic epiphenomena, absorbs what actually took place territorially, and introduces the politics of the time, the main conclusion is irresistible.

The 1925 deference to Uzbek, Kazakh, Kirghiz or Turkmen "nations" represented more a goal of the Bolsheviks than it did a Bolshevik response to local reality and native demands. It would be more accurate to characterize the process as the establishment of State units in order to encourage *emergent* or *artificial* nations rather than to argue—as Russian commentators did—that it was a reaction to crystallized Uzbek, Turkmen, Tajik, and Kirghiz national consciousness.

The specific authors of the national delimitation scenario remained anonymous, though Stalin's and his agents' roles must have been substantial. On the local scene in Central Asia, Faizulla Khojaev and his allies who should be singled out. The 1920 proposal for a division of Turkestan must have provided the basic outline, but it had to be augmented by Faizulla Khojaev's proposals as to how to deal with Bukhara and Khiva.

A local native role and interest in the outcome must be explored and there is no question that the key figure and the main proponent of ethnic and territorial realignment was Faizulla Khojaev. Turar Ryskulov and like-minded people committed to larger multinational units were surely as opposed to a partition in 1924 as they were in 1920. The main losers were the Turkestan idea and Turkestan's politicans. The major beneficiaries were Bukhara and its Jadid leaders.

The impulse behind Moscow's partition could be explained as its response to recent unsettling experiences. "There is little doubt," wrote Alexandre Bennigsen, "that the wish to forestall the fashioning of a pan-Turkestan national consciousness around the hub of a common language—Chagatay—was central to the 1924 decision. One need only to recall that the Bolshevik leaders had to combat at the same period the ideas of Sultangaliev and his followers on the union of all Turks of Russia into a single republic, Turan."[20]

But it should also be clear that this did not constitute a mass movement; the tendencies were vigorous only among the remnants of the old Jadid intelligentsia or the native Communists, who were often the same people. The native peoples certainly had not been attached to Soviet Turkestan, and no patriotism had emerged that would throw road-blocks in the path of Moscow's fragmentation and reformation scheme. Native loyalties had never been linked to formal political boundaries drawn by Tsarist officials or by their Communist successors. These feelings flourished, rather at local tribal levels, were manifest in the *mahallah* and the *kishlak,* and were also expressed in an amorphous although powerful Islamic identification. However, this religious tie uniting the region's

Muslims had little political relevance unless directly tested and challenged by inept Russian policies. Bolshevik delimitation policy—or what has been termed "parcelization of their ancient territory" into artificial "tribal republics"—did not produce widespread mass opposition since no direct attack was mounted against Islam or local traditions.

Few but the local Russian functionaries and die-hard pan-Turks seemed upset by the disappearance of the larger entity, the Turkestan ASSR. Some Russian officials argued that it was economically unsound to move from the large unit to a series of smaller republics. They were silenced by the charge that this smacked of "Great Russian chauvinism" and by the reassurance that economic plans would be coordinated. Paskutskiĭ, the Chairman of the Central Asian Economic Council, wanted all three Central Asian Republics joined into a single unit. A Soviet source tells us that some centralists had an even tighter form of unity in mind since "deviationists and Great Power chauvinists tried to use the formation of the USSR as a step to the liquidation of national republics, demanding their complete merging with the Russian Federation in a unitary State."

Ironically, the relative ease with which the 1924–25 national division was accomplished was an indication of the long-term difficulties that each Republic would confront in internal integration and in creating a viable *national* cohesion. Grouping diverse people with primarily local loyalties under the label "Uzbek" had the effect of circumscribing them within boundaries of a Republic of which they had little understanding. It had a definite rationale and internal logic for it drew together under one umbrella many who shared "objective" common traits. But *subjective* consciousness is something different. This amalgamation process did not automatically erase the tribal, historical, economic, and regional cleavages that divided native communities, nor did it eradicate religious loyalties that reached across the new boundaries. Bitter native tribal feuds that had played a major role in defeating the Basmachi movement were no less obstacles to future Communist nation-building. Labelling as "uzbeks" the diverse and distant inhabitants of Ferghana, Zarafshan (Zeravshan), parts of Bukhara, Khiva, Syr Darya, and Kashka Darya provinces was no magic incantation leading to immediate integration and new identity.[21]

In 1937 when celebrating the achievements of Soviet nationalities policy, Uzbekistan's Communist leader, Akmal Ikramov, testified how muddled in 1924 was the ethnic terrain that the Soviet regime sought to simplify through national consolidation. He observed:

> The Uzbek people up to the October socialist revolution were not yet fully developed and consolidated as a nation. The Uzbek toiling masses had not then recognized themselves as a single nationality. The Ferghana uzbeks usually were called kokandists, according to the name of the khanate; the Zarafshan, Kashka Darya, and Surkhan Darya peoples were not considered uzbeks (by the Uzbeks of that time). Khorezmians, for example, when travelling elsewhere were for some reason called Tajiks. And the Russian colonialists called all of them Sarts.[22]

Uzbeks as Politicians and "Elder Brothers"

While reform was not overtly resisted by the native population, within Turkestan's Communist elite there was intense controversy and heated disagreement. Although ethnic cohorts in some places formed distinct and compact masses, they were also scattered throughout the territory and intermeshed, making the drawing of boundaries on so-called "national" grounds no simple endeavor. There were various alternative proposals suggested, much negotiation involved, and considerable flexibility finally displayed in applying the test of national affiliation.

In January 1924 in Moscow the *Orgbyuro* (The Communist Party's Organizational Bureau) of the Central Committee had discussed the Turkestan situation and the projected partition. Ian Rudzutak was delegated to introduce the question during his forthcoming visit to Central Asia. It is evident that this project was an updated version of the 1920 plan to separate the Uzbek, Turkmen, and Kirghiz (Kazakh) peoples. On February 25, Faizulla Khojaev presented this at a Plenum of the Bukharan Party and it approved the scheme for national republics and the creation of Uzbekistan. Later Soviet authors admitted that the question of national division led to a "sharp struggle, lively discussions." Supposedly, "bourgeois nationalists" took this opportunity to kindle national passions and national feuds. Reconciling the various positions and adjudicating contradictory claims was no simple task. One can conjecture as to whether Moscow did or did not welcome "the sharp struggle, lively discussion". Some native Communist leaders lobbied in general against creation of smaller units and argued for an enlarged Turkestan, or pushed for a "Central Asian Federation" that would have encompassed the large Kazakhstan republic which was already part of the RSFSR.

There were also contentious issues as to allocation of specific territory and the drawing of concrete boundaries. Native Communists argued over the future of the large Syr Darya region which would be divided between the new Uzbek Republic and the older Kazakh Republic. The latter, an autonomous Republic within the RSFSR since 1921, would enter into an even tighter future embrace with Moscow. Turkestani political figures argued against the dissection of Syr Darya and the loss of substantial territory to the Kazakh unit. From their side, the Kazakh leadership was unreconciled to the likely loss of the strategic Tashkent region and the Kazakhs located there who would be included in Uzbekistan. These Turkestani politicians of Kazakh background surfaced a counterproposal to create something like the existing Trancausasus Federation. calling on the RSFSR to surrender its Kazakh territory and to allow its merger with kazakh regions of Turkestan.

The centuries-old antagonism between uzbeks and tajiks had been mitigated by the gradual "turkification" of the tajiks. In Bukhara, for instance, as in the

Samarkand region not only uzbek and tajik but numerous other peoples were able to live side by side, not in perfect harmony and not without periodic difficulties, but, nonetheless, they had adjusted to one another. The national delimitation undercut the ongoing assimilation process. It marked the tajiks out as one of the primary ethnic formations to be preserved and this probably saved them from sublimation in other formations and absorption through "Turkification." The national delimitation singled them out for distinction and a special political status. However, until 1929, Uzbekistan's authorities were in fact to exercise a kind of hegemony over the whole region inhabited by tajiks. Within the confines of overt and covert Uzbek hegemony, there was continued conflict between uzbeks and tajiks. Apparently Tajik spokesmen presented cultural, ethnic, and historical justification for including the renowned city of Samarkand (and Bukhara) within Tajikistan. Their petition was rejected and Samarkand was in fact named the capital of the Uzbek SSR. Another Tajik-Uzbek bone of contention was the Khojand region. Although at first allocated to the Uzbeks, it was transferred in 1929 to Stalinabad's (formerly Dushambe) jurisdiction.

Discord was evident at what must have been a raucous Plenum of the Turkestan Party's Central Committee which met at Tashkent in March 1924:

> . . . at the plenum differing points of view on the national delimitation were unveiled. There was advanced the proposition of creating from the Turkestan ASSR several autonomous national republics; conducting the division only in the Turkestan ASSR—not touching Bukhara or Khorezm; creating a Central Asian Federation; transforming the Turkmen oblast into a Turkmen Autonomous Republic. The representatives of Bukhara proposed that the Uzbek Republic consist of Bukhara plus the Uzbek parts of Turkestan and Khorezm. They proposed to designate as the capital of Uzbekistan either Bukhara or Samarkand and as the capital of Turkmenistan, Charjui. There was an argument as to which republic was to be allocated Tashkent, etc.
>
> At a meeting of the Central Asian Bureau of the Central Committee of the RKP on April 28, 1924, during discussion of the delimitation, again the opinion was put forward that several autonomous republics should be formed in Central Asia and joined together in a federation of Central Asian republics on the model of the RSFSR.[23]

The Central Asian Bureau's "National-Territorial Commission" established three sub-commissions. The "Kirghiz" (actually the Kazakh) and also a "Kara-Kirghiz" (in fact, the Kirghiz) bodies later met. They approved the proposal for a Central Asian Federation that would incorporate the Kazakh Autonomous Republic which since 1920 had functioned within the RSFSR. This Federation was to comprise three Republics (Kazakh, Uzbek, and Turkmen) and two autonomous *oblast's* ("Kara-Kirghiz" and Tajik).

The Bukharan uzbek leaders would have none of this and torpedoed the Federation idea. On May 10, the Uzbek sub-commission convened with Faizulla Khojaev and Rajabov also present. It rejected the Federation proposal and called for a distinct and separate Uzbek Republic. The sub-commission approved a resolution ("Concerning the Formation of an Independent Uzbek Republic") which stated:

1. An independent Uzbek Republic is to be formed consisting of: *Ferghana Oblast'* with the exclusion of *raions* with a predominantly Kara-Kirghiz population; the *Bukharan Republic,* with the exclusion of the area beyond the left bank of the Amu Darya (parts of Charju and Kerinsk *vilayets*); *Samarkand Oblast'* with the exception of the five nomad *volosts* of Jizaezd *Uezd;* the *Khorezm Republic* with the exception of raions with Turkmen and Kirghiz population; and the city of *Tashkent* and Mirzachul *uezd* of Syr Darya *Oblast'*.
2. It is an unconditional necessity for an independent Uzbek Republic to enter the Union of Soviet Socialist Republics on the same basis as the Ukraine Republic and other Soviet Republics.
3. Within the Uzbek Republic there will be formed a Tajik autonomous oblast out of the Pamirs, Matchinsk *raion* of Samarkand *oblast'*, and Garm, Darbaz and Kulab of the Bukharan Peoples Soviet Republic . . . [24]

Surely no interested party had more solid grounds for complaint than the Khorezm republic. While the Bukharan state was to disappear as a separate entity, it would be resurrected within the Uzbek SSR and its leaders raised to new political heights there. However, Khorezm was truly to be erased from the map and no compensation was in the offing. The Khorezm leaders refused to commit political suicide willingly or to accept the unfolding verdict of history. On May 8, 1924 they opposed the national partition and submitted a counter-proposal. It called for continued existence of the Khorezm SSR and its future expansion through the addition of Turkestan's Amu Darya region!

This attempt failed dismally. After Karklin, the Secretary of the Central Asian Bureau, made a trip to Khorezm, Sultan Kari—the Chairman of Khorezm's Central Executive Committee—capitulated and announced willingness to be absorbed into Uzbekistan.[25] While Karklin's persuasive powers could not be underestimated, neither should the concomitant arrival there of G.I. Bokiĭ, the veteran Chekist, be ignored.

Although it was fundamentally the Uzbek sub-commission's design that won out over the objections of other native Communists, the victory was neither quick nor easy. Determining national boundaries was no simple task. The final resolution of difficulties was complicated by the fact that the so-called ethnic boundaries seldom coincided with preferred economic borders. The Kazakhs in particular kept the boundary controversy alive. Unlike the Khorezm comrades, they did not meekly submit, as the following account illustrates:

> In terms of population the city of Tashkent itself was Uzbek but the rest of the district was predominantly Kazakh. The Kazakh commission therefore insisted that the whole district be included in Kazakhstan. The demand was rejected on the grounds that it violated the national principle . . . The Kazakhs then entered a claim for three volosts (rural districts) of the district. But the second proposal was also unacceptable, this time for economic reasons. It was rejected on two counts: (1) that the headwaters of the Boz-su and Salara canals which served the city of Tashkent would be in Kazakh territory while their lower courses would be in Uzbekistan; and (2) that the Central Asiatic Railway which terminated in Tashkent would be cut by a wedge of Kazakh territory eleven miles south of the city.
>
> Under pressure the Kazakhs were forced to a compromise solution which placed most of the Tashkent district in Uzbek territory. This did not end the dispute. In the fall of 1924, the Kazakhs appealed their case to the All-Russian Central Executive. In a bitter denunciation of the settlement, the Kazakh delegate charged that the very principle of the delimitation would be defeated if the ethnic principle was not strictly adhered to. He was ruled out of order. And in the final settlement, Tashkent and its environs were included in Uzbekistan.[26]

Whether it was through Faizulla Khojaev's skills, the weight of the Bukhara uzbek lobby, the influence at the "Center" of Khojaev's patrons like Kuibyshev, or the correlation of his project with Stalin's objectives, Uzbekistan emerged from the delimitation as the strongest unit. This was true not only in terms of population, resources, and territory; in addition, Uzbekistan incorporated most of the prize area at stake—the fertile Ferghana region. Further, both ancient historical and cultural centers—Bukhara and Samarkand—were to fall within Uzbekistan's boundaries. The major strategic center and Russian stronghold-Tashkent-was also allocated to the Uzbeks, not to the Kazakhs. That this latter victory was to prove more bane than boon became evident.

That Moscow recognized Uzbekistan's preeminent position within Central Asia was made abundantly clear in February 1925 by Kalinin's remarks at Bukhara when he addressed the First Congress of the Republic's Communist Party:

> Naturally, Uzbekistan must play a large role in Central Asia, a role, one might even say, of hegemony. This role must not be lost sight of, Comrades, leaders of the Central Committee of Uzbekistan. I consider this proper. Certainly, Uzbekistan has available sufficiently large cultural forces, it has available great material possibilities, a large population, it has the most wealthy cities. I consider it a fully valid and natural desire to play first violin in Central Asia. But, if comrades want to play first violin, then it is reasonable that this will be achieved in the Soviet Union only by increased labors, great generosity, huge work, and sacrifices for the neighboring republics, which will come in contact with you. For when you are strong, because you are mighty, then from you will be demanded great compliance toward these republics. In a word, you must be related to them as Moscow is related to you.[27]

Although the area originally designated for the Tajiks was raised from a mere *oblast'* to an autonomous republic, it remained within the Uzbek SSR until 1929, and the Uzbeks were to emerge as something like their "elder brothers." Tajikistan's lowly position and Uzbekistan's preeminent one was also evident in the Party sphere, and until 1929 the Tajiks' Party organization remained a mere *oblast'* branch subordinated to Uzbekistan's authorities. Tajik economic affairs were considered intimately linked to Uzbekistan and they were treated as such in discussions and resolutions of the Party Congresses throughout the twenties. This tutelary position seemed to encompass all realms of Tajik life.

There was persistent evidence of ethnic tension, cultural conflict, and condescending Russian colonial treatment of the native peoples—especially during the 1930s. At the same time, among the Muslims themselves, there was group strife and similar problems of superior and inferior. Uzbek/turkmen conflicts had plagued Khiva's rulers in the past. There was evidence that the Uzbek could play the tyrant and display a chauvinist attitude toward his national minorities and native compatriots, especially the turkmen and tajiks. Moscow's repeated warnings throughout the twenties regarding "Great Power chauvinism" were directed not only at local Russians but also at the Uzbeks. A resolution of Uzbekistan's Fourth Party Congress (1929) stressed the failure to implement directives on the nationality question. Soon after, Tajikistan was named a separate Union Republic and Uzbekistan was territorially diminished. Evidently Faizulla Khojaev opposed this move, and in fact in 1929 he resurrected the idea of a Central Asian Federation, perhaps as a last-ditch effort to avoid losing territory.

One might argue that a second phase of national delimitation was launched in 1929—one that undercut the former Bukharan politicians' grand design of 1925. Indeed there was evidence that considerable additional territory held by the Uzbek SSR was about to be transferred to Stalinabad's jurisdiction in 1929, but this project was abandoned.[28] Evidence points to an effort in Uzbek politics at that time to undermine Khojaev and the Bukhara lobby. The separation of Tajikistan was something of a political punishment dealt out to him.

There was now also a shift in the center of gravity from Uzbekistan's western and central regions to its northeast and eastern sector through the transfer in September 1930 of its capital from Samarkand to Tashkent. This was a deadly blow to the hopes of uzbeks like Faizulla Khojaev and his Bukharan colleagues. It apparently was part of the attempt to discipline him and to move the center of political gravity in Uzbekistan from a Bukhara/Samarkand axis to the Tashkent/Ferghana orientation. Stalin used other uzbek politicians—initially Akmal Ikramov and his Tashkent/Ferghana cadres—against the Bukhara/Samarkand Jadids. Moscow's manipulation of political cleavages and regional differences provides a major key to the divisive game it played during the twenties and early thirties; the First Secretary of Uzbekistan's Party organization, Ikramov, was Stalin's main man in exploiting the various feuds and the local natives' ambitions. Later he too would be jettisoned by Stalin and replaced by Usman Iusupov and a more authentic Stalinist clique—also, by the way, based in the Tashkent/Ferghana nexus that served Moscow's interests.[29]

Faizulla Khojaev's Fate and Uzbekistan's Future

In the wake of the 1925 national delimitation, Faizulla Khojaev had moved his base of operations from Bukhara to Samarkand. He was instrumental in the choice of Samarkand as capital and the rejection of Tashkent, the main Russian stronghold since the Tsarist conquest, which had also been the capital of Soviet Turkestan. During the Samarkand years (1925–1930), as Chairman of Uzbekistan's Government, he was the republic's primary political figure, but he increasingly ran into stiff competition from Akmal Ikramov, leader of the anti-Bukhara wing of Uzbekistan's Communist party. In 1927 Faizulla Khojaev could still observe optimistically:

> If you desire to see what we have achieved as a result of national-state delimitation, look upon the territory of the present Uzbek Republic, see how the relations between the various nationalities are established, see how wide strata of workers and peasants have been associated with the entire administration in the Republic; see and tell us who rules this country. Look at the number of schools which the Soviet Government has established and also the work it is carrying out in the educational sphere; look at the mutual relations which have evolved between the Soviet republics and the Soviet Union into which Uzbekistan, of its own free volition, has entered as an equal member; look at the complete national peace which now prevails, the growth of our industries, agriculture and trade, which have already attained the prewar level (of development). See all these and be convinced about all that national delimitation has given to Central Asia.[30]

Unfortunately, Khojaev's prognostic powers did not prove equal to his journalistic and rhetorical gifts, which we are told were considerable. By late 1929 Moscow was to launch the collectivization and cotton mono-culture offensives which along with other campaigns were to attack and disrupt traditional Muslim society. Soon the "continuous purge" and the Great Terror of the thirties struck Central Asia, eliminating the generation of Jadid reformers and budding nationalists who had adopted the Bolshevik banner. Faizulla Khojaev, Tursun Khojaev, Akmal Ikramov, as well as Turar Ryskulov and his followers and many others, were liquidated. From Bukhara to Samarkand, then to Tashkent—and finally to Moscow—Faizulla Khojaev's route from minor to major power centers represented formally increased authority; actually each move brought decreased power and increased personal vulnerability as well as declining autonomy for the land he governed. The journey finally terminated in 1938 with his public trial at Moscow and his death. For nearly thirty years Faizulla Khojaev remained a non-person whose life and career were "blank pages" in Uzbekistan's history; finally, in 1966 he was posthumously rehabilitated.[31]

Khojaev's post-Stalin era return to good graces followed a tortuous path but represented something of a political resurrection and personal vindication. It is not farfetched to contend that this turn of events with its many twists portended, although not immediately, the revitalization of Uzbekistan itself. Today a fully independent and sovereign state, Uzbekistan has arrived at a juncture that is closer to the original 1925 point of departure when the future had appeared open, but now with real possibilities for achieving Khojaev's objective of a national renaissance.

But one must be cautious as to predictions about Uzbekistan's future path. Whether it will continue on an exclusive journey alone as an Uzbek state or embark on a more inclusive path, travelling in unison with the region's other peoples, is not yet determined. There are reasons to believe that Ryskulov's original, inclusive, pan-Turkic design has a future in Central Asia and may prove as viable as Faizulla's Khojaev's more restricted notion of a nation-based state.[32]

After 1938 the national dimensions of Uzbekistan's development were sublimated in Moscow-oriented endeavors and subordinated to a Stalinist totalitarian enterprise. Nonetheless, almost seventy years later, the framework created in 1925, making national identity the basis for state integration, remained in place, and could provide the wherewithal for a nation-state. Most important, an Uzbek national intelligentsia and State middle class were spawned in the intervening years. These were in place, ready to come center stage, when the Soviet imperial system entered on its terminal crisis in the 1980s.

But what of the 1990s and beyond? Uzbekistan's future is problematic: national identity and the nation-state as conceptualized in the West cannot be considered as sole paradigms for understanding what may be emerging in Central Asia. Equally unrealistic are expectations of a Islamic fundamentalist revival. This fundamentalist-revival scenario is an illusion based on a misreading of local Turkic (and even Tajik) societies as simply mirror-images of some Middle East based abstractions. More likely to emerge is a long-term competition between the two views of identity and statecraft that have surfaced as the dominant patterns in our case studies: on the one hand, a modernized version of Ryskulov's vision of a greater Turkestan encompassing most of Central Asia; and, on the other, the narrower nation-state vistas of Faizulla Khojaev manifest in a separate Uzbekistan and in other independent national republics.

Notes

1. Hugh Seton-Watson, *Nations and States,* Westview Press, Boulder, Colorado, 1977 , p.l. For an insightful treatment of Nation and State during and after colonial rule, see Rupert Emerson, *From Empire to Nation,* Harvard University Press, Cambridge, Mass., 1959.

2. The origins of the "uzbeks/Uzbeks" is treated in Edward A. Allworth, *The Modern Uzbeks,* Hoover Institution Press, Stanford, California, 1990, especially pp. 30–43. My position is that the history of Soviet Central Asia should be viewed as an attempt to create modern nations (Uzbek, Tajik, etc.) where previously there were unconsolidated tribal/clan cohorts or, at best, ethnic groups (i.e. uzbeks as opposed to Uzbeks; tajiks in contrast to Tajiks).

The major corollary to this nation-in-the-making approach is that, in Uzbekistan, pre-1924 realities lived on during the Soviet period and proved as salient as the artificially-contrived State created for the not-yet existent Nation: thus the argument is that sub-national and pre-national allegiances superseded "Uzbek" and "Uzbekistan" as primary realities. In various guises, pre-revolutionary Kokand, Khiva, Bukhara, and Turkestan persisted. To drive home this point, I will often use lower-case letters (uzbek and tajik) as opposed to capitals (Uzbek, Tajik) to suggest pre-national conditions or non-national phenomena.

3. For an analysis of the so-called "national delimitation" which produced Uzbekistan, Turkmenistan, and eventually Tajikistan and Kirgizia, see Alexander G. Park, *Bolshevism in Turkestan, 1917–1927,* Columbia University Press, New York, 1957, especially Chapter II. A comprehensive study that too often seems satisfied with the official Soviet view is R. Vaidyanath, *The Formation of the Soviet Central Asian Republics,* Peoples Publishing House, New Delhi, 1967.

4. The best comprehensive treatment of Moscow's policies toward the Muslims during this period is A. Bennigsen and C. Lemercier-Quelquejay, *Islam in the Soviet Union,* Frederick A. Praeger, New York, 1967. Turar Ryskulov's life and political career are discussed in V.M. Ustinov, *Sluzhenye Narody,* Izdatel'stvo "Kazakhstan," Alma Ata, 1984. For many of his speeches and publications, see T.R. Ryskulov, *Izbrannye trudy,* Izdatel'stvo "Kazakhstan," Alma Ata, 1984.

5. Sagdulla Tursun Khojaev (1891–1940) must not be confused with Faizulla Khojaev who will have a prominent place in this study. Both men were Jadids who broke with traditional Islam. But Sagdulla worked in Russian Turkestan, especially in Tashkent, while Faizulla was born and raised in the distant Bukharan Emirate. However, their paths were to cross, for Sagdulla served as Party Secretary in Soviet Bukhara in 1921–22, assisting Faizulla—who was then head of the new Government—to tame obscurantist forces. Later in Uzbekistan during the twenties, they again worked together.

6. The "Basmachi" was the name given to the native partisans who waged guerilla war against the Bolsheviks in Central Asia from 1918 through at least 1922, and in some locales even later.

7. Georgii Safarov, *Kolonial'naia revoliutsia; opyt Turkestana,* Moscow, 1921, p. 123.

8. This important document and a fascinating account by one of the participants is found in D.I. Manzhara, *Revoliutsionnoe dvizhenie v Sredneĭ Azii 1905–1920, vospominaniia,* Tashkent, 1934.

9. The tale is told in Ustinov, *op.cit.,* pp. 62–78.

10. *Op.cit.*

11. The text was published for the first time in *Inostrannaya voennaya interventsiia i grazhdanskaia voina v Sredneĭ Azii i Kazakhstanĭ, tom vtoro, sentiabr' 1919—dekabr' 1920 g.),* Alma Ata, 1964, p. 564.

12. For the text of the document, with Lenin's rejection of the three-fold ethnic division, see *Leninskiĭ sbornik,* tom XXXIV, pp. 323–326.

13. See Serge Zenkovsky, "The Tataro-Baskhir Feud of 1917–20" in *Indiana Slavic Studies,* Volume II (1958); and Richard Pipes, "The First Experiment in Soviet Nationality Policy: The Bashkir Republic, 1917–1920" in *The Russian Review,* October, 1950, pp 303–319.

14. Faizulla Khojaev was born in Bukhara in 1898. While having early training in religious schools, he received a European education and spent time in St. Petersburg where his father had business connections. He was drawn to the Jadid reform movement at Bukhara—his uncle Usman Khojaev was one of its leaders—and joined its secret underground organization. When in 1917 the movement divided into moderate and radical wings, he became the leader of the latter group which was called the "Young Bukharans." (See also F. Khojaev, *K istorii revolyutsii v Bukhare,* Gosudarstvennoe izdatel'stvo, Uz SSR, Tashkent, 1932.)

The best books published in the West on Bukhara are Seymour Becker, *Russia's Protectorates in Central Asia: Bukhara and Khiva, 1865–1924,* Harvard University Press, Cambridge, Ma., 1968, and Hélène Carrère D'Encausse, *Islam and the Russian Empire: Reform and Revolution in Central Asia,* University of California Press, 1988 (originally published in 1966 under the title, *Réforme et révolution chez les musulmans de l'empire russe),* and for the history of Bukhara after 1917, A.I. Ishanov, *Bukharskaia narodnaia sovetskaia respublika,* Izdatel'stvo "Uzbekistan," Tashkent, 1969.

15. For Faizulla Khojaev's personal account, see his *K istorii revolyutsii v Bukhare.* To supplement this account, consult A.I. Ishanov's *Bukharskaia narodnaia sovetskaia respublika.* Ishanov provides indispensable information regarding the differences within the Soviet camp as to whether the Young Bukharans or the local Communist party should be supported. We learn how important was the support of Kuibyshev—after September 1920 the Comintern and Soviet Government's representative in Bukhara—to Khojaev in his consolidation of power. He remained until his death in 1935 Khojaev's main political patron in Moscow. Ishanov, *op.cit.,* pp. 236–238.

16. Alexander Barmine, *One Who Survived* (G. P. Putnam Sons: New York, 1945), pp. 104–105, 123.

17. While in command in Soviet Bukhara, Khojaev began the process of political differentiation on ethnic grounds that would later produce Turkmenistan. In 1921 he consolidated Bukhara's western desert areas—where nomadic turkmen tribes predominated—into a distinct oblast within the Bukharan State. This was an early attempt to separate uzbek and turkmen and it became the central feature of the national delimitation which resulted in 1925 in the Uzbek and Turkmen Union Republics.

18. Maps 5.1 and 5.2 are redrawn from Akademia Nauk Uzbekskoĭ SSR, *Istoriia Uzbekskoî SSR,* Tom V, Izdatel'stvo Akademii Nauk Uzbekskoî SSR, Tashkent, 1957, and are to be found before p. 210. While Map 5.2 is correct in showing Uzbekistan's 1957 shape and dimensions, it is not an entirely accurate guide to the 1925 situation; it shows as part of Uzbekistan in the north a sharp pointed wedge of territory cutting into Kazakhstan. This was not the contour of the 1925 northern border between Uzbekistan and Kazakhstan—it did not extend as far north and was curved or crescent-shaped. This additional territory was added to Uzbekistan only in the 1950s. Map 5.2 is also somewhat misleading in the way it depicts Karakalpakia, which abuts the Aral Sea: true, in 1957 it was contained within Uzbekistan's boundaries, having been transferred to Uzbek jurisdiction after 1932. But until then, it was part of Kazakhstan.

However, the usefulness of Maps 5.1 and 5.2 for comparative purposes is not diminished by these corrections: the important point is that Map 5.2 correctly shows that in

1925 Tajik regions were distinct but incorporated within Uzbekistan; furthermore, and most important, Map 5.2 can be juxtaposed to Map 5.1 and Bukhara's relation to Uzbekistan is made visible and the argument in the text illustrated.

19. There have been an extraordinary number of Soviet monographs and articles detailing the process. The initial major publication was F. Ksenofontov's *Uzbekistan i Turkmenistan,* Gosudarstvennoe izdatel'stvo, Moscow-Leningrad, 1925. Typical of the official version as of the mid-fifties was Kh.T. Tursunov's *Obrazovanie uzbekskoĭ sovetskoĭ sotsialisticheskoĭ respubliki,* Tashkent, 1957. Since Faizulla Khojaev then was still considered an "enemy of the people," neither his major contribution nor the central role of Bukhara, before and after 1925, could be admitted.

The first Soviet author to concede the fundamental points in print and partially adopt my view is Amabai Ishanov in his *Rol' kompartii i sovetskogo pravitel'stva v sozdanii natsional'noĭ gosudarstvennosti uzbekskogo naroda,* Izdatel'stvo "Uzbekistan," Tashkent, 1978. For instance, he writes (p. 224) that on February 25, 1924 the Plenum of the Bukharan CP adopted the proposal:

". . . that the Uzbek SSR be created *on the basis of the Bukhara SSR by joining to it* part of the territory of the Khorezm SSR as well as the Ferghana, Samarkand, and Syr Darya oblasts of the Turkestan ASSR. . . ." (My emphasis added—DSC)

20. Bennigsen and Lemercier-Quelquejay, *op.cit.,* p. 134.

21. We have no idea what specific standards were used to determine who was an Uzbek, a Kazakh, a Turkmen, a Kirghiz, or a Tajik for the purpose of "national delimitation." Was linguistic practice decisive or were residence patterns and style of life given priority? How were the multiple tribal and clan identifications reduced to the few national identities that deserved political recognition as republics? Was self-identification or other means used? Where intermingling of uzbeks, tajiks, kazakhs, and other peoples in convoluted patterns produced ethnic puzzles, how were they solved?

22. *Pravda vostoka,* February 13, 1937, p. 1.

23. R.Kh. Abdushukirov, *Oktiabr'skaia revoliutsiia rastsvet Uzbekskoĭ sotsialisticheskoĭ natsii i sblizhenie ee c natsiiami SSSR,* Gosudarstvennoe izdatel'stvo Uzbekskoĭ SSR, Tashkent, 1962, pp. 196–7.

24. Cited in Kh. T. Tursunov, *Obrazovanie Uzbekskoĭ sovetskoĭ sotsialisticheskoĭ respubliki,* Izdatel'stvo Akademii nauk Uzbekskoî SSR, Tashkent, 1957, pp. 117–8.

25. For historical materials and relevant documents, see *Istoriia khorezmskoĭ narodnoĭ sovetskoĭ respubliki (1920–1924), Sbornik dokumentov,* Tashkent, 1976.

26. Park, *op.cit.,* pp. 95–6.

27. M.I. Kalinin, *Izbrannye proizvedeniia,* Tom 1 (1917–1925), Moscow, 1960, p. 630.

28. Dr. Reinhard Eisener observes that in 1924–25 the Tajiks had been mere passive objects during the first stage of the delimitation; however, he has seen a document testifying to their political activity as the second phase began to take shape. He writes that: ". . . as early as 1928 a lengthy letter signed by 19 members of the local political leadership of the Tadzhik ASSR was sent to the Politbureau in Moscow. In this letter are claimed all those districts of Uzbekistan which, by certain statistical evidence, were mainly inhabited by Tadzhiks. These were among others, the cities and districts of Samarkand, Bukhara, and Khodzhent.

As a consequence of this demand, the Tadzhik ASSR was joined with Khodzhent in 1929, and she became the Tadzhik SSR. Thus, the claims of Tadzhikistan were not all fulfilled, and they endure until the present day."

Eisener, "Some Problems of Research Concerning the National Delimitation of Soviet Central Asia in 1924," paper presented at *The 4th European Seminar on Central Asian Studies at Bamberg,* October 8th, 1991, pp. 8–9.

29. See Donald S. Carlisle. "Power and Politics in Soviet Uzbekistan: From Stalin to Gorbachev" in William Fierman (ed.), *Soviet Central Asia: The Failed Transformation,* Westview Press, 1991, p. 121; 109–110.

30. Faizulla Khojaev, *Izbrannye trudy,* tom II, Izdatel'stvo "FAN," Tashkent 1972, p. 158.

31. For his trial, death, and subsequent rehabilitation, see my review-article, "Faizulla Khodzhaev," in *Kritika,* Volume VIII, No.1 (Fall 1971), pp. 43–71.

32. This argument—and its limitations—are spelled out in Donald S. Carlisle, "Uzbekistan and the Uzbeks," *Problems of Communism,* Vol. XL, September-October 1991, especially pp. 23–25; 39–44.

CHAPTER 6

Tajiks and the Persian World

Muriel Atkin

Although "Turkestan" is an historically well-established name for the region which includes what is now Soviet Central Asia, its inhabitants are not now, nor were they in the past, exclusively Turkic. Notable among the region's other inhabitants are the various Iranian peoples who have lived there from prehistoric times to the present and who have profoundly influenced its politics and culture. "Iranian" in this sense does not refer solely to the modern state of Iran or the Persian-speakers who are the dominant nationality there but to the larger group of speakers of various languages in the Iranian family who have at different times in history lived over a wide area, including the Eurasian steppes, Central Asia's oases and mountains, and a broad zone across south Asia. In Central Asia, Persian did not prevail over the local Iranian languages until a few centuries after the Arab-Islamic conquest (although it had already been known in the region long before that). In both the medieval and modern periods, Persian has also been used at times by non-native speakers, in Central Asia and parts of South Asia from Anatolia to India, as a language of literature, learning, and government. With the use of the language came the influence of Persian culture and traditions that were expressed through it. The transformation of the non-nomadic population of Central Asia from predominantly Iranian to predominantly Turkic dates from after the Arab conquest, especially from the eleventh century, although scholars disagree on the pace of the change.[1]

By far the most numerous and self-assertive of the Iranian peoples in contemporary Central Asia are the Tajiks, who speak an eastern variety of Persian. At least for many of the educated and politically active among them, their Iranianness, and particularly their Persianness are essential parts of what defines them as a nationality and justifies their unwillingness to be assimilated by their Turkic neighbors or become homogenized, Russified "new Soviet men." This does not mean that they have made Persian connections an overriding obsession. As the advent of *perestroika* and *glasnost'* in the Soviet Union made possible the more frank discussion of problems and the consideration of new solutions, educated Tajiks showed considerable interest in how other Soviet republics grappled with change and also expressed an interest in the West without having to couch that in the critical terms that had formerly been required when discussing it. Nonetheless, educated Tajiks see their links to the wider Iranian/ Persian world, past and present, as vital to their survival as a people.

The Development of Soviet-Tajik Identity

The various peoples of Central Asia have long known that there were differences among them in their origins, language, way of life, culture, and so forth. However, the notion that the inhabitants of Central Asia ought to be categorized by nationality and that the political and cultural institutions of the region ought to be organized on that basis is a twentieth-century innovation. In the nineteenth and early twentieth centuries, most Central Asians customarily identified themselves according to supranational categories, especially Islam, or subnational ones, especially a locale or a tribe. Another important distinction was the one between the nomadic and sedentary populations. Even the name "Tajik," which has been used on occasion for about a millennium to distinguish Persian-speakers (in general, not only in Central Asia) from Turks, came to be used in modern Central Asia for sedentary Uzbeks as well as Persian speakers. In the realm of the Uzbek Emirs of Bukhara, Persian was widely used as a language of literature, scholarship, and government, while Persian speakers often knew Uzbek as well, and various Persian dialects were influenced by Turkic languages.

The nationally-defined political and cultural institutions in contemporary Central Asia are contrivances of the Soviet regime, for the purpose of political control, and were imposed on the region by Moscow's fiat in the 1920s and 1930s. What was artificial then has since taken on a life of its own. National identity became a factor in the competition for advancement within the Soviet system. In the past few years it became even more important as the Soviet Union collapsed and people looked for alternative political programs. For many nationalities this also entailed, as a crucial component, redefining the national identity, which had been subject to manipulation for decades by the Soviet regime. The Tajiks offer one striking example of the complexity of this phenomenon. Contemporary Tajik nationalist[2] rhetoric encompasses, as nationalist movements typically do, both the differentiation from other groups (and, with that, the implicit or explicit assertion of superiority to those others) and the assertion of the inherent worth of this particular nationality. In the case of the Tajiks, the perception of their place in the Persian world contributes to the rhetoric on the first point and is vital to the rhetoric on the second.

Most of the elements of this approach to the Tajiks' national identity began developing in the 1940s but found more open and forceful expression in the Gorbachev and post-Gorbachev eras, with the greater latitude in public debate and also the increased political uncertainty. In the Soviet period, the redefinition process concentrated on cultural issues. Despite the Stalinist formulation of nationality policy, which justified the regime in defining national identity according to "objective" criteria, without regard for the perceptions of the people being categorized, there is, in the ways national identity actually evolves, no single, absolute formula which specifies an inflexible set of qualifications for nationhood (such as politics, economics, customs, religion, language, history, etc.) and determines their fixed proportions. The process of national self-definition that begins with culture and expands to other spheres has been one of the patterns followed by various peoples historically (as in nineteenth-century Central and Eastern Europe) and in the present, including among several Soviet nationalities. In the latter case, the Soviet regime's willingness to allow officially recognized nationalities at least the outward trappings of cultural autonomy helps explain the initial emphasis on that sphere in the process.

Some of the Tajik nationalists' attention is directed towards non-Persian components of the Iranian world, especially the Eastern Iranian peoples of Central Asia. For example, a mass-circulation newspaper pointed out, perhaps as a counterweight to the tendency to equate the Persians of the Iranian plateau with the standard of Iranianness, that the definition of what constitutes "Iran" applies to much more than the individual country which now bears that name. Instead, it refers to a larger region, including southern Central Asia, from the Syr Darya River southward, and all of the speakers of Iranian languages who ever lived in this broad zone.[3]

This linkage between Tajiks and other Iranian peoples besides the Persian-speakers applies above all to the Soghdians, one of the most powerful, civilized peoples of ancient Central Asia. (Several of Central Asia's major cities, including Bukhara, Samarkand, in what is now Uzbekistan, and, in what is now Tajikistan, Panjakent and Khojand [Leninabad], have Soghdian origins.) Various officially sponsored publications in recent years have discussed the achievements of the Soghdians. When a group of Tajiks established an unofficial cultural organization in Moscow in 1989, they chose to call it Sughdiana [in Russian, Sogdiana]. The small groups of Eastern Iranian peoples who live in contemporary Tajikistan have also begun to receive more attention from advocates of Tajik national interests, after years of official policies aimed at the Tajikicization of these peoples. This is especially true of the Yaghnobs, descendants of the Soghdians. Thus, protecting their language was one of the issues raised during the debate over a bill to make Tajik the official language of Tajikistan. The advocates of this were strong supporters of the bill, which means it is unlikely that they were following orders from Moscow to undermine Tajik national assertiveness by encouraging the assertiveness of ethnic minorities within the republic.[4] However, such interests do not compare in extent or intensity with the interest in the Persian component of the Iranian world.

An important point to note is that much of the discussion by the Tajik intelligentsia and political figures about their place in the Iranian world reflects a sense of weakness and vulnerability. In contrast to much of the contemporary Uzbek nationalist rhetoric, which often conveys a sense of pride based on strength, the discussion among the Tajiks has a tone of alarm about it—that the

Tajiks are in danger of losing their very identity, in large part because their ties to the Persian world are weak.

Tajik nationalists see the majority of Tajiks as ignorant of their own heritage, language, and national identity. Many people outside the educated elite are said to define their identity in terms of a particular locale within Tajikistan rather than thinking of themselves as belonging to a nation which encompasses people from all these locales, still less people beyond the republic's borders.[5] Many Tajiks are alleged not to know their own history.[6] It is common for Tajiks, including members of the elite, to know their mother tongue poorly; by the late 1980s, many had ceased to use it outside the home.[7] Not only is Tajik literature taught badly in the schools but also few publications of Tajik or pre-revolutionary Persian-language literature have been available in Tajikistan's bookstores. Examples of twentieth-century Persian literature, such as the works of two of its most important authors, Sadiq Hidayat and Muhammad Ali Jamalzadah, are available in Russian translation, but a "Great Wall of China" prevented their publication in Tajik in Tajikistan.[8]

Much of the blame for these problems lies, according to the Tajik nationalists, with the artificial isolation of the Tajiks from the wider Persian-speaking world. The nationalists' approach to medieval Tajik history and to Tajik literature and the arts before 1917 treats the Tajiks of Central Asia as inseparable from Persian-speakers everywhere, including those in what are now Iran, Afghanistan, northern India, and Pakistan. This enables the nationalists to claim for their people a past in which they were stronger and more esteemed than they were in the Soviet Union or are in post-Soviet Central Asia, with not only a rich and widely influential cultural heritage but also powerful rulers. According to this argument, the insufficient attention which the Tajiks' heritage now receives has facilitated a disregard for their legitimate interests both in Central Asia and Moscow. Similarly, the 1929 dropping of the Arabic alphabet for writing the Tajik language (on Moscow's orders) cut Tajiks off from direct access to their own heritage, as one Tajik poet remarked, making them illiterate, and weakened the language itself, by isolating its speakers from speakers of the same language in Iran and Afghanistan. As a result, Tajiks became increasingly inclined to use other languages, while Tajik was corrupted by intrusions from foreign tongues.[9]

A central component of the nationalists' remedy for their people's declining fortunes is to look to the Persian-speaking world beyond the borders of the Soviet Union and to the Persian, and broader Iranian, past as well as present. For years, Tajiks tried to counter Soviet efforts to depict them as distinct from Persians by simply relabeling ancient and medieval Persians as Tajiks. The underlying intent was pragmatic: to make it politically acceptable for educated Tajiks to show an interest in Persian cultural achievements, which they considered part of their heritage, while appearing to comply with Moscow's policy of separating nationalities from kindred peoples abroad. This remained a widespread approach even under the conditions of *glasnost'*. A prime example of "relabeling" can be found in a work from the pre-Gorbachev era, a history of the Tajiks by Bobojon Ghafurov (1908–1977), a former head of the Communist Party of Tajikistan and subsequent cultural arbiter of the republic. The work has remained in good standing with the Tajik elite since his death and was republished in a Tajik-language edition during the 1980s (the original was in Russian). However, nationalists now go much further. They openly declare the Persianness of the Tajiks and are keenly interested in the millions of Persian-speakers outside the Soviet Union. Some of this interest expresses itself in a generalized curiosity about the activities of any Persian speakers wherever they live, such as singers of Persian popular music living in exile in Western Europe and young Iranians studying there. More importantly, it involves the desire to draw on Persian culture abroad to strengthen Tajik culture in Central Asia, especially in the areas of language and literature.

In 1989, the government of Tajikistan enacted a law which made Tajik the state language. Several other Soviet republics took comparable steps at about the same time. What is distinctive about Tajikistan's case is that the definition of the national language linked it explicitly with a language spoken by a much larger number of people beyond Soviet borders. The language law and the republic's constitution, which was revised as a consequence of the language law's enactment, equate Tajik and Persian, as in the expression used to describe the language, "Tajik (Persian)" ("tojiki (forsi)").[10] Standard Tajik, Tehran Persian, and Dari (Kabul Persian) can all be considered dialects or closely related languages classed as Persian. (At the level of everyday spoken language, these are subdivided into numerous dialects, some of which vary considerably from the written standard.) All derive from New Persian, which evolved as a literary language in the region from Central Asia to Sistan (in southeastern Iran) in the ninth and tenth centuries and spread widely from there. Although the three have much in common and are mutually comprehensible to a substantial degree, Tajik and Dari share some differences of pronunciation from Tehran Persian. In addition, modern Tajik shows some influence in its grammar from Uzbek and in its vocabulary from local Persian dialects. Soviet language policy led to the incorporation of a significant number of Russian words. Dari is distinguished from other varieties of Persian because it preserved some features of New Persian (especially in verb forms) that the other varieties did not and incorporated loan words from India.

Furthermore, the language law calls for the teaching of the Arabic alphabet for use in writing Tajik and for the republic's presses to provide publications in that script.[11] (The alphabet in question is a slightly modified form of the Arabic that contains four additional letters to represent consonants which exist in Persian but not in classical Arabic.) In 1989, one of Tajikistan's publishing houses produced a university-level textbook of medieval Tajik (i.e., Persian) literature in the Arabic alphabet. The teachers' newspaper (*Omuzgor*) and the literature and arts newspaper (*Adabiyot va san"at*) published a series of articles to teach the Arabic alphabet to their readers and included small excerpts from Persian literary works as study pieces. By 1989, more than 1,000 people were said to have graduated from courses teaching the Arabic alphabet.[12] Schools are now supposed to teach required courses on the Arabic alphabet in the sixth grade and above but as of the time of writing Tajikistan does not yet have any children's books in that type. It is too soon to tell how well people will adjust to the alphabet change or even whether Tajikistan can overcome the logistical problems of publishing on a large scale using a completely different type font. For the present, that is a serious problem, since Tajikistan has just begun to acquire the equipment for publishing in the Arabic alphabet. It had to use a press in Lithuania for some Arabic-font publishing in 1990.[13]

This approach toward the national language is not solely the province of the Communist leadership of Tajikistan. Rather, it is an example of the way the Communists, adapting to the new political conditions of the Gorbachev era, used issues of broader public concern to strengthen their own position. Nationalist organizations not controlled by the Communist leadership express similar views on the closeness of Persian and Tajik and the significance of the Arabic alphabet.[14]

Tajik nationalists also urge drawing upon Persian as it is used in Iran and Afghanistan to enrich the Tajik language by providing both examples of good usage that Tajik has lost in its current, degraded state and neologisms, including scientific and technical terminology adopted in Iran as it underwent rapid development in the 1960s and 1970s, the unstated consequence being that these would replace the words which have come into Tajik from Russian.[15] The vocabulary of written Tajik is now in transition, as official publications are replacing Russian words with Persian ones (including many Arabic words that became part of Persian over the centuries). It would be natural for this transition period to include a certain amount of trial and error before the vocabulary stabilizes. Some of the new terms are the same as those used in standard written Persian in Iran for decades, such as *shuravi* (Persian: *shawravi*) for "soviet," *bemoriston* (Persian: *bimaristan*) for "hospital" (Russian: *bol'nitsa*), or avomfireb (Persian: *'avamfirib*) for "demagogue" (Russian: *demagog*). Other choices are less clear cut, as in the case of "compromise" (Russian: *kompromiss*), for which there are at least three alternatives proposed: *musoliha* (Persian: *musaliha*), which would be the standard choice in written Persian; but also *sozish* (Persian: *sazish*), which can mean "accord" but also "composition" or "collusion" in Persian; and *madoro* (Persian: *mudara*), which expresses moderation, caution, or leniency; both *sozish* and *madoro* have connotations that the Russian loan-word *kompromiss* does not have.

There is a movement to replace Soviet place names with historic ones. The same process is at work elsewhere in the former Soviet Union, including the Russian Republic. All the changes have political overtones but in the non-Russian republics they have stronger ethnic connotations than when the citizens of Leningrad voted, as they did in June 1991, to restore its original name, St. Petersburg. For example, in early 1991, Tajikistan's government decided that the republic's second largest city, Leninabad, a settlement of ancient Soghdian and Greek origins, important over the centuries as a trading center and, at times, an administrative and military center as well, should henceforth be known by its historic name, Khojand. Some educated Tajiks have also become open about their dislike for the Russianized spelling of Tajik personal names and the addition of the suffix "ov" to their last names.

Relations with Iran

As changing conditions in the USSR made it possible for individual Union republics to negotiate direct agreements with foreign states (as well as other Soviet republics) Tajikistan and Iran exchanged several official visits in 1989, 1990, and 1991, and declared their intention to cooperate in a variety of spheres, including the economy, scholarship, and culture. For example, the Tajikistan Cultural Foundation made agreements in 1990 with several Iranian publishers to sell books and magazines in Tajikistan, among them dictionaries, the Qur'an (with a Persian translation), literary and political works, and educational materials. Iran's President, Ali Akbar Hashemi-Rafsanjani, authorized the gift of Arabic-font printing equipment to the Tajikistan Cultural Foundation.[16] Dushanbe (Tajikistan's capital) held both an Iranian film festival and an Iranian book exhibit and sale in late autumn 1990. The films were shown in the Persian original, without subtitles, even though not all of the vocabulary was comprehensible to a Tajik audience. Personnel from Iran's Ministry of Culture and Islamic Guidance as well as the Voice and Vision of the Islamic Republic of Iran (the radio and television agency) traveled to Tajikistan for the two events.[17]

Tajikistani visitors to Iran received an enthusiastic response from President Hashemi-Rafsanjani to their proposal to establish consulates in each other's capitals. The sudden collapse of the Soviet state at the end of 1991 and the creation of independent republics in its wake created an unanticipated opportunity to establish relations at a higher level. Therefore, in January 1992, Iran opened an embassy in Tajikistan. Rafsanjani also encouraged the establishment of direct airline service between Dushanbe and the northeastern Iranian city of Mashhad. Representatives of Iran and Tajikistan have discussed the possibility of joint economic ventures in Tajikistan, particularly in spinning and weaving cotton, Tajikistan's leading agricultural product. (Under the Soviet centrally-planned economy, the vast majority of Tajikistan's cotton output was processed outside the republic.)[18] As the Soviet Union and post-Soviet republics grappled with economic reform, at least a few Tajik nationalists were interested in using Iran as a model of economic self-sufficiency and prosperity[19] though other Tajikistanis considered the use of Western economic expertise.

In another reflection of changing political conditions, an official Tajikistani delegation, led by the vice-chairman of the Council of Ministers, Otakhon Latifi, joined representatives of many other countries in Tehran in June 1990 to observe the first anniversary of Ayatollah Khomeini's death. President Hashemi Rafsanjani chose to recognize a Tajik reporter who was part of the delegation to ask two questions at a press conference. Both questions dealt with Iranian-Tajikistani relations and stressed the cultural bonds of the two lands. The president's response (as reported in Tajikistan) discussed the potential for increased economic and other relations between Iran and the Soviet Union. He also voiced an eagerness for cooperation with Tajikistan and other republics with Muslim populations. He indicated that the invitation of the Tajikistani delegation to the Khomeini memorial was evidence of that interest.[20] Nongovernmental Tajik organizations also urge the development of relations with speakers of the same language living in other countries.[21]

An exchange at a still higher level was planned to start on August 25, 1991, when Qahhor Mahkamov, head of both Tajikistan's government and Communist Party, had been scheduled to visit Iran. That visit never took place because of the attempt by Communist hard-liners to seize power in Moscow between August 19 and 21, 1991, and Mahkamov's fall from power soon thereafter. Early in December 1991, Iranian Foreign Minister 'Ali Akbar Velayati paid a brief visit to Tajikistan as part of his trip to various places in the Soviet Union. He called for increased relations between Iran and Tajikistan and met with Tajikistan's newly elected president, Rahmon Nabiev, a member of the Communist old guard, as well as various government officials and academic personnel.[22] The Nabiev regime followed the general orientation of the Mahkamov regime, which entailed promoting contacts with Iran and with *any* country, regardless of political or economic system or religious orientation, that might be able to help Tajikistan.

Iran's open interest in increasing its dealings with and influence in Tajikistan matters but should not be exaggerated. In the 1980s and early 1990s, the Iranian government had higher priorities elsewhere, including Iraq and other Persian Gulf states, Afghanistan, Lebanon, the Arab-Israeli dispute, Algeria, and its troubled relations with United States. Even when it has looked northward, the Tehran leadership has seen the Soviet central government and, in the post-Soviet era, Russian, as quite useful to Iran's interests in a variety of areas, including military purchases, trade, access to transportation routes, and diplomatic cooperation (particularly as regards Iraq and Afghanistan.) The importance Iran ascribes to good relations with whoever rules in Moscow was reflected symbolically in Foreign Minister Velayati's trip to the Soviet Union in late November and early December 1991. He went first to Moscow before proceeding to the Central Asian republics. (Russia's Vice President, Alexander Rutskoĭ, reciprocated with a visit to Tehran soon after.) After the Soviet Union dissolved at the end of 1991, Iran quickly recognized all the successor states, without giving priority to those with large numbers of Muslim inhabitants.

In dealing with the Central Asian republics, Iran does not place disproportionate emphasis on the Tajiks. The Tehran government has been particularly attentive to developing contacts with Turkmenistan, with which it shares a long border; dealings between the two have focused especially on cross-border trade and transportation as well as access for Iranian ships to port facilities on Turkmenistan's Caspian coast. One Central Asian undertaking of particular interest to Iran is the construction of additional railroads to link the Chinese, Russian, and Central Asian systems with Iran's. The hope of developing lucrative trade routes make Turkmenistan and Kazakhstan particularly important to Iran now. However, Tajikistan would not be directly on the route and would play at most a subsidiary role in developing the rail network.

Iran also has hopes of gaining influence in Central Asia by playing on Islamic and cultural themes. It has been directing religious propaganda toward the region since the early years of the Islamic Republic's existence but the concrete results of these efforts are unclear.

The collapse of the Soviet Union has intensified the ambition of the Tehran regime to create and lead a coalition of Muslims from many lands in pursuit of Iran's foreign policy objectives. Tehran would like the Muslims of the Central Asian republics and Azerbaijan to join this coalition and, in so doing, accept Tehran's definition of international priorities. Iran's leadership and press voiced such sentiments at a February 1992 meeting in Tehran of the representatives of all five Central Asian republics as well as Azerbaijan with officials from Iran, Turkey, and Pakistan. While Iran's President, Ali Akbar Hashemi Rafsanjani, and Pakistan's Prime Minister, Nawaz Sharif, described the meeting in terms of Islamic solidarity, they joined with secular, though predominantly Muslim, Turkey to facilitate economic relations among the participating states. The methods proposed to accomplish this included lowering tariffs, disseminating expertise, and creating a bank to fund economic development projects in Central Asia, in direct competition with fellow-Muslim Saudi Arabia. Non-Muslim Romania also seeks admission to this economic association.[23] Evidently, Muslim solidarity is a concept subject to varying interpretations.

One suggestion of the reasons the great majority of Central Asians have not yet sought to follow Iran's lead can be found in Foreign Minister Velayati's observations on his return from his late-1991 visit to the Soviet Union. He noted that the Central Asian nationalities (in general, not just the Tajiks) are striving

> to return to their roots, . . . and since the illustrious figures of the history of Islam, Iran, and civilization are the symbols of the revival of the national identity of these republics, we thought it would be appropriate for us to participate with the very little we can offer.[24]

In an era when nationalism is a powerful force in Central Asia, including among Islamic activists, it is unlikely that any of the major nationalities there want to be told by anyone else what constitutes their identity or how they should interpret their own heritage. In addition, the vast majority of Central Asia's indigenous inhabitants are Sunni Muslims, which makes them heirs to a tradition of estrangement from Iran dating from the sixteenth century, when Shi'ite Islam became the state religion there. Moreover, except for the Tajiks, all of the larger indigenous nationalities of Central Asia are Turkic. Their contemporary nationalist movements have minimized the influence on them of Persian or other Iranian cultures. Even the Tajiks want to use the cultural heritage they share with Iran to aid them in recovering and redefining their identity as a distinct and accomplished people in their own right, not as passive recipients of enlightenment from the Iranian plateau. One illustration of the Tajiks' desire not to become dependent on Iran can be found in an area in which Iran is well placed to play a prominent role: the change of alphabet from Cyrillic to Arabic in writing Tajik. When the leading Islamic religious figure in contemporary Tajikistan, Qadi Akbar Turajonzoda, visited Pakistan in November 1991, one of his objectives was to obtain printing equipment from that country.[25]

Not all the contacts between Tajikistan and Iran or Afghanistan were intended to invigorate Tajik culture. Some were designed by the Soviet regime for its own political ends. For example, beginning in the 1920s, the Soviets published propaganda materials in Persian in Central Asia for distribution to Persian-speakers in Iran and Afghanistan. In the 1960s and 1970s, Soviet citizens studied Persian at Tajikistan State University before being sent to Iran to work as teachers or in economic development projects. Under the directed research plans that existed in the Soviet Union, scholars at the Institute of Oriental Studies of Tajikistan's Academy of Sciences worked on topical issues regarding Iran and Afghanistan; a Department of Socio-Economic and Political Religious Problems was added to the Institute in 1980 in response to developments in Iran and Afghanistan. Tajiks from the Soviet Union served in Afghanistan in the Soviet military from the 1979 invasion to the withdrawal in 1988, and in various civilian positions. Afghanistani students were taken to Tajikistan for their education. In late 1989, Tajikistan's Academy of Sciences established the Paivand (Link) Society, with its own publications and radio broadcasts, to explain to Tajiks (*sic.*) outside the Soviet Union how well Tajikistan fared under Soviet rule and to laud *perestroika* and *glasnost'*.

The Revival of Tajik Culture Under Perestroika

After years of official efforts to undermine the observance of the ancient Persian new year's celebrations, Naw Ruz (which despite its pre-Islamic origins has survived to the present among Persian speakers and others), or at least reprocess it into a bland spring festival devoid of its traditional associations, Tajikistan's government has declared it a state holiday. Although this has special significance for educated Tajiks concerned about reasserting their Persian heritage, this kind of move has broader connotations for the cultural traditions of the Turco-Persian borderlands. Both the Uzbekistan and Azerbaijan republics also declared Naw Ruz an official holiday; the titular nationalities of both republics, though influenced by centuries of exposure to Persian culture, are Turkic peoples with a strong sense of their distinct identities.

In 1989 and 1990, Tajikistan's cultural establishment voiced repeated panegyrics to Bārbad, a Middle-Persian bard (active around 600 AD), said to be the founder of Persian music, and who lived before the Arab-Islamic conquest of Iran and Central Asia. These celebrations were capped by an international gathering in Dushanbe in April 1990, with delegates from Iran among those attending. The message which ordinary Tajiks were intended to derive from this is that Bārbad, though he lived before any Persian-speakers were ever called Tajiks, was a great contributor to the Tajik poetic and musical heritage, and an artist of international significance, whose influence extended from Greece to India.[26]

This commemoration is part of a larger trend among the Tajik elite today of praising the achievements of pre-Islamic Iranian civilization as part of the Tajiks' rightful heritage and a source of pride. (Iranian nationalism under the two shahs of the Pahlavi dynasty [1925–1979] extolled Iran's pre-Islamic past. However, there is no indication that that directly inspired the current Tajik nationalist interest in Zoroaster, Bārbad, or the Soghdians.) Thus, Zoroaster and Zoroastrian writings are hailed as Tajik contributions to world civilization.[27] A Tajik scholar remarked in this author's presence in early 1991 that there is now a strong interest in Zoroastrianism in Tajikistan. One example is the publication of a translated excerpt of a book on the subject by a distinguished British scholar in the field, Mary Boyce, in the first issue (March 18, 1990) of *Sukhan,* the weekly paper of Tajikistan's Writers' Union. This interest is cultural rather than religious. For example, a Tajik to whom Islam is important has nonetheless urged the publication of the *Avesta,* the Zoroastrian holy book, written in an ancient Iranian language, and compares it to a national epic as well as praising it for espousing admirable values. The *Avesta* has also received praise from other Tajiks for various other reasons.[28]

A similar attitude underlies the favorable treatment of the Isma'ili form of Shi'ism and its explicit linkage to the eastern part of the medieval Persian-speaking world, especially Central Asia. This includes positive discussions of Nasir-i Khusraw (1004 to c. 1072), a Persian-speaker from Central Asia who was important both as an accomplished writer of poetry and prose and as a crucial figure in the spread of Isma'ilism in the Persian-speaking world. He receives praise in contemporary Tajikistan for his cultural contributions and as a humanist philosopher, just as Isma'ili doctrines are praised for their advocacy of "free thinking" and their challenge to the medieval Islamic establishment.[29] Although this reflects an enthusiasm for the Persian cultural heritage as a whole, it is not in any way symptomatic of admiration for the Shi'i regime in contemporary Iran. The kind of Shi'ism which prevails in Iran, Imami or "Twelver"

Shi'ism, is very different from and hostile towards Isma'ili or "Sevener" Shi'ism. Both forms of Shi'ism agree that the leadership of the Islamic community ought to have been vested in certain infallible personages, Ali (Muhammad's cousin and son-in-law as well as the fourth caliph of the early Islamic state) and his descendants. However, the Imamis and the Isma'ilis disagree on which particular descendants deserved to lead, and on much else besides.

This brings us to another important consideration about the Tajiks' interest in their cultural links abroad. For the vast majority of the nationalists, this has not reflected a desire to become part of the Islamic Republic of Iran or to set up an imitative Islamic republic in Tajikistan. Rather, they have been attracted by such secular considerations as the Persian-speaking Iranians' cultural development and independence. In fact, some educated Tajiks were concerned lest the vaunted fears of Islamic "spillover" from Iran be used by the Soviet government to deny them cultural contacts with that country. As two writers complained, this fear was based on the assumptions that Tajiks had no legal right to have religious beliefs and that such belief in Islam as did exist could only be the result of pernicious Iranian influence. As they noted derisively, Dushanbe was already the sister city of Boulder, Colorado and yet the inhabitants of Tajikistan's capital had not become Christian converts or blindly pro-American.[30]

Many contemporary Tajiks do consider Islam important, but they interpret this in a variety of ways; it certainly should not be equated automatically with an unwavering admiration for the Islamic Republic. For one thing, Iran's leadership is militantly Shi'ite and has earned the disfavor of many among its Sunni minorities, and most Tajiks are also Sunni. Besides, an interest in the achievements of the Iranian peoples before their conversion to Islam is at odds with the ideology of Iran's Islamic Republic. For many Tajiks, Islam is an integral part of their national identity; therefore, they want to preserve it, or, in the case of some, learn more about it now that religious instruction is tolerated by the authorities, as part of their national pride, their way of life, and as an alternative system of values to the discredited Marxism-Leninism. Tajiks who learn to read Persian as written in the Arabic alphabet will still not be able to read the Qur'an or other works in the Arabic language with comprehension, only to sound out words and recognize those which Persian has assimilated.

There is very little reliable information about those Tajiks who go much further and advocate a radical Islamicization of society, especially since virtually all the information about them which has become public comes from official sources opposed to them, especially Communist hard-liners and Russian chauvinists who never reconciled themeselves to the passing of the old Soviet system of dominance. The main Islamic challenge perceived by Tajikistani officials at the end of the Soviet era came not from admirers of Iran's Islamic Republic but from alleged Wahhabis. (Wahhabism is a form of Islam which seeks to reestablish the norms of practice of the early Islamic community; it is the predominant form of Islam in Saudi Arabia and had acquired some followers in Central Asia before 1917.) The people who are now being called Wahhabis in Tajikistan appear to have been given that designation initially by their opponents, who may have chosen the term for polemical purposes, to imply foreign-inspired subversion, or used it as a loose description for people who are strictly observant Muslims and who criticize those Islamic figures who worked in the Soviet-sanctioned religious bureaucracy.[31] No irrefutable case has been made that these people are literally Wahhabis, but to the extent that they share Wahhabi views they are necessarily opposed to the variety of Islam advocated by Iran. In the post-Soviet era, Communist hard-liners applied the term "Islamic fundamentalist" indiscriminately to advocates of political change.

Tajiks also use their Persian and Iranian links in a combative or at least a competitive sense in opposition to perceived offenses against their national dignity by others. Within the Soviet Union one target was the Russified Soviet establishment, with its long-standing rhetoric that the Tajiks, and other Central Asians, are "formerly backward peoples," who owed all their progress to the Soviet regime, in which whatever was Russian was routinely treated as the equivalent of what was progressive. Another target is the Turkic peoples of Central Asia, especially the most numerous of them, the Uzbeks, whom Tajiks accuse of decades of discrimination against Tajiks. To both groups of disparagers, Tajiks respond by presenting themselves as heirs to 2,500 years of Iranian civilization, in both its Persian and eastern Iranian incarnations. The Tajiks' antagonism towards the Uzbeks is even more deeply felt and more vehemently expressed than their resentment of the Russians. By claiming *both* the eastern Iranian and Persian legacies, the Tajik nationalists can present their people as the only authentically indigenous Central Asians and the region's only truly civilized people. In this argument, the Turkic peoples are outside conquerors, destroyers, and oppressors while the Tajiks and their ancestors are the ones who made great contributions to world civilization.[32]

Tajik nationalists play on the same themes to uphold their own importance within the Persian-speaking world. The concern in this case is defense against the inclination of Persian-speakers in Iran to regard Tajiks as mere provincials, while asserting that the focal point of Persian culture is the Iranian plateau. Part of the Tajiks' response is to invoke the ancient achievements of the Iranian peoples of Central Asia, especially the Soghdians, and to call many Persian-language writers of the past Tajiks rather than Persians, even if they made their careers far from Central Asia. Thus Firdawsi, author of the best-known and much loved version of the Persian national epic, the *Shah-namah* (Book of Kings), a native of Tus, in what is now northeastern Iran, is called a Tajik. So are the poets Nizami, who was born in what is now the Azerbaijan Republic, Sa'di and Hafiz, of Shiraz, in southwestern Iran, and Khosrow, Bidal, and Iqbal, of the Indian subcontinent. However, the fundamental counter-argument is that Central Asia is the birthplace of New Persian culture (i.e., what developed after the Arab conquest). The same argument Tajiks make against Uzbeks, that the

Tajiks are the heirs of a Persian-eastern Iranian synthesis with deep roots in Central Asia, also works against the Persians of Iran. According to this argument, after the Arab conquest and, with it, the eclipse of written Middle Persian, New Persian developed as a literary language in Central Asia, with some influence from the eastern Iranian languages also spoken there. Although this polemic would be challenged on some points by many non-Tajik scholars, it is true that the first flowering of New Persian literature occurred in the Samanid realm, which ruled much of Central Asia and Eastern Iran from its capital at Bukhara from 874 to 999. In the Tajik nationalist interpretation, the Persians of Iran owe their language and literature to the Tajiks.[33] Tajikistan's Minister of Culture from 1987 to 1990, Nur Tabarov, who had a reputation for encouraging Tajiks' opportunities in the arts, remarked in the context of the debate over the bill to make Tajik the state language that its passage would enable Tajiks to take pride in saying to inhabitants of Iran and Afghanistan that the language of the great medieval Persian poets is the state language of Tajikistan.[34]

As Tajikistan began to seek increased contacts with Iran, some educated Iranians reciprocated the interest, ironically for some of the same reasons: seeing Tajikistan as part of a formerly large and imposing Iranian world and source of information for recapturing what the domestic culture has lost because of foreign influences. For example, Dr. Muhammad Rajabi, head of the National Library of Iran, was a member of the Iranian delegation that attended the Bārbad observances in Dushanbe and, after his return, gave an enthusiastic, lengthy interview about his thoughts on Persian-Tajik kinship to an Iranian newspaper. He noted that Tajiks live in an area that was once part of Iran, speak Persian—and do so more fluently than the inhabitants of some parts of Iran—and that they have preserved the language of the early classics of medieval Persian literature as well as Iranian customs which have been forgotten in Iran proper as a consequence of prolonged Western influence. The head of an Iranian publishing house (Suruzh), Dr. Mahdi Firuzan, expressed a similar view of the Tajik language's usefulness to Persian.[35] From the Iranian perspective, there are also the more conventional attractions of extending Iran's influence and helping a kindred people who seek that help and, by doing so, imply recognition of Iran's superiority.

The Tajik nationalists' view of where the wellspring of Persian creativity lies is undercut by their current eagerness to reinvigorate their own culture by borrowing from Persian-speakers elsewhere. Although some try to reconcile this disparity by arguing that the borrowing entails reclaiming what the Tajiks formerly possessed but lost in the recent past, it is too soon to predict the ultimate outcome of this contradictory approach.

Conclusion

In many parts of the former Soviet Union today, nationalism is a more powerful force than it has been for decades. For the larger nationalities in Central Asia, its strength is without precedent. It now seems possible that this rallying point, unlike others in the past, may, within specific nationalities, bring urban elites and the rural majority, as well as urban workers, together in a common cause.

The nationalists' main competition comes from two quite different sources: Communist hard-liners and, potentially, Islamic activists. The Communist establishment's highest priority is preserving its own power and privileges at a time when these have been vigorously disputed in the successor states to the Soviet Union, including Tajikistan. Toward that end, it has tried to use to its own advantage themes which are currently popular. In the case of Tajikistan, these include nationalism, tolerance of Islam, and the quest for economic improvement. In addition, Tajikistan's Communist old guard still has at its disposal powerful means to influence public opinion in the republic: the state radio and television systems; many (though no longer all) of the republic's newspapers and magazines; the extensive party machine; reconstituted security forces; and an improvised militia. After Tajikistan became independent, the old guard used repression and outright warfare against its citizens to stifle all opposition. The Islamic activists are an amorphous group; they do not speak with a single voice and appear to be comprised of a number of different movements with followings that vary considerably in number. The two most prominent advocates of Islamic interests in contemporary Tajikistan are Qadi Turajonzoda and the Islamic Rebirth Party. The Qadi has repeatedly voiced his support for complete religious freedom for Muslims in Tajikistan but on several occasions has opposed the establishment of an "Islamic republic" there (in the sense of a state governed by Islamic law.)[36] The leaders of the Islamic Rebirth Party have not been consistent on this point but at least on some occasions they have taken a stance similar to Turajonzoda's.[37] The struggle against the Communist establishment for the sake of greater change led both the Qadi and the Islamic Rebirth Party into a coalition with secular nationalist, Communist, and ex-Communist reformers (who also took account of the current appeal of nationalism), all of whom acknowledge the importance of Islam in Tajik life. The coalition showed its resolve in the large demonstrations it organized in Dushanbe between late August and early October 1991 against Communist hard-liners. The coalition continued to hold together through the presidential election (Novemeber 1991), the anti-government demonstrations of early 1992, and the civil war, which led to a victory by the communist hard-liners in December 1992. Although the hard-liners have used massive force to ensure their control of the government it is nationalism, linked to political and economic reforms and religious freedom, which enjoyed broad-based support in Tajikistan.

Tajik nationalists, who tried to formulate what the national identity means, do not want to be submerged in the much larger population of Persian-speakers beyond the Soviet border. However, they want at least to borrow selectively from that wider sphere in order to strengthen their cultural identity, after decades of Soviet dominance. For Tajik nationalists have decided that they have no future as Tajiks unless they also are Persians—but on their own terms.

Notes

1. Y. Bregel, "Turko-Mongol Influences in Central Asia," in *Turko-Persia in Historical Perspective,* ed. R.L. Canfield (Cambridge: Cambridge University Press, 1991), pp. 54–64.

2. For the sake of brevity, "nationalism" and "nationalist" will be used in this paper, when referring to the Soviet period, to denote advocates of Tajik national pride and increased autonomy for Tajikistan, within the Soviet system.

3. R. Dodkhudoev, "Eronu Turon chī ma"nī dorand?", *Adabiyot va san"at,* November 13, 1986, p. 15.

4. T.K. Varki, "Iazyk-est' ispoved' naroda," *Komsomolets Tadzhikistana,* June 30, 1989, p. 2; "Muzokira az rūi ma"rūzai 'Dar borai loihai qonuni zaboni respublikai sovetii sotsialistii Tojikiston'," *Tojikistoni sovetī,* July 26, 1989, p. 1.

5. B. Berdieva, "Hama rostī jūyu mardonagī," *Omūzgor,* July 25, 1989, p. 7.

6. I. Qalandarov, "Bozsozī va ba"ze problemahoi munosibathoi millī," *Omūzgor,* August 22, 1989, p. 11; A. Mukhtorov, "Ta"rikhdonī khudshinosist," *Gazetai muallimon,* March 4, 1989, p. 3; A. Mirboboev, "Ta"rikhdonī khudshinosist," *Tojikistoni sovetī,* August 18, 1987, p. 3.

7. "Kalomi navisanda—vositai muhimi tarbiyai internatsionali" *Adabiyot va san"at,* June 11, 1987, p. 3; "Dar borai loihai qonuni zaboni RSS Tojikiston," *Tojikistoni sovetī,* July 23, 1989, p. 1; "Mas"uliyati buzurg meboyad," *Tojikistoni sovetī,* July 25, 1989, p. 2, 3.

8. G. Faizullozoda, "Nohamvorihoi roh," *Omūzgor,* Aug. 15, 1989, p. 5.

9. *Ibid.;* S. Halimsho, "Darakhti jovidonkhirad," *Adabiyot va san"at,* August 24, 1989, p. 5; A. Istad, "Ba ki ta"na mezanem?". *Tojikistoni sovetī,* July 1, 1989, p. 3; "Muzokira az rūi ma"rūzai . . . ," p. 1.

10. "Qonuni zaboni Respublikai Sovetii Sotsialistii Tojikiston," *Tojikistoni soveti,* July 30, 1989, p. 1.

11. *Ibid.*

12. "Muzokira az rūi ma"rūzai . . .," p. 1.

13. M. Olimpur, "Tehronu Dushanbe baradarshahr meshavand," *Adabiyot va san"at,* August 30, 1990, p. 12; ibid., "'Paivand' dar Eron tabligh meshavad," *Adabiyot va san"at,* October 11, 1990, p. 12; "Tājikistān, jazirah-yi zabān-i pārsī dar miyān-i tork hast," *Kayhān-i hava-i,* January 23, 1991 (Bahman 3, 1369), p. 14. The author wishes to thank Dr. Patrick Clawson for bringing this article to her attention.

14. "Pora obnovleniia," *Sogdiana,* no. 1, 1990 (February), p. 1; "Na ruinakh ambitsii," ibid., p. 3; "Izhoroti ishtirokkhunandagoni konferentsiyai ta"sisii sozmoni umumimillii tojikon 'Mehr'," ibid., no. 3, 1990 (October), p. 1; "Ustav i programma organizatsii 'Rastokhez' (Vozrozhdenie) Tadzhikskoî SSR," *Rastokhez,* no. 5, 1990, p. 3.

15. M. Qurbon and S. Ayub, "Tehron, Kobul, Dushanbe," *Adabiyot va san"at,* August 10, 1989, p. 2; "Muzokira az rūi ma"rūzai . . . ," p. 3.

16. Olimpur, "Tehronu Dushanbe," p. 12; *idem,* "'Paivand'," p. 12; Nasrullo, "Muhabbati Eron," *ibid.,* November 8, 1990, p. 3; "Tajikistān, jazirah-yi zabāni pārsī," p. 14.

17. "Jashnovorai filmhoi eroni," *Adabiyot va san'at,* November 22, 1990, p. 6; Olimpur, "Namoishi kitobhoi Eron," *ibid.,* December 13, 1990, p. 11.

18. Nasrullo, "Muhabbati Eron," p. 3; TadzhikTA, "Mehmoni eronī dar Tojikiston," *Tojikistoni sovetī,* October 20, 1989, p. 2.

19. Nasrullo, "Muhabbati Eron," p. 14.

20. "Eron—Ittihodi Shuravī—Tojikiston," *Adabiyot va san"at*, June 14, 1990, p. 1.

21. "Izhoroti ishtirokkunandagoni . . . ," p. 1; "Ustav," p. 3.

22. Dushanbe radio, December 2, 1991, as quoted in Foriegn Broadcast Information Service [hereafter FBIS], *Daily Report. Soviet Union*, December 4, 1991, p. 83.

23. "Muslim Regional Group Welcomes Ex-Soviet Asians," *New York Times*, February 17, 1992, p. A9.

24. Tehran television, December 8, 1991, as quoted in FBIS, *Daily Report. Near East and South Asia*, December 9, 1991, p. 76.

25. Interfax (Moscow), November 11, 1991, as quoted in FBIS, *Daily Report. Soviet Union*, November 13, 1991, p. 86.

26. Representative of the numerous articles on such themes are: A. Rajabov, "Nazare ba oghozgohi hunar," *Sadoi Sharq*, no. 3, 1989, pp. 123–131, *passim.;* A. Yuldoshev, "Rūzgori Borbadi Romishgar," *ibid.*, pp. 102–4, 110; I. Hidoyatov, "Lahnu ghazali Borbad," *Omūzgor*, July 18, 1989, p. 11; A. Abdullo, "Bar sari sarv zanad 'Pardai ushshoq' tazarv," *Adabiyot va san"at*, April 19, 1990, p. 5.

27. Halimsho, "Darakhti jovidonkhirad," August 24, 1989, p. 5.

28. Representative of these themes are: E. Subhon, "Az ajdod chī burda ba avlod chī dodem?", *Omūzgor*, July 11, 1989, p. 4 and R. Sharofzoda, "Kitob va farhang," *Adabiyot va san"at*, June 14, 1990, p. 11.

29. Representative of this are N. Arabzoda, "Gumanizmi Nosiri Khusrav," *Adabiyot va san"at*, September 14, 1989, p. 6 and Kh. Dodkhudoev, *Ismoiliya va ozodandeshii sharq* (Dushanbe: Irfon, 1989).

30. Qurbon and S. Ayub, "Tehron, Kobul, Dushanbe," p. 2.

31. M. Atkin, "Islamic Assertiveness and the Waning of the Old Soviet Order," *Nationalities Papers*, vol. 20 #1 (spring, 1992), pp. 55–72.

32. M. Atkin, "Religious, National, and Other Identities in Central Asia," in Jo-Ann Gross, ed., *Muslims in Central Asia: Expressions of Identity and Change* (Duke University Press, 1992), pp. 51–53.

33. B. Gh. Ghafurov, *Tojikon*, vol. 1, pp. 496–501, 504–508, 510; M. Asimov, "Slavnyĭ syn tadzhikskogo naroda," *Kommunist Tadzhikistana*, no. 5, 1989 (May), p. 93.

34. "Muzokira az rūi ma"rūzai . . . ," p. 3.

35. "Tājikistān, jazirah-yi zabāni Pārsī," p. 14; Olimpur, "'Paivand'," p. 12.

36. V. Vyzhutovich, "Krasnoe znamia kommunizma ili zelenoe znamia islama?", *Izvestiia*, October 5, 1991, p. 2; *Berliner Zeitung* November 22, 1991, as quoted in FBIS, *Daily Report. Soviet Union*, November 27, 1991, p. 73–74.

37. Interfax, December 9, 1991, as quoted in FBIS, *Daily Report. Soviet Union*, December 10, 1991 p. 10; TASS, December 9, 1991, as quoted in *ibid*, p. 74.

CHAPTER 7

Underdevelopment and Ethnic Relations in Central Asia

A. M. Khazanov

Of all the numerous problems that Central Asia and Kazakhstan are facing now, the most important one remains their underdevelopment. Modernization was pursued in this area with minimal participation by the native population, and none of its processes—industrialization, urbanization, the demographic revolution, the revolution in education, and occupational mobility—were fully implemented there. Limited industrialization was accompanied not so much by the creation of an indigenous working class as by the attraction of a work force from the European parts of the USSR. During the construction of industrial complexes neither local needs nor local traditions were taken into account. As a result, at the end of the Soviet period the area contained large heavy industry enterprises, even entire cities with the indigenous population comprising the minority and industrial revenues never reaching the local budget.[1] People from the western USSR remained the backbone of the skilled work force and scientific-technical personnel. The large enterprises, electric stations, oil wells, mines, railroads, aviation, and means of mass communications created during the Soviet period were still served by engineers, technicians and skilled workers from industrial centers of Russia, Ukraine and Belorussia, attracted to Central Asia by higher wages, the possibility of receiving an apartment, and good promotion possibilities.[2]

The local population, even those who wished to take blue-collar jobs, were often passed over and had limited opportunities to learn a trade.[3] Until recently, in the cities of Ferghana Oblast' it was even forbidden to employ rural people.[4]

Sixty to sixty-five percent of the indigenous population in Central Asia was still employed in agriculture, and there were frequent complaints that the movement of the rural population to the cities was hampered by the number of Russians and other people from western republics settled there.[5] In Kirgizia the Kirghiz made up only 20 percent of the industrial workers and a much smaller proportion in management and engineering.[6] In Kazakhstan, Kazakhs provided

The author wishes to express his gratitude to the Wenner-Gren Foundation for Anthropological Research for supporting the research reflected in this chapter.

18 percent of the industrial work force, and the 71 districts (raions) of Kazakhstan with a predominantly Kazakh population were economically the most backward. The results of this situation were demonstrated by the 1989 interethnic conflict in Novyĭ Uzen', the center of oil industry in Western Kazakhstan.[7] The Soviet authorities had pumped oil there for decades and, in order not to build schools, hospitals and day-care centers preferred to bring in temporary workers from the North Caucasus. Every quarter planes brought in a new shift of twelve thousand people. These shifts included not only skilled workers, but also secretaries, cooks, and even office cleaners. In addition, migrants from the Caucasus managed to seize many lucrative positions in trade and service.[8] Eighteen thousand Kazakh youth remained unemployed with nowhere to go.[9] As a result, they began to demand the expulsion of all the settlers and workers from the Caucasus and the provision of jobs for unemployed Kazakhs. Mobs went on a rampage, which resulted in several deaths, numerous injuries, and great damage to various consumer enterprises and services.

A good command of Russian remained a necessary requirement for social advancement and career promotion in almost all spheres of professional activity in Central Asia; this placed members of Central Asian ethnic groups in an even more subordinate position to Russians, and intensified ethnic competition. In 1988 the capital of Kirgizia, Frunze, (now Bishkek), had only one Kirghiz-language school, and by 1990 there were three.[10] In Tashkent, it was impossible to send a telegram or call an ambulance in the Uzbek language. Even employment applications had to be written in Russian.[11]

In agriculture also, labor was divided along ethnic lines. While the native population supplied most unskilled labor in cotton cultivation and for pastoral production, ethnic minorities like Russians, Ukrainians, Koreans, and Tatars were occupied in other more mechanized branches of agriculture demanding skilled labor.[12] Thus, the virgin land campaign in Kazakhstan was not only conducted at the Kazakhs' expense; they were practically prevented from becoming involved in grain production.

A shortage of land and water and ethnic competition for a limited number of jobs resulted in growing tension in regions with a mixed population, not only between indigenous population and settlers or migrants of European origin, but with Muslim ethnic minorities from outside, like Crimean Tatars and Meskhetian Turks,[13] and among different native ethnic groups. Two examples are the violent conflict over land and water rights between Tajiks and Kirghiz on the border between the two republics in summer 1989 in which thousands of people became involved,[14] and the brutal and bloody fighting between Kirghiz and Uzbeks in the Osh Oblast' of Kirghizia in summer 1990 which took at least several hundred lives.[15]

Education in Central Asia remained inferior to that in other parts of the Soviet Union. One of the reasons why the mechanization of cotton production remained low was the regime's ability to mobilize the almost unpaid labor of school children and students forced to bend their backs in the field at the time when their counterparts in other areas of the Soviet Union enjoyed their vacations or attended classes. As a result of this practice and of neglected school systems the quality of secondary education in the rural areas was very low.[16]

This situation was further aggravated by a demographic explosion. The birthrates of most of Central Asian ethnic groups have remained very high and correspond not to the Western model but to that of the Third World countries.[17] There are many reasons for this situation, including low urbanization, a tradition of support of elders by younger members of the family, the influence of Islam, and, last but not least, the pressure of tradition-oriented public opinion. From my field-work in different parts of Central Asia I know that some women and men there would like to use contraceptives and to limit the number of their children, but they were afraid to do it because this would expose them to condemnation by their relatives and neighbors.

Taking all these factors into account, it should not be surprising that the area was affected by another social scourge of the Third World countries—growing underemployment and unemployment. Although Soviet statistics were not particularly precise, they revealed that in the late 1880s Central Asia and Kazakhstan had several million unemployed.[18] In Ferghana Oblast' alone one out of five youngsters entering the job market could not find employment.[19] In 1990 in Turkmenia unemployment was 18.8 percent,[20] in Tajikistan even higher. Already in the 1970s the work force in Uzbekistan was growing by 250,000 persons a year, while the number of jobs outside the agricultural sector increased by only 100,000 a year.[21] Nevertheless, the Soviet leadership acknowledged that it could not (or would not) create jobs fast enough to keep pace with the population growth.

The rural population of Central Asia and Kazakhstan is usually characterized by low mobility even within their own republics. Thus, for example, in Uzbekistan in 1989 only 9 out of each 1,000 people moved from rural areas to cities, while in the Soviet Union in general this figure amounted to 33.[22] However, figures are sometimes deceptive. It is true that from 1980–90 the ratio between rural and urban population remained almost the same. But given higher birthrates in rural regions, in practice this means that hundreds of thousands of people migrated to cities. In both professional and educational spheres new migrants to Central Asian cities were at a disadvantage and met strong competition from other ethnic groups. However, if they failed in the cities, they usually could not return back because their jobs, if they had any, were already taken by other people.

It was just these people, unemployed and often homeless, who came to constitute a new and growing underclass in Central Asian cities.[23] Dissatisfied, alienated, angry and sometimes desperate, they were often hostile towards the Russians and other ethnic minorities and have proved to be particularly prone to extremism, violence, and crime. The result is a tense situation in which some social differences take on ethnic colors, and social mobility strikes against ethnic boundaries. All this has contributed to a general deterioration of inter-ethnic relations in the area.

Ethnic Identities and Political Structure

The ethnic and socio-political situation in Central Asia resembles to a certain extent that in many Third World countries, although the idea that Central Asia still lacks clear ethnic divisions, or that these divisions are unimportant, which was argued particularly strongly by the late Professor Bennigsen,[24] seems to me mistaken. With all my respect for his scholarship and erudition, I believe that his insistence on a common Turkestan and/or Muslim identity as still prevailing in the area was largely an armchair speculation. From my own field work in Central Asia I have no doubt that Uzbeks and Tajiks, Kazakhs and Turkmen, Karakalpaks and Kirghiz now constitute separate ethnic groups with distinct self-consciousness and self-identification, and in most of the cases with clear ethnic borders. The number of inter-marriages among indigenous Muslim groups in Central Asia is very low and is continuing to decline.

An Uzbek poet and a leader of the "Erk" party, Muhammad Salih, recently characterized the ethnic situation in Central Asia in very sober words: "A unified Turkestan today is a 'political dream.' The peoples of Turkestan are already divided into five republics, and in each a national identity has been formed. One can't deny this process that began even during the colonial period some hundred years ago."[25]

It is true that the Soviets contributed much to the process of ethnic differentiation in Central Asia by the national delineation, and subsequent educational, cultural, and social policies, creating new political and educational elites which do not have a vested interest in a unified Turkestan, but on the contrary, are interested in the separate political existence of their ethnic groups. However, it would be an exaggeration to call this policy artificial ethnic engineering. The relative ease with which it was accomplished indicates that some of the preconditions had already existed before the revolution.

Central Asia was always an ethnically and linguistically diverse region, and political unity occurred only for relatively short periods.[26] The circulation of pan-Turkist and pan-Islamist ideas was limited there and they never held sway over the souls and minds of ordinary people. There were over 20 bloody inter-ethnic conflicts in the nineteenth century within the Kokand Khanate and even more in the Khivan khanate.[27]

However, in spite of the noticeable ethnic diversity of Central Asia, and the important role it has played in political life, the process of nation building is far from complete. Ethnic consciousness still has a hierarchical character. An individual considers himself to belong to a given ethnic group vis-à-vis other ones, but in internal ethnic relations his parochial and/or kin-based tribal and clan affiliations still play an important role. Parochial divisions are particularly conspicuous in Tajikistan and Uzbekistan, while in other Central Asian republics one meets with rather pure forms of tribalism.

Turkmenistan can be taken as an example. Before the revolution, the Turkmen people consisted of many tribes such as the Yomud, Teke, Göklen and Ersari. In the Soviet period, the war on tribalism was more than once declared victorious. But tribalism in fact continues to play a very important role in Turkmen politics, social consciousness, and everyday life. Tribal affiliation is always taken into account in personal relations, marriage arrangements, career promotion and in-fighting among the ruling elite. In the Soviet period it was a common practice for the First secretary of the Communist party to put his tribesmen into prominent positions in government, administration, and even in the scientific and cultural establishment, while regional party organizations sometimes resembled tribal fiefdoms. A Turkmen who settles in the territory of an alien tribe has no prospects for social and economic advancement. In everyday life he feels the scornful attitude of his neighbors.[28] Curiously enough, President Niiazov claims that he is an orphan and, therefore, does not have strong affiliation with any particular tribe.

In Kazakhstan, belonging to a certain horde or "zhuz" (something similar to a tribal confederation) is still important. There are many members of the Middle (Sredniĭ) *Zhuz* among the Kazakh intelligentsia, and in the 1920–1930s their predominance was even more significant. At the same time, the long-term first secretary of the Communist party of Kazakhstan in the Brezhnev period, Kunaev, tried to put his fellow tribesmen from the southern regions of Kazakhstan, i.e. from the Great (Starshiiĭ) *Zhuz,* into positions of power. This practice was officially condemned after Kunaev lost power. His successor, Kolbin, tried to eliminate favoritism towards Kazakhs from the Great *Zhuz* but after 18 months abandoned this attempt. Some Kazakhs complained to the author that today's leader of Kazakhstan, Nazarbaev, who owes his career to Kunaev continues the policy of encouraging members of the Great *Zhuz.*[29]

Clan and tribal membership has retained great importance in Kyrgyzstan as well, although the former First secretary of the republican Communist party, Usubaliev, insisted that tribalism no longer existed in his republic anymore and that appointments on the basis of tribe or clan had no place there.[30] In fact, in the 1930–1950s, the majority of leading positions were occupied by southern Kirghiz from the Kipchak tribe; then the balance of power began to change in favor of the northern Sary-Bagysh tribe. When in October 1990 the moderate reformist, A. Akaev, became the President of Kirgizia, his election was connected with a struggle not only between reformists and conservatives, but even more between northern and southern Kirghiz. The rivalry was so intense that in the opinion of some Soviet observers it put the republic on the brink of schism or even civil war.[31] Being a southerner president Akaev still meets the strongest opposition in the northern regions of Kyrgyzstan.[32]

One example more. In the 1991 contest over the presidency in Tajikistan, the candidate of the democratic and moderate Islamic forces was defeated by the candidate of the Communists, because the latter belonged to the so-called "Khojand (Leninabad) clan" which had been in power in the Republic since the late 1930s. All the northern Tajiks, in spite of their political differences, preferred to support their fellow countryman.[33] Regional identities are stronger than differences between the Communists and opposition. Even many Muslim activists are divided along regional lines.[34] The ongoing civil war in Tajikistan, which is often explained in terms of the struggle between secular communists and Islamic fundamentalists, may be better conceived as the struggle of regional factions that for historical and political reasons have chosen different ideological garments. (These factions are usually called "clans," which is wrong because they are not based on kinship.)

Soviet policy towards Central Asia actually helped to preserve or even to revive tribalism and parochialism, in spite of lip-service paid to the need to fight them. During the purges of the 1920s and 1930s, all of the political elites of the indigenous peoples were physically destroyed, not only the populists and enlighteners of the pre-revolutionary period and the national Bolsheviks of the revolution and civil war generation, but also those who had been promoted to positions of leadership in the 1920s. The cultural elites were also destroyed. The Soviets created new political elites whose privileged positions in local structures of power were connected not with the interests of their republics and peoples, but rather with their compliance with all of Moscow's demands and goals, and their capability to implement policies dictated by the center. The positions of the top-level regional leaders depended also on their personal reputation in the center and on their allegiance to the most powerful figures in the Moscow hierarchy. When the center was pleased with regional leaders, they were given a right to run internal affairs in their republics and to distribute preferential treatment and high level jobs, a percentage of which were reserved for the non-Russian elites in Central Asia and Kazakhstan in order to secure their support for the Soviet regime.

The undemocratic pyramidal structures of power built with Moscow's consent and support, and complete absence of civil society in Central Asia inevitably led to a situation in which the actual dispensation of power was connected to a network of personal trust, patronage and clientage. One of the important focuses of any individual's loyalty remains the groupings in which he has grown up and lived. These are the foundations of trust and thus the channels through which power is mediated and social advancement can be achieved. In these conditions it is natural that the leadership in Central Asia would woo the support of tribesmen or fellow countrymen.

The ordinary population, which was denied participation in political life and was unprotected in legal and social respects by state-imposed and state-supported institutions, also tended to rely on the traditional ties of kin-groups and neighborhoods with their old traditions of reciprocity. These institutions have also helped to play down social differences and promote local loyalties. Local particularism which was ruthlessly exploited by ruling elites then inhibited the emergence of a liberal and democratic consensus. So the Soviets failed to create a *homo sovieticus* from ordinary Central Asians. Not without reason, the structures that evolved in Central Asia were sometimes called in the Soviet Union "Communism in its eastern feudal understanding." With equal correctness they might be called the Asian mode of production in its eastern Communist understanding.

It is no wonder that the social structure of the Central Asian ethnic groups in many respects could also be characterized as pre-modern. It consisted of an upper class which included a Communist party hierarchy and people involved in government and administration, and a large lower class, the peasantry. Members of the working class and of the middle class from the indigenous population were small in number; most of the latter were white-collar workers or people involved in humanitarian professions. Blue-collar workers and a majority of the middle class were recruited from other ethnic groups—the Russians, Ukrainians, Tatars, Germans, Jews, Koreans, and several others.

The Early Impact of Perestroika

In the beginning of *perestroika* (1986–1987) the policy of openness and restructuring took an anti-Central Asian overtone. The Soviet leadership was clearly disappointed with the situation there and with the regional political elites.[35] First, the Moscow center was concerned because the regional leadership in Central Asia was unable or unwilling to fight effectively against nationalism. The events in Alma-Ata in December 1986 had significant repercussions.[36] They were characterized as nationalistic riots, and the leadership of Kazakhstan was commanded to take immediate measures to combat Kazakh nationalism. In the following repressions, hundreds of people were sentenced to prison, fined, or fired from work. About 3,000 students were expelled from the universities and other educational institutions.

Second, the Soviet leadership began to seriously fear the influence of Islamic fundamentalism on the Muslim peoples of the USSR. In its fight against Islam, it did not take into consideration the characteristics of this religion, thus making all measures taken against it ineffective. In particular, it ignored the strength of so-called parallel or unofficial Islam. While official Muslim spiritual authorities were under control by the state and were as servile as their Christian Orthodox colleagues, unregistered clergy also conducted religious rites, such as circumcision, weddings, and funerals, as well as organizing underground studies and even mosques. Although most Muslims of Central Asia could not consistently follow the obligations of Islam and regularly visit a mosque, they continued to consider themselves Muslims. Insofar as traditional institutions, attitudes and practices in Central Asia have survived, or even revived as byproducts of Soviet policy towards the area, the role of popular Islam remains invincible because it is inseparably linked with them.[37]

The Soviet leadership looked on with alarm as the observation of religious rites in Central Asia continued to grow.[38] In November 1986, Gorbachev while stopping in Tashkent on his way to India ordered the local leaders to conduct an "uncompromising fight against religion."[39] The Central Asian leadership demonstrated its inability, and often its lack of desire, to seriously oppose Islam. Many officials, especially from the ranks of the lower leadership, combined an outward devotion to Communist dogma with the observation of many Islamic practices in their private lives.[40] I heard many stories from Communists in Central Asia about how they bypassed the prohibition on circumcising children, the violation of which could have meant being excluded from the Party or being fired from work. Usually they sent their children to older relatives, or went away on business trips and then explained that their irresponsible kinsmen had performed the rite without their knowledge and consent.

The threat of Islamic fundamentalism was overestimated by the Soviet leadership in the early 1980s. But events in Iran and Afghanistan actually had an influence on the Muslims in Central Asia, who came to identify Islam with anti-colonial liberation movements. From the end of the 1970s a growing number of people in Central Asia began to listen to broadcasts of Teheran radio, and audio cassettes with recording of Khomeini speeches were circulated.[41]

Third, the central government began to consider the political elites in Central Asia and Kazakhstan as too conservative to put reforms into practice. The anti-corruption campaign and the so-called "Uzbek affair" which had been secretly initiated during the Andropov reign, was made public under Chernenko[42] and revived by Gorbachev, excoriated their complete corruption, incompetence, and ineffectiveness. However, this state of affairs was to a significant extent the result of the Moscow's own policy towards Central Asia. While corruption there is endemic, the population is used to it and considered it as a normal state of things, and the central leadership for a long time closed their eyes to it, particularly because some of its members received their share of bribes.

Cotton production in Uzbekistan had been in decline from the early 1980s.[43] However, Moscow's demand remained the same: "Cotton at any cost." In consequence, a bitter joke became popular in Uzbekistan: "If you don't plant cotton, you will be planted in jail; if you don't bring it in, you will be put out" (in colloquial Russian the verb *posadit'* means simultaneously "to plant" and "to imprison," while the verb *ubrat'* means "to harvest" and "to sack").[44] The local leadership, unable to meet Moscow's constantly increased demands, resorted to different types of deception, including falsification of cotton production figures and bribes.

In 1986 the "Uzbek affair" reverberated across the entire Soviet Union. Ninety percent of the personnel of the Central Committee of the Communist party of Uzbekistan was changed. Major personnel changes were also made in Uzbekistan's Council of Ministers, the Presidium of the Supreme Soviet, the militia, the regional party apparatus and government, and ministries. A massive wave of arrests and dismissals affected different strata of Uzbek society. Thousands of foremen, agronomists, kolkhoz and sovkhoz directors, and lower level specialists and administrators involved with cotton were subjected to punitive measures.[45] To a lesser but still significant degree repression was carried out in other Central Asian republics as well.

The decisions made at the January plenum of the Soviet Communist Party Central Committee in 1987 and subsequent measures definitely put the republics of Central Asia and Kazakhstan at a disadvantage. Central Asian leaders were told that while the center was too short of capital to contribute much to the development of the area, they should give the center an even larger part of their financial and material resources. "A decisive strike must be made against any attempt to place local interests over all-state interests," stated Pravda.[46] Central Asian republics were even told that their population lived too well at the expense of subsidies from the center.[47]

Another demand was to get rid of obstacles to the introduction of Russians into the local elites and the migration of Russians into the area. A growing outmigration of Slavic population from Central Asia and Kazakhstan sounded an alarm to the Soviet leadership which tried to change the situation, although without positive results. Pravda was upset that "the most prestigious professions were in several republics turned into a unique privilege for persons of one or another nationality."[48] The campaign involved a number of concrete measures. Hundreds of officials in the Party and administrative apparatus were taken from the center, moved to Uzbekistan and given substantial promotions. They were locally nicknamed the "landing force of the limited contingent"[49]—a clear allusion to the occupation troops in Afghanistan, which the Soviet press always called the "limited contingent." Moscow also expressed dissatisfaction with the fact that the national intelligentsia and student population of Central Asia were becoming too numerous and exceeded the ratios for the native ethnic groups.[50] Some practical measures followed. For example, the number of Kazakh students entering institutions of higher education in Kazakhstan was limited.[51]

For a long time many Central Asians had high hopes for improving agricultural yields through a plan to divert Siberian rivers to Central Asia, no matter how impractical the plan was ecologically and economically. When in 1986 the center shelved the plan without any appropriate reconsideration of Central Asian ecological policy,[52] this was perceived there as one more manifestation of a colonial policy that strangled the interests of the periphery for the benefit of the Russian center.[53]

It became clear that Gorbachev's leadership was not going to help the Central Asian republics to overcome their economic hardships. Instead, the central government recommended the same solutions to the problem that had been advocated in vain in the Brezhnev period: reducing the birth rate and transferring a part of the Central Asian population to unpopulated or underpopulated parts of Russia—to the non-black earth zone, the Urals, or even Siberia.

One may suspect that these suggestions had strong political connotations. Due to differences in birth rates and the out-migration of Slavs from Central Asia, the ratio of natives to Russians there was changing to the advantage of the former. Moscow was afraid that this tendency would result in the growth of nationalism. Thus, one of the champions of the policy of Russification, the Soviet demographer V.I. Kozlov, admitted quite frankly his alarm concerning the danger presented by the ethnic homogeneity of Central Asian republics to the position of Russians in the Soviet Union.[54]

However, the suggestions of the center failed. Ordinary people in Central Asia simply ignored the family planning campaign, whereas many intellectuals there publicly denounced it.[55] Attempts to persuade or lure the Central Asians to migrate to Russia likewise brought no significant results.[56]

The Emergence of National Movements

Central Asian public opinion reacted acutely against what it considered as the colonialist policy of the center. Because vertical social structures with widespread patronage and clientage are still characteristic of Central Asian society, economic and other benefits there are distributed not only in accordance with an individual's general standing in the society, but also depending on his position in these structures. When the power of a *patrone* is diminishing, his clients are at a disadvantage. By 1988 growing discontent with existing conditions affected all strata in Central Asia and Kazakhstan. National groups and organizations began to emerge in different republics in which the intelligentsia and the educated urban middle classes played the most active role in articulating political goals and actions.[57]

Of all these movements, the largest was Birlik (Unity), the Movement for Preserving the Natural, Material and Spiritual Wealth in Uzbekistan, formed in November 1988 by 18 intellectuals. Among its original demands were the end of "cultural imperialism" and colonial exploitation in Uzbekistan, the democratization of political life, and finally, the sovereignty of the republic. Its popularity quickly grew in 1989, despite active opposition. Similar, though less successful, attempts were made in other Central Asian republics.

While some Russian scholars still explain nationalism in Central Asia and Kazakhstan by the fact that society remains traditional, in my opinion, the opposite is true, and nationalism there is more connected with still insufficient but ongoing modernization and with the emergence of new urban social strata. As in many Third World countries, the competitive advantage of such elites has depended on their privileged positions in their republics, and they have become the main promoters of ethnic nationalism, much more than Communist political elites. Thus, issues of rights and identity have become closely intertwined, and a liberal democratic system based on individual merit and competence, which would guarantee equal rights to all citizens regardless of ethnic membership, is considered detrimental to the interests of the politically strong but economically disadvantaged indiginous ethnic groups.

However, the formation of mass national movements in Central Asia and Kazakhstan took place under significantly more difficult conditions than in many other regions of the Soviet Union. The national intelligentsia there is a rather new phenomenon. Although its members now demonstrate the same "colonial ingratitude" that other colonial powers have faced in the recent past, they are a creation of the Soviet regime.[58] They lack a common tradition of democratic political process and often lack a clear vision of the political future for their republics, whether in the form of Western-type liberal democracies or another system. Instead, they tend to incline towards ethnic nationalism because they regard the dominance of their own ethnic groups in corresponding republics as the best safeguard of their own positions in society.

Moreover, the national intelligentsia in Central Asia is still not numerous, and has been tied to the old political elite and official power structure more closely than in other parts of the former Soviet Union. Most of its members are involved in culture, education, and the humanitarian professions, which were always under strict control by the Communist Party. Until recently, most of them were obedient servants of the Communist leadership, particularly because a significant part of the system of higher education was turned into a marketplace where admission to a university and even a university diploma, as well as professional positions, could be acquired for money or through patronage. It is notable that during *perestroika* most of the leaders of the informal national organizations in Central Asian republics were moderate in their political demands, preferred to avoid anti-Communist slogans, and were willing to collaborate with local political elites. Often their criticism of the latter was leveled more at personalities than at institutions.

It is significant that on January 17, 1992, when the leader of the "Erk" party Muhammad Salih tried to ease the atmosphere at the university campus in Tashkent, after a student demonstration had been dispersed by police the previous day, participants of a protest rally booed him because of his moderate stand toward the government.[59] Even such influential and internationally known figures in the Central Asian cultural elite as the Kirghiz writer Chingiz Aitmatov, or the Kazakh poet Olzhas Suleimenov, never openly sided with the opposition and preferred to maintain good relations with the political elite.

No wonder that during the restructuring period the opposition in Central Asia and Kazakhstan turned out not to be influential enough to lead broad national movements with clear social and political goals. From time to time they were temporarily able to inspire the urban underclass and part of rural population with nationalistic slogans but they often failed to suggest to them an attractive alternative, or to control them. Furthermore, they began to face competition from groups with an Islamic orientation. Attempts have already been made to organize various Islamic parties within the borders of separate republics, or even the whole area,[60] although most of these groups have primarily local participation. However, they definitely have an influence among certain strata of Central Asian society, particularly on issues connected with cultural identification and ethnic nationalism.

The underclass and the rural population proved particularly prone to extreme forms of ethnic nationalism and to slogans like "Down with cotton," "Uzbekistan for Uzbeks," "Russians out of Tajikistan," or "Priority to the indigenous people in Kazakhstan."

Inter-ethnic relations in Central Asia and Kazakhstan deteriorated during *perestroika.* After unrest in Ashkhabad and Nebit-Dag (May 1 and 9, 1989) there followed pogroms against the Meskhetian Turks in the Ferghana valley (June 1989), riots in Novyĭ Uzen' and Mangyshlak (June 17–20, 1989), clashes in Buka and Parkent (March 3, 1989), unrest in Dushanbe (February 11–14, 1990), a pogrom in Andijan (May 2, 1990), fighting between Kirghiz and Uzbek in the Osh oblast' (Spring–Summer 1990), and clashes in Namangan (December 2, 1990).

For a long time everything was blamed on various subversive forces. The central government liked to point to extremists, Islamic fundamentalists, "enemies of *perestroika,*" corrupt local political elites, the mafia, etc. The regional leadership preferred to blame informal organizations, like "Birlik" in Uzbekistan, or "Kirghizia" in Kirgizia. The opposition in Central Asia also claimed that the violence was the result of outside instigation; but it pointed in the opposite direction—to local and central authorities and the KGB. Thus, one of the opposition leaders in Uzbekistan, Muhammad Salih, made the following claims about the pogroms in the Ferghana valley: "the violence that occurred was instigated. Which organ instigated it—the KGB, the Central Committee [of the Uzbek Communist Party], or the center—we cannot say with certainty, but it is very clear that all of the actions were planned in advance."[61]

So far only one thing is clear: there are different forces in Central Asia, which in spite of their contradictory interests are ready to play with the fire of ethnic conflicts, and in an atmosphere of overall crisis they can always find a receptive and explosive social environment.

Because the political culture of the masses in Central Asia and Kazakhstan is undeveloped, conservative political elites still hold power there. While in the Baltics or Moldavia people who could be called national communists came to power for a time, in Central Asia leadership was taken by groups best characterized as the national *nomenklatura.* In spite of all their grievances against the center most of them clearly preferred to side with Moscow against democratic movements in the Soviet Union in general, and against opposition movements in their republics. Thus, all of them were in favor of preserving the Soviet Union and of a new Union Treaty. It was not by chance that the Central Asian deputies at the sessions of the USSR Congress of People's Deputies and Supreme Soviet were the most docile in the Union and always voted the way the central leadership wished.

Although the political elites in Central Asia had nothing against strengthening their power at the expense of the central Soviet leadership, they were unwilling to implement political and socio-economic reforms which might jeopardize their own privileged positions. It is not surprising that in 1988–1990, all attempts to organize national movements and parties in Turkmenistan immediately met with opposition from the Turkmen leadership, which more than once announced that the creation of unofficial organizations in the republic would be a "blind, absurd mimicry."[62] In 1988, the First Secretary of the Communist Party of Tajikistan also spoke out against the creation of a People's Front in his republic. The same policy was practiced by the Kirghiz leadership. In Uzbekistan, the political elite used all its organizational capabilities and administrative pressure to defeat the opposition in the election to the republic's parliament in February—March 1990.[63] In Kazakhstan, the leadership adopted a more subtle tactic, trying to patronize and tame those organizations that were not involved in the political process, and avoided pressing national problems.[64]

To remain in power, the political elites in Central Asia did not hesitate to resort to violence, or even to instigate it. There is some reason to believe that the unrest in Dushanbe in February 1990 was provoked by the local elite who knew how strong the dissatisfaction was and feared losing power in the upcoming election to the supreme soviet of the republic.[65] The unrest had a nationalistic character and was directed against the European or Europeanized population, however simultaneously a demand was put forth for the resignation of the local leadership. The leaders promised to comply, but this seemed no more than a tactical maneuver. Control over the situation was restored with the help of the Army. Elections took place under a state of emergency, and the Communist elite was victorious.[66]

The events in Kirgizia in 1990 provide a similar example. The political elite there also refused to enter into constructive dialogue with the opposition, represented by the movement "Kirghizia" which appeared in early 1990. At the same time, the leadership tried to play along with nationalism by placing the Kirghiz in a privileged position in the republic. The explosive situation that had developed in the Osh Oblast' was not a secret to anyone, but there were no measures taken to alleviate the situation.[67] The congress of the Kirghiz Communist Party, which took place during the Kirghiz-Uzbek fighting and during a state of emergency in the capital of the republic, tried to place the blame for the bloody events in the Osh Oblast' on the "Kirghizia" movement and reelected almost all of the old leaders headed by First Secretary Masaliev.[68] In July 1990, at the time when "Kirghizia" was being persecuted, news began coming from Kirgizia that the ruling powers, including the KGB, were secretly supporting extremist organizations: the Kirghiz "Osh Aimagy" and the Uzbek "Adolat."[69] As a result, many representatives of the party apparatus were elected that summer to the Supreme Soviet of the Republic.[70]

Nevertheless, the Osh events upset the situation in Kirgizia, and put Masaliev's position in jeopardy. His desire to preserve the compromised leaders and to incite tribal passions turned out to be extreme even for the less conservative members of the local elite, and the candidate from the reformist circles, Akaev, was elected president of the republic on October 27, 1990.

In its turn, the Soviet center clearly expressed to the political elites in Central Asia its support and again demonstrated readiness to close its eyes on their old and new sins, as long as they controlled the situation in their republics and did not insist on a fundamental transformation of the Soviet Union. Beginning in late 1987 attempts to introduce ethnic Russians into the political elites and administrative apparatus of the Central Asian republics were curtailed and then practically abandoned. Thus in July 1989, Kolbin, whose name had been indelibly connected with the events in December 1986, was recalled from Kazakhstan. In 1989 Moscow called out of Central Asia the "landing force"—those Russians whom it had sent into leadership positions there during the anti-corruption campaign. Scathing attacks on the command-control apparatus in Central Asia turned into growing reliance on it.

Prospects for the Near Future

Because of the region's economic weakness and political instability the Central Asian leaders to the very end were the most persistent champions of keeping the Soviet Union intact, and its dissolution has confronted them with many new problems. At present, they spare no efforts to secure their power. In Uzbekistan, Tajikistan, Turkmenistan, and to a large extent in Kazakhstan power is still in the hands of the old Communist parties existing under different party names. Even in Kyrgyzstan, the only Central Asian republic where the Communist Party and the state ceased to be one, President Akaev is still very susceptible to pressure from the former Communist Party functionaries.

It is obvious that Central Asia is a long way from Western-type liberal democracy, and many political scientists in Russia foresee only two possible developments there: a dictatorship by former Communist leaders, or a dictatorship by Muslim fundamentalists. The first development has taken place in Uzbekistan and Turkmenistan. The Uzbek president Karimov imposed a strict censorship over the press and mass media, banned all opposition parties and organizations, and put their leaders into jail or forced them to emigrate. The president of Turkmenistan, Niiazov, expressed his attitude towards democracy in his country by stating: "for our people democracy is not a good system."

The second development looks at present less plausible, at any rate in the short run, because it would meet with resistance from both the ruling political elites and their more liberal-minded opponents. Besides, a movement to disseminate knowledge about scripturalist Islam and dogmatic religious practice can be seen as an attempt to recreate and reintegrate this religion as a component of the local national culture and identity. Even many of those who consider themselves fundamentalists are rather traditionalists; most of them do not support the creation of an Islamic state.

Although some Central Asian leaders and their Moscow allies are trying to justify their dictatorship by pointing out that otherwise the Islamic fundamentalists would come to power, actually the opposite may become true. In conditions when secular opposition is weak and suppressed, disillusioned and dissatisfied ordinary people may turn to fundamentalism as a political force against their corrupt, oppressive and inefficient rulers.

The international situation also should be taken into account. Different Muslim countries—Turkey, Iran, and Pakistan—have already begun to compete for influence in Central Asia. Except for Tajikistan, which has strong historical, cultural, and linguistic ties with Iran (though the majority of Tajiks are Sunni, not Shi'i) the republics so far consider Turkey as their most desirable and attractive partner. At the same time, the "Chinese model," i.e. the combination of a strict political control with a limited economic liberalization, looks very attractive to some Central Asian leaders, like President Karimov of Uzbekistan, or even President Nazarbaev of Kazakhstan.

In this situation, I would not rule out completely a third possible development: autocratic or semi-autocratic regimes led by moderate reformers, such as Nazarbaev in Kazakhstan and particularly Akaev in Kyrgyzstan. One should have no illusions. These men are quite authoritarian, in no way democrats. (In this respect a joke about Akaev, at present popular in Kyrgyzstan, is quite significant: "Communism has gone, Keminism has come"—Kemin is the birthplace of Akaev.) Nevertheless, in the current situation they are certainly a lesser evil.

The possibility of political or even economic unity for the Central Asian republics and Kazakhstan also does not seem feasible. Some preliminary attempts made in this direction were not particularly successful, and President Nazarbaev publicly called it "unrealistic."[71] The economies of these republics are to a large extent not complementary. When in the beginning of 1992 Turkmenistan increased prices on its gas fifty-fold, without any consideration for its neighbors' financial situation, this action put Tajikistan and Kyrgyzstan on the brink of energy starvation.[72]

The idea of Turkestan unity is now alive, or rather resuscitated, only in narrow circles of the Uzbek ruling elite and intelligentsia, who hope that Uzbeks will dominate in a united Turkestan.[73] Uzbek troops are strongly involved in the civil war in Tajikistan. Turkmens, Kirghiz, and particularly Tajiks do not wish even to hear about unity. In any case, territorial claims and counter-claims between Tajiks and Uzbeks (on Bukhara, Samarkand, the Zarafshan oasis, parts of the Ferghana valley, and some other territories), Uzbeks and Kirghiz (on the Kirghiz part of the Ferghana valley), Uzbeks and Kazakhs (on some territories along the Syr-Darya and Arys rivers), Kirghiz and Tajiks (on the Northern Pamirs, the alpine pastures in the Alay and Transalay ranges, and some other territories), Turkmens and Kazakhs (on the Mangyshlak peninsula), etc., water disputes between Uzbekistan and Turkmenistan, and other tensions among different Central Asian ethnic groups do not facilitate their unity.

In Central Asia and Kazakhstan the ideology of ethnic nationalism, of nationalism by blood, is now replacing Communist ideology. It is true that the political leaders of Kazakhstan and Kyrgyzstan, the most multi-ethnic republics in the area, have declared their allegiance to "nationalism by soil" and their desire to achieve nation-state consolidation in their republics. However, in these republics also ethnic nationalism has turned out to be the trump card in the political game. Even democratic parties and organizations in Kazakhstan and Kyrgyzstan have been organized, or split, along ethnic lines.[74]

Meanwhile Russians and other non-indigenous people are leaving the area in growing numbers, thus creating shortages in the professional and skilled labor force. In 1989, 94,000 people left Uzbekistan.[75] In the first half of 1990, 34,000 people left Kirgizia.[76] During the first nine months of 1990, 65,000 people left Tajikistan.[77] According to one opinion poll, in 1991, at least 130,000 Russians in Uzbekistan, over 50,000 in Tajikistan and about 20,000 in Kirgizia were prepared to flee from the area.[78]

There is no improvement in the ecological situation and the economy of the area remains in a serious crisis. With the possible exception of Turkmenistan rich in gas and oil, this crisis can hardly be overcome in the near future. The transition to a market economy, the reduction in cotton production and its intensification will not change the situation drastically or help Central Asia out of poverty. Thus, considering the fact that one-fifth of all labor used to produce cotton is connected to water, a reduction in water consumption could reduce the labor force by 6–12 percent.[79] This and similar developments will inevitably lead to an increase in unemployment and to further pauperization of a significant part of a population plagued with ethnic and social unrest. When the Uzbek government removed control over prices on January 16, 1992, this action immediately resulted in a spontaneous student protest in Tashkent, cruelly suppressed by force.[80]

Timid attempts to attract foreign capital so far have not brought any significant results, and one may doubt that they will be successful in the future given the geographic location of the area, its shortage of infrastructure, material and skilled labor, and its completely corrupt and inefficient administration.

All in all, the future of the area does not look particularly bright and the possibility of more social disorder, and even violent riots in spontaneous and sometimes very unpleasant forms, is definitely present.

Notes

1. Z. Kh. Arikhanova, "Ne prenebregat' etnicheskim faktorom," *Voprosy istorii,* 1989, N 5; see also M. Rywkin, *Moscow's Muslim Challenge, Soviet Central Asia* (London: C. Hurst & Co., 1982) pp. 52–54.

2. T. Pulatov, "Mass Exodus Hits Central Asia," *Moscow News,* October 21–28, 1990, p. 7.

3. "Sredniaia Aziia i Kazakhstan: prioritety i al'ternativy razvitiia," *Kommunist,* 1989, N 15, pp. 24, 26, 41.

4. *Pravda,* October 14, 1989.

5. A. M. Khazanov, "Ethnic Stratification in Kazakhstan" forthcoming in *Ethnic and Racial Studies.*

6. J. Soper, "Nationality Issues Under Review in Kirgizia," *Radio Liberty Research,* January 29, 1988, 49/48, p. 4.

7. *Izvestiia,* June 20, 21, 23, 1989; *Pravda,* June 22, 23, 1989; A. Sheehy, "Interethnic Disturbances in Western Kazakhstan," *Radio Liberty Report on the USSR,* vol. 1, N 27, July 7, 1989; 11–14; A. A. Rorlich, "Novyi Uzen': A Small City with Major Problems," *Radio Liberty Report on the USSR,* vol 1, N42, October 20, 1989: 22–24, p. 14.

8. A. Samoilenko, "I opiat' Komendantskiĭ chas," *Literaturnaia gazeta,* June 28, 1989.

9. D.A. Zhambulov, "Problemy sotsial'nogo razvitiia v Kazakhstane," in: *Mezhnatsional'nye problemy i konflikty: poiski puteĭ ikh resheniia,* ch. 1. (Bishkek, 1991): p. 98.

10. *Izvestiia,* March 21, 1988.

11. *Izvestiia,* July 22, 1989.

12. O. I. Brusina. "Mnogonatsional'nye sela Uzbekistana i Kazakhstana osen'iu 1989 g. (migratsii korennogo naseleniia)," *Sovetskaia etnografiia,* 1990, N 3, pp. 20 ff.

13. For more information see A. M. Khazanov, "Meskhetian Turks in a Search of Self-Identity," *Central Asian Survey,* vol. II, no. 4 (1992), p. 1H.

14. *Kommunist Tajikistana,* May 31, June 28, July 15, 1989; *Pravda,* July 16, 1989.

15. B. Brown, "Ethnic Unrest Claims More Lives in Fergana Valley," *Radio Liberty Report on the USSR,* vol. 2, N 24, June 15, 1990, pp. 16–18; A. Stepovoĭ, G. Shipit'ko, "Predskazannyĭ vzryv," *Izvestiia,* June 25, 1990.

16. M. B. Olcott, "Central Asia: The Reformers Challenge a Traditional Society," in L. Hajda and M. Beissinger, eds. *The Nationalities Factor in Soviet Politics and Society* (Boulder: Westview Press, 1990), pp. 266–7.

17. M. B. Olcott, *op. cit.,* pp. 262–3, table IA–IC.

18. D. J. Peterson, "Unemployment in the USSR," *Radio Liberty Report on the USSR,* August 25, 1987, pp. 5, 7, n. 27.

19. A. Bekker, "Chornyĭ rynok Chorsu," *Moskovskie novosti,* September 3, 1989.

20. C. Carlson, "Inching Towards Democratization," *Radio Liberty Report on the USSR,* vol. 3, N 1, January 4, 1991, p. 35.

21. B. Rumer, "Central Asia's Cotton: The Picture Now," *Central Asian Survey,* 1987, vol. 6, N4, p. 86.

22. O. I. Brusina, *op. cit.,* N 7, p. 30.

23. A. V. Galiev, "Bezrabotitsa v Sredneĭ Azii i Kazakhstane na sovremennom

etape," *Vsesoiuznaia nauchnaia sessiia po itogam polevykh etnograficheskikh i antropologicheskikh issledovanii 1988–1989 gg.* (Alma Ata, 1990), ch. I, pp. 127–28.

24. See for example: A. Bennigsen and M. Broxup, *The Islamic Threat to the Soviet Union* (London: Croom Helm, 1983); A. Bennigsen and S. Enders Wimbush, *Muslims of the Soviet Empire* (London: C. Hurst & Co., 1985).

25. A. Bohr, "Inside the Uzbek Parliamentary Opposition: An Interview with Mukhammad Salikh," *Radio Liberty Report on the USSR,* November 16, 1990, vol. 2, N 46, p. 20.

26. A. M. Khazanov, "Nomads and Oases in Central Asia," in John A. Hall and I. C. Jarvine, eds., *Transition to Modernity* (Cambridge: Cambridge University Press, 1992), pp. 74 ff.

27. T. Pulatov, "Osh: Classical Central Asian Conflict," *Moscow News,* N 26, June 1990.

28. Olga B. Naumova. "Evolution of Nomadic Culture Under Modern Conditions: Traditions and Innovations in Kazakh Culture," in Gary Seaman and Daniel Marks, eds., *Rulers from the Steppe: State Formation on the Eurasian Periphery* (Los Angeles: Ethnographic Press, University of Southern California, 1991), pp. 302-3.

29. On the other hand, some articles in the Soviet press claim that Nazarbaev belongs to the Junior (Mladshiǐ) *zhuz* and, therefore, could not be regarded favorably by Kunaev—see for example, "Moscow News File," *Moscow News,* N 3, January 19–26, 1992.

30. *Sovetskaia Kirgiziia,* June 26, 1988 (an interview with S. Tabyshaliev).

31. I. Rotar', "Volneniia v Dzhelal-Abade," *Nezavisimaia gazeta,* October 28, 1992, p. 1; I. Rotar', "Ugroza parlamentsko-prezidentskogo krizisa," *Nezavisimaia gazeta,* April 17, 1993, p. 3.

32. V. Ponomarev, *Kirgiziia: Spetsial'nyǐ vypusk informatsionnogo tsentra Moskovskogo Narodnogo Fronta* (Moscow, 1989) p. 9–10; K. Baialiev, "'Shelkovaia revolutsiia,' ili 'Zagovor demokratov?'" *Komsomol'skaia pravda,* November 21, 1990.

33. V.L. Bushkov, *O nekotorykh aspektakh mezhnatsional'nykh otnoshenii v Tadzhikskoǐ SSR.* Institut etnografii AN SSSR. Issledovaniia po prikladnoǐ i neotlozhnoǐ etnologii, seriia A, dokument N9 (Moscow, 1990;); V.L. Bushkov, D.V. Mikul'skiǐ, *Obshchestvenno-politicheskaia situatsiia v Tadjikistane: ianvar' 1992g,* Institut etnologii i antropologii RAN. *Issledovaniia po prikladnoǐ i neotlozhnoǐ etnologii,* seriia A, dokument N29 (Moscow, 1992).

34. I. Rotar', "Kinorezhisser protiv byvshego pervogo sekretaria," *Nezavisimaia gazeta,* November 9, 1991; V. Vyzhutovich, "Nabiev-Khodonazarov, 57: 31," *Izvestiia,* November 26, 1991.

35. A. Khazanov, "The Current Ethnic Situation in the USSR: Perennial Problems in the Period of 'Restructuring'," *Nationalities Papers,* 1988, vol. XVI, N 2, pp. 157 ff.

36. *Izvestiia,* November 15, 1989; September 27, 1990; *Kazakhstanskaia pravda,* November 18, 1985; *Radio svoboda, Arkhiv samizdata,* N 6434, 6435, 6436; "Focus on Kazakhstan," *Central Asia and Caucasus Chronicle,* 1990, vol. 9, N 1, pp. 3–6; B. Brown, "Alma-Ata Commission of Inquiry Publishes Report," *Radio Liberty Report on the USSR,* October 19, 1990, vol. 2, N 42, pp. 20–21.

37. *Pravda Vostoka,* November 25, 1986.

38. S. Enders Wimbush, "The Soviet Muslim Borderlands," in R. Conquest, ed., *The*

Last Empire: Nationality and the Soviet Future (Stanford: Hoover Institution Press, 1986), pp. 227 ff.

39. *Pravda,* November 16, 1985; February 5, 1988; *Literaturnaia gazeta,* May 13, 1987; *Pravda Vostoka,* August 13, 1987; *Komsomol'skaia gazeta,* March 25, 1988; *Kommunist Tajikistana,* September 3, 1988; *Izvestiia,* September 13, 1988; Anotoly M. Khazanov. *Soviet Nationality Policy during Perestroika* (Falls Church, VA: Delphic, 1991), pp. 64-7.

40. *Pravda,* November 16, 1985; *Pravda vostoka,* August 13, 1987.

41. "Spillover Effects of Religious Broadcasts in Iran on Soviet Muslims," *Radio Liberty,* 142/80. April 14, 1980; "Iranian Religious Propaganda in Turkmenistan," *Radio Liberty,* 375/87, September 22, 1987.

42. V.A. Pechenev, "Kremlevskie tainy—Vverkh po lestnitse vedushcheǐ vniz," *Literaturnaia gazeta,* January 30, 1991.

43. S. Ziiadullaev, "Razvitie proizvoditel'nykh sil Uzbekistana," *Voprosy ekonomiki,* 1989, N5, p. 31.

44. A. Minkin, "Zaraza ubiistvennaia," *Ogonek,* N 13, 1988, p. 26.

45. T. Gdlian, "Piramida," *Strana i mir,* N 4/58/, 1989, pp. 88–89.

46. *Pravda,* December 28, 1986.

47. *Pravda,* February 13, 1987.

48. *Pravda,* September 27, 1987.

49. S. Rizaev, "Za kompleksnuiu sistemu v rabote s kadrami," *Voprosy istorii KPSS,* N 10, 1990, p. 32.

50. *Pravda,* February 13, 1987.

51. A. Alimdzhanov, "Gor'kie uroki," *Druzhba narodov,* N 12, 1989, p. 217.

52. P. P. Micklin, "The Fate of Sibaral: Soviet Water Policies in the Gorbachev Era," *Central Asian Survey,* vol. 6, N 2, 1987, pp. 67–8.

53. B. Atchabarov, T. Sharmanov, "Voda dlia regiona," *Zvezda vostoka,* N 4, 1990, pp. 117 ff.

54. V. I. Kozlov, "Osobennosti etnodemograficheskikh problem v Sredneǐ Azii i puti ikh resheniia," *Istoriia SSSR,* N 1, 1988; Kozlov, "Natsional'nyǐ vopros: paradigmy, teoriia i politika," *Istoriia SSSR,* N 1, 1990.

55. A. Sheehy, "Opposition to Family Planning in Uzbekistan and Tajikistan," *Radio Liberty Research on the USSR,* April 5, 1988, pp. 1–7.

56. M. Rywkin, *op. cit.,* pp. 76 ff.

57. For more details see Anatoly M. Khazanov, *Soviet Nationality Policy during Perestroika,* pp. 82 ff.

58. E. Allworth, "The Changing Intellectual and Literary Community," in E. Allworth (ed.), *Central Asia: 120 Years of Russian Rule* (Durham: Duke University Press, 1989), p. 380.

59. A. Usmanov, "Guns Fired at Hungry Crowds," *Moscow News,* N 4, January 26–February 2, 1992, p. 3.

60. B. Brown, "The Islamic Renaissance Party in Central Asia," *Radio Liberty Report on the USSR,* vol. 3, N 19, May 10, 1991, p. 12.

61. A. Bohr, "Inside the Uzbek Parliamentary Opposition": 22.

62. *Turkmenskaia iskra,* April 29, 1989.

63. *Izvestiia,* February 16, 1990.

64. V. Ponomarev, "Samodeiatel'nye obshchestvennye organizatsii Kazakhstana i

Kirgizii 1987–1991 (opyt spravochnika)," Moscow: *Institut issledovaniia ekstremal'nykh protsessov,* 1991, pp. 11 ff.

65. *Kommunist Tajikistana,* February 1, 1990; M. Mirrakhimov, "Glavnye Prichiny ne lezhat sverkhy," *Moskovskie novosti,* N 30, June 29, 1990, p. 2.

66. *Pravda,* February 25, 1990.

67. *Sobesednik,* N 4, January 1990; *Izvestiia,* June 25, 1990.

68. *Pravda,* June 19, 1990.

69. *Novoe Russkoe Slovo,* August 6, 1990.

70. *Ekspress-khronika,* N 26, June 26, 1990.

71. *Komsomol'skaia pravda,* September 24, 1991.

72. R. Narzikulov, "Vostok—delo slishkom tsvetistoe," *Nezavisimaia gazeta,* February 5, 1992, p. 4.

73. *Radio Liberty Report on the USSR,* vol. 2, N 24, June 29, 1990.

74. V. Ponomarev, *op. cit.*, pp. 27 ff, 84 ff.

75. T. Pulatov, *op. cit.*, p. 7; *Radio Liberty Report on the USSR,* vol. 2, N 37, September 14, 1990 gives a much higher figure—170,000.

76. *Izvestiia,* September 17, 1990.

77. "Tajikistan: Firm Hand Needed?," *Moscow News,* N 51, December 30–January 6, 1991, p. 6. However, *Izvestiia* (August 5, 1990) claimed that during the first seven months of 1990 only 23,000 people left the republic.

78. *Moscow News,* N 5, February 3–10, 1991, p. 11.

79. Z. Wolfson, "Central Asian Environment: A Dead End," *Environmental Policy Review,* 1990, Vol. 4, N 1, pp. 32–33.

80. *Ekspress-khronika,* N 3/233, January 1992.

CHAPTER 8

The Influence of Islam in Post-Soviet Kazakhstan

Reef Altoma

The collapse of the Soviet Union has raised the question of which paths of political development the newly independent Central Asian states will now choose. Until the sovietization of the twentieth century, which resulted in the penetration of the state into nearly every field of human endeavor, Islam had been the most durable cultural phenomenon to influence these lands. More than just a faith, Islam was very much associated with learning and the arts, and religion became closely intertwined with the cultural traditions of the peoples of this region. Will Islam shape the national identity and state institutions of the newly independent Central Asian states? The fate of the republic Kazakhstan is of particular interest to many observers, due to the presence on its territory of rich natural resources, a share of the former Soviet nuclear forces, and a large Russian minority concentrated along the country's northern border with the Russian Federation.[1] As Kazakhstan struggles to recover from the ill effects of the Soviet command economy and establishes its place in the world community, is it returning to its Islamic roots?

Many observers would give an affirmative answer, based upon their view of Kazakhstan's interaction with the Muslim world in recent years. Since May 1990, leaders from Kazakhstan and the other Central Asian republics have met several times to discuss various forms of cooperation. Western and Slav commentators alike use buzzwords like "pan-Islamism" and "Islamic-Turkic bloc" to describe these contacts. Due to its Islamic heritage, Central Asia is often assumed to be "an arc of instability," and the new states are presented as passive pawns in a great game being played out by Turkey, Iran, and other nations of the Islamic world.[2] When the dissolution of the USSR in December 1991 led to the realization that Soviet nuclear forces were located on the territory of four independent states, calls "to [rid] the Mideast of the Islamic bomb" suddenly arose, as did unsubstantiated rumors that Kazakhstan was selling nuclear technology to Iran.[3] Meanwhile, the President of Kazakhstan, Nursultan Nazarbaev, could be quoted as saying "We do not forget that we are a Muslim people, and I believe that our relations with the Arab states will grow and improve constantly and that a long period of estrangement and separation from our Islamic world will be ended."[4]

What is the reality behind the rhetoric? Is Islam a significant element of the post-Soviet national identity taking shape in Kazakhstan, which is home to nearly equal numbers of Kazakhs and Russians? Does Kazakhstan follow some form of pan-Islamic ideology in establishing its place in the world community, or does it simply pursue its national interests? Ideally, a discussion of a nation's identification with a religion would call for an examination of the beliefs and practices of the general public. Since inadequate evidence exists, however, for a rigorous discussion of the actual level of adherence to religion, this chapter concentrates on evidence of interest in the republic's Islamic heritage as reflected in foreign policy, official religious institutions, independent political parties, and governing institutions and ideology.

The author finds that since the inception of the *glasnost'* policies of the late 1980s, official efforts to forge ties with countries of the Islamic world have increased, as has the role for Islamic-oriented institutions in domestic politics. But due perhaps to the peculiarities of Islamicization among the steppe nomads and the heterogeneous ethnic make-up of the contemporary state, the Kazakhstan government maintains a cautious view of the role of religion in politics. Pragmatic interests better explain Kazakhstan's foreign policy, and in domestic affairs, the leadership strives to mold the identity of independent Kazakhstan into a secular, stable multiconfessional and multiethnic entity. Before looking more closely at the influence of Islam in the areas of politics mentioned above, a review of the historical process of Islamicization and its present influence on society is in order.

Islam in the Kazakh Lands from the Eighth Century to the Present

The first messengers of Islam appeared in the southern reaches of Kazakhstan in the eighth century, after Qutayba Muslim's opening of Transoxiana in 714. At this time a number of religions flourished in the region—shamanism, Buddhism, Christianity, and Zoroastrianism, among others. In most of the south and in Semirechie, the Arab conquests did not result in the adaption of Islam or the Arabic language and script until the tenth and eleventh centuries.[5] In the Kipchak steppe, Islam came relatively late, with Naqshabandi and Yasawi Sufi missionaries making the first significant numbers of converts in the fifteenth and sixteenth centuries.

It is generally believed that Islam made little impression on the Kazakh hordes, who lived far from urban centers of Islam, until the Russian conquests of the eighteenth century.[6] The conquest of Kazan and the policy followed by Ivan IV and a number of his successors to forcibly convert the Tatar population to Christianity began to spread (Sunni) Islam; to escape persecution, Tatar merchants and *mullahs* fled toward Bukhara and the Kazakh steppes and started to build mosques and *madrasas*, or religious schools, among the nomads.

Beginning in 1773 the propagation of religion in Kazakhstan was further strengthened by Catherine the Great's use of Tatar missionaries to spread Islam in Kazakhstan and to "civilize" the nomads.[7] Nevertheless as late as the 1860s, the celebrated Kazakh scholar Chokhan Valikhanov wrote that Islam still had not been absorbed into the Kazakh "flesh and blood"; he admitted that due to the influence of Tatar mullahs, the steppe peoples were increasingly adopting Islamic customs, but stated that among the Kazakhs "there are still many who do not know even the name of Muhammad, and in many places our shamans have still not lost significance."[8] Thus the scholarly consensus maintains that the nomadic Kazakh population was largely resistant to Islam, and that the Kazakh adaptation of Islam reflects a mixture of steppe spirit cult and practices.[9]

Nevertheless, by the time of the Bolshevik revolution, Central Asia, including the Kazakh lands, was predominantly Muslim, and the Soviet regime consequently attacked religion in order to assimilate the various nationalities to the new Soviet political order. Not only was separation of church and state proclaimed, but independent religious organizations were practically eliminated. The *waqfs*, or religious endowments, were taken under state control, mosques were closed, and Muslim courts and schools virtually disappeared. During World War II, a system of muftiates, or spiritual boards, was established. (John Voll discusses this creation of "official Islam" in Chapter 3.) Kazakhstan came under the jurisdiction of the Spiritual Board for Muslims of Central Asia and Kazakhstan (DUMSAK), which, like the other boards, established sanctioned channels of Muslim religious activity, administered what few Muslim religious institutions were allowed to function, and regulated religious training and the activities of the official clergy.

The *glasnost'* policies of the late 1980s provided an opening for peoples all over the Soviet empire to express an interest in the language, customs, and religion of their past. In Kazakhstan, the rights of the titular nationality have been receiving long overdue attention; a strong movement to revitalize the Kazakh language has developed, and numerous literary and historical associations have formed with the aim of educating the public about little-known Kazakh writers and political figures, restoring Kazakh cultural monuments, and rehabilitating victims of Stalinist repressions.[10] At the same time, Kazakhstan has witnessed an increase in mosque attendance and the visibility of religious activities. Religious literature has become more accessible to the general public; the Koran has been translated into Kazakh, and Kazakh as well as Russian and Arabic versions of the Koran are sold openly. Histories of the Prophet Muhammad and Islam, pamphlets containing selected *suras*, explanations of the five pillars of Islam, and descriptions of how to pray are widely available in kiosks and bookstores. In addition, the spiritual board of Kazakhstan has begun issuing an Islamic calendar in Kazakh which specifies the times for the five prayers in Alma Ata and other cities, and identifies religious holidays.[11] The instructive nature of the literature, it should be noted, suggests that the Muslim population of Kazakhstan is just getting reacquainted, or perhaps acquainted for the first time, with the basic principles of the faith.

It is very difficult to determine the level of adherence to Islam among the general population since no rigorous public opinion data reflecting the influence of religious belief is presently available. During an extended stay primarily in the Alma-Ata region during 1992–93, the author found that most Kazakhs will identify themselves as Muslim, but this "Muslimness" seems to signify more of a cultural identity than a commitment to observing the faith. Kazakhs are careful to differentiate themselves from the neighboring Uzbeks, whom they view as (religious) "fanatics," and pride themselves on the fact that women were never veiled in traditional Kazakh nomadic society. Raushan Mustafina, a Kazakh ethnologist who recently conducted a study of religion in southern Kazakhstan, supports the notion of limited religious observance. Mustafina finds that many Kazakhs consider Muslim ceremonies part of their "national" rather than religious heritage.[12] There does exist an "older generation," the members of which consider themselves to be true believers, but younger and middle-aged individuals usually have a sketchy knowledge of tradition. Moreover, even *observant* Kazakhs often deviate from formal fasting and prayer requirements.[13]

Foreign Policy

The historical ties of Kazakhstan with the Islamic world and remnants of Muslim identification among the Kazakh public are leaving an imprint on the republic's foreign policy. High-level contacts between Kazakhstan and Turkey began multiplying before the August 1991 coup attempt, with officials on both sides repeatedly stressing common linguistic, religious, and cultural bonds between the two nations. In the spring of 1991, Kazakhstan's minister of culture called President Turgut Ozal's visit to Kazakhstan a turning point in Kazakhstan-Turkish relations, remarking, "We have a common language, religion, culture, and history. We had been apart for a while, we are now reunited." Similarly, President Ozal explained that his interest in visiting Kazakhstan and Azerbaijan stemmed from "Turkey's historic ties with the peoples of these republics."[14] By September 1991, President Nazarbaev was being received in Turkey with the fanfare usually reserved for a head of state; at the end of the Kazakhstan delegation's visit, the two governments signed agreements in the fields of transportation and telecommunications, and a memorandum of intent about further contacts.[15] The May 1992 visit of Turkish Prime Minister Demirel brought more concrete results; a wide range of agreements were signed—on the issuing of credit lines, the establishment of automobile and aviation transport links, and the development of small and medium enterprises. According to protocols signed at this meeting, Turkish firms would cooperate with Kazakhstan partners to develop oil facilities and an electric power station in Aktiubinsk, to reconstruct the port of Atyrau (former Gur'ev), and to facilitate the transport of exports from Kazakhstan across the Caspian, Black and Baltic seas.[16]

Kazakhstan has also made efforts to establish links with other Muslim countries. In December 1991, Kazakhstan and Azerbaijan became the first of the Soviet Muslim republics to send delegations in an observer capacity to the annual summit of the Organization of the Islamic Conference, held in Dakar that year. At the summit the representative from Kazakhstan, Sailau Batirsha-uly, a deputy foreign minister who was educated in Syria and speaks Arabic, commented, "Kazakhstan, like the Central Asian republics which were part of the USSR, has for many years been cut off from the outside world and even from its neighbors in terms of economic, cultural, and other ties in the Islamic world. . . . We are now on a sure road to openness and integration with the entire world community which, naturally, includes the Arab world."[17] Kazakhstan officials have been exchanging visits with banking and trade officials from numerous Islamic countries, including Saudi Arabia, Iran, and Pakistan; the Saudis have already opened an equity joint venture Islamic bank in Alma-Ata. Al-Baraka Bank actually operates on the basis of Islamic law; that is, in accordance with the shariah's injunction against usury, the bank allows no interest to be earned on the loans it issues.[18] By early 1992 Iran had signed agreements to open an Iranian bank in Kazakhstan as well, and to assist in oil exploration and the transportation of goods between Kazakhstan and Iranian Caspian Sea ports.[19] Similarly, Nazarbaev's visit to Pakistan, during which the president stressed that ties with the Islamic world are one of Alma-Ata's priorities, resulted in the signing of numerous protocols for cooperation in the fields of trade and economics, science and technology, culture, sports and tourism.[20]

In cooperating with countries of the Islamic world, the government of Kazakhstan has not neglected its Central Asian counterparts. Since the summer of 1990, the leaders of the Central Asian republics have met several times all together, and bilaterally, to discuss various forms of cooperation. These contacts have led to discomfort in some Russian political circles, and have been described as efforts to set up an "Islamic" or "Turkic" bloc. Some mild play is given to the common historical and spiritual ties shared by the Central Asian peoples (not all of whom are Turkic, of course), but the most striking evidence of a role for Islam as the basis for forming a political or economic community is held to be the symbolism of the meetings: for example, the May 1992 meeting between Kazakhstan and Uzbekistan was held in the Kazakh city of Turkestan, home to the mausoleum of Sheikh Ahmad Yasavi, the Sufi saint who played a major role in bringing Islam to the region.[21]

Why this interest in developing ties with Muslim nations? One should recognize that the outside Muslim world is to a certain extent courting Kazakhstan. Exploring the motives of Turkey or Iran requires separate treatment, but some general assumptions can be made here. Religious and cultural-ethnic ties probably encourage greater interest in this part of the world, as compared to a culturally very distinct and geographically distant South America for example, but there are also adequate pragmatic considerations for Muslim nations to be interested. After all, Kazakhstan and the other Central Asian republics represent a new market for consumer goods, and a new source of valuable raw materials. But what are the main reasons for the interest displayed on the Kazakhstan side?

To some extent, we can take the expressions of spiritual and cultural bonds at face value; the leadership of Kazakhstan is acting upon a natural interest in reconnecting with a part of the world with which it shares religious, cultural and ethnic bonds. The main determinant of Kazakhstan foreign and trade policy, however, seems to be pragmatic, national interest. First, developing diplomatic and trade relations with the Islamic world has helped to legitimize Kazakhstan's new sovereign status; while Western nations reacted cautiously to post-August 1991 developments, Iran and Turkey were among the first governments to provide much-needed international recognition to Kazakhstan. In this way, ties with the Islamic world can be viewed as strengthening sovereign Kazakhstan's entry into the world community.

Secondly, economic interest guides Kazakhstan's policies towards Muslim neighbors; establishing friendly ties and regular trade with regional neighbors is a matter of national interest for any state, and as an essentially land-locked nation, Kazakhstan needs to develop close ties with its regional neighbors in order to develop transportation routes and facilities for anticipated increases in raw material exports. Turkey, Iran, and Pakistan can all provide access to warm-water ports.[22] Furthermore, some of the Muslim nations are relatively convenient suppliers of much-needed consumer goods, and Turkish goods, especially apparel, toiletries, and some food items have flooded markets in Kazakhstan.

As for Kazakhstan's special relationship with the rest of former Soviet Central Asia, Kazakh statements and press releases about Central Asian cooperation rarely mention common religious or ethnic roots as a basis for cooperation. What the agreements *do* stress, however, are the problems the republics share on their way to a difficult economic and political transformation in a region which shares many daunting problems, with environmental problems receiving much attention.[23] Nazarbaev's chief motivation for working closely with the other former Soviet Muslim republics, even in considering membership in the Economic Cooperation Organization, is not to "strengthen the position of Islam," but rather to preserve the links of integration crucial to the functioning of the Kazakhstan economy and establish new trade relations to facilitate the transition to the market economy.[24] Moreover, the development of greater coordination of policies with other Central Asian states should not be seen as directed against the non-Muslim states of the CIS. The Kazakhstan leadership, more than any other in Central Asia, and possibly the entire Commonwealth, has worked hard to improve the links of the CIS and clearly views close relations with Russia as the best way to limit the damage of the collapsed union economy;

Nazarbaev has on numerous occasions made constructive proposals to maintain the ruble zone and improve the overall coordination of economic policy among the countries of the CIS.[25]

As further proof that pragmatic national interest guides Kazakhstan's relationship with the Islamic world, we should recognize that Kazakh leaders look to these countries for clues on political and economic development, and that in doing so, they express a preference for secular Turkey. The leadership of Kazakhstan, like the leadership of other Central Asian states, views Turkey as a successful, secular political system with a measure of economic viability that can be feasibly attained in conditions of post-Soviet independence.[26] Iran's theocracy is *not* a preferred model for Kazakhstan; when asked in an interview about the strength of religion in Kazakhstan, President Nazarbaev flatly denied any threat of Islamic fundamentalism due to the secular bent of the Kazakh people; and he further stressed, "Let us again turn to Turkey. We regard its secular system as a model for Kazakhstan . . . State and religious affairs are separate. This reveals why Turkey is so important for Kazakhstan."[27] Furthermore, Turkey provides the lens through which Western capitalist development in general is viewed. In an interview published in the Turkish newspaper, *Cumhuriyet,* in December 1991, President Nazarbaev stressed, "I must emphasize that we regard Turkey as our economic hope . . . our historic ties with Turkey and its achievements in a short period have convinced us we should give priority to the Western world."[28] During this challenging transition period, Kazakhstan needs capital, a strong private sector, and contact with international business and financial circles, which is precisely what the isolated Iranian economy could use itself; Turkey, on the other hand, has good, established trading and financial links with Europe and the United States and can facilitate Kazakhstan's entry to the world economy.

Aside from recognizing the strong influence pragmatic political and economic considerations have for Kazakhstan's establishment of ties with the Islamic world, it is important to look at the broader picture: the leadership of Kazakhstan is looking not to Turkey and the Islamic world alone for trade and cultural links and clues to development. The Republic of Korea is one of the models Nazarbaev publicly praised early on, and a delegation from Kazakhstan visited Seoul back in November 1990 in search of foreign investment. Pleased with his visit, then Prime Minister Nazarbaev stated, "Over the past 30 years, the Koreans have rapidly developed their economy with little natural resources . . . We think that these assets and the entire course of Korea's economic growth are a very proper experience for our republic. We plan to employ this experience in our republic."[29] Nazarbaev also enlisted a Korean-American businessman and professor, Chan Young Bang, as an economic advisor, and interest in the ROK has found a place among parliamentarians' debates and in the press. Indeed, many individual Kazakhs, businessmen and ordinary workers alike, maintain that their country could become the fifth "Dragon" or "Tiger."[30]

The leadership of Kazakhstan has been considering numerous models, hoping to incorporate the best features of all of them. Singaporean authoritarianism, Swiss consociationalism, and China's free trade zones all receive attention. Whatever links Kazakhstan *does* have with the Islamic world, they have no ill effect on relations with Israel. Israeli expertise in agriculture has not been overlooked; direct communication links were established with Israel in early January 1992, and plans for further cooperation were laid out during Prime Minister Sergeĭ Tereshchenko's visit to Israel in fall 1992.[31] National newspapers have published sections of the U.S. constitution for debate, speeches of the American ambassador, and U.S. Information Agency essays describing democratic ideals and principles of market economy. Furthermore, while Kazakhstan tries to avail itself of the expertise and credit capacities of the countries of the Islamic world, the biggest deals contracted by the Kazakhstan government have been with Western energy giants such as Chevron, British Gas, Agip, and Elf-Aquitaine.[32] Rather than trying to choose between worlds, then, Kazakhstan pursues foreign and trade policies largely based on national economic interest. As one official in the presidential apparatus told the author, "We will turn in whatever direction is beneficial—whether to China, Pakistan, Turkey, or Russia."

Kazakhstan's balanced and eclectic approach in developing foreign relations has not taken shape in an ideological vacuum; external relations are reflective of domestic developments, as the leadership of Kazakhstan strives to maintain a balance among the different religions and ethnicities represented in the population.

"Official" Islam Today— The Spiritual Board of Muslims of Kazakhstan

One of the most obvious signs of a heightened role for Islam in the national identity of Kazakhstan was the establishment in January 1990 of the Spiritual Board for the Muslims of Kazakhstan (DUMK), separate from the original Central Asian spiritual board which had determined Kazakh religious affairs for nearly half a century. This development may be viewed as a response to, or anticipation of greater religious adherence among the local Muslim population. In the last several years, ethnic Kazakhs have been displaying a greater interest in Islam. The Chief Mufti of Kazakhstan, Ratbek Hajji Nysanbai-uly, views this growing interest in religion as natural, considering the weight of Islam in Kazakh history and the ideological vacuum formed with the discrediting of the Soviet regime.[33] A locally-based muftiate will be better placed to determine and meet the needs of growing numbers of believers, to organize and finance the construction of mosques and the training of mullahs to administer circumcision, marriage, and burial rites, and so forth.

Yet beyond the logical goal of DUMK to provide for growing spiritual needs among the local population, the establishment of an independent spiritual board in Kazakhstan accomplishes at least two major objectives. First, the DUMK apparatus facilitates greater government influence over any process of Islamic revival taking place. The board is officially independent and self-financing, claiming to operate entirely on the contributions of believers. In fact, the new law on religious organizations declares that the state cannot finance such organizations. Yet the activities of the spiritual board are clearly still sanctioned from above to some extent, though how the actual lines of command work in post-Soviet Kazakhstan today is a difficult question to answer. The new law on freedom of religion specifies the formation by the president of Kazakhstan of a state organ maintaining ties with religious associations. Presumably it is at least in part through the liaison and advising functions of this organ that the government influences DUMK.[34]

Second, the independent muftiate acts as a symbol of sovereignty; had the directorate not been established before independence, the Kazakhs certainly would have scrambled (as did the Kirghiz and the Turkmens) to establish one after independence. More specifically, the creation of DUMK may be viewed as an outcome of Kazakh-Uzbek rivalry. Indeed, Mufti Nysanbai-uly has stated that the concentration of political and economic authority in Tashkent at the expense of the Kazakhs and the cultural differences between Kazakh and Uzbek Muslims were the main reasons for the establishment of a separate Kazakh board. In the 47 years of the existence of a joint Central Asian and Kazakh spiritual directorate, Nysanbai-uly complained, not a single Kazakh was elevated to the position of head of the directorate, and in general, Kazakhs were poorly represented among the officials of the directorate.[35] The Kazakh Qadi Kalan had little control over Muslim financial contributions in the form of *zakat* and *sadaka* (religious almsgiving); over the decades millions of rubles were sent off to Tashkent's coffers, with the Kazakh Muslim community having little to say about their subsequent use. Furthermore, the Mufti stressed that the Kazakh language, traditions and customs differ greatly from those of the Uzbeks; in particular, he complained that DUMSAK *fatwas* (legal opinions) were issued entirely "according to Uzbek tradition."[36] The establishment of DUMK has had the added benefit of eliminating Tashkent's monopoly on religious education for the Kazakh Muslim community: it facilitated the establishment of the Higher Islamic Institute, from which the first class of 30 graduated in 1991.[37]

While the Kazakhstan spiritual board still maintains links with the board in Tashkent, greater effort has been made to establish ties with non-CIS Muslim countries. Relations have been established with the official religious establishments or ministries of Egypt, Turkey, Saudi Arabia, and Pakistan. One of the guests of honor at the second regular congress of Kazakhstan Muslims was an emissary from UAE and Kuwait (who offered one million rubles for the construction of a new mosque); also attending were delegates from the Turkish and Egyptian muftiates, Saudi Arabia, Pakistan, Iran, and Mongolia.[38] It is instructive to note that among representatives from the peoples of the CIS present at the conference, no Central Asians were enumerated, nor were they mentioned in Mufti Nysanbai-uly's speech. Rather, the Mufti talked about the gains of independence and the benefits of international status such as that achieved by membership in the United Nations, and described the development of ties with non-CIS Muslim states.

Islam in Political Party Platforms

If the creation of DUMK reflects a sanctioned role for the Islamic religion in Kazakh identity today, the most prominent unsanctioned incorporation of religion is manifested by the Alash Party. Founded as a national independence party in the spring of 1990, though still not registered with the Ministry of Justice, the Alash Party acts as an opposition movement to the official Islamic functionaries and openly criticizes the Nazarbaev regime.[39] Alash activists promote ideas that many Kazakhstani and Western observers have called Turkish chauvinist and Islamic fundamentalist.[40] Alash has attracted mostly Kazakh and only Muslim followers, though the party program calls for freedom of worship and the right to representation on the part of members of all religions and ethnicities in the republic.[41] But clauses on freedom of worship do not allay the fears of many Russians and more secularly-oriented Kazakhs who attribute to the party purely chauvinistic intentions, since the rights of the titular nationality of the republic occupy a special place in the Alash program. More precisely, the Kazakh nation possesses "priority rights in the observation of its national traditions, the development of language and culture, and concerns over the rational and economical use of its natural riches." Moreover, Islam, as the religion of the Kazakh people, occupies a priority position among religions of the land.

In terms of concrete influence, however, it should be stressed that the Alash party relies on a small core of members and sympathizers; the State Committee on Youth has estimated that Alash represents the views of 3–5% of youth.[42] Alash gained fame—or notoriety—when a group of activists took over the Alma-Ata mosque for a couple of days in December 1991. Blockading the mosque after the mid-day prayer, the Alashists accused Mufti Nysanbai-uly of having KGB ties and pilfering the religious community's contributions toward the construction of a new mosque in Alma Ata. One of the group apparently assaulted the mufti before he left the premises; several Alash leaders were later arrested and charged with inciting mass disorder.[43] While some of the views expressed by Alashists, especially criticisms of the chief mufti, are echoed by ordinary citizens, the aggressiveness and illegality of some of Alash's actions apparently find little resonance among the patient and unpoliticized bulk of Kazakhstani society.

Most larger parties and movements formed since the collapse of the USSR claim a secular and ethnically neutral orientation, and their programs use strikingly similar rhetoric in calling for economic reform and national ethnic and spiritual accord. The first large political movement to gain currency in Kazakhstan society was the environmental social movement Nevada-Semipalatinsk, the name reflecting a commitment to ridding the world of nuclear testing sites. The creation of the popular writer, Olzhas Suleimenov, Nevada-Semipalatinsk Anti-Nuclear Movement provided the base from which the political party People's Congress of Kazakhstan emerged in the fall of 1991; the party "expresses the interests of the citizen of Kazakhstan independent of his national, class or religious affiliation. . . . We call and will be calling all Kazakhstanis to [observe] mutual tolerance in interethnic relations."[44] The People's Congress Party, for which President Nazarbaev indicated strong support at the opening congress, and the Socialist Party of Kazakhstan, the direct successor to the Communist Party of Kazakhstan, have elicited support among former CPSU members and members of the governing elite; both are committed to a gradual establishment of a democratic, multi-party political system and market reform, and exhibit no signs of radicalism. Most recently, a new political force with a platform not dissimilar to that of People's Congress and similarly endorsed by Nazarbaev has emerged—the Union for National Unity of Kazakhstan (SNEK). Headed by People's Deputy Serik Abdrakhmanov, SNEK is actually the brainchild of an accomplished group of intellectuals, political scientists and sociologists who have a solid commitment to maintaining an atmosphere of religious tolerance and ethnic calm and understanding in sovereign Kazakhstan.[45] It should be noted that even representatives of the Alash party, in recognition of the country's unique demographic composition, argue that only a secular model like that of the Republic of Turkey could be implemented in Kazakhstan.[46]

When we analyze the platform and followings of Kazakh political parties, we see that the larger story of political demands in Kazakhstan revolves not around Islam, or any religion, but rather around nationalism. Since many parties and movements adhere to a similar ideology in their commitment to the sovereignty and market reform ideals proclaimed by the government, constituencies have broken down along ethnic, rather than class or ideological lines. In fact, Alash should be viewed as appealing not so much to a religious as to a nationalist audience, since many of its stances reflect a concern about improving the situation of the Kazakh people. The Civil Democratic Movement "Azat," which merged with other parties and movements to form the Republican Party–Azat in fall 1992, in theory stands for "liberty, equality, fraternity, and a decent life for all citizens of Kazakhstan."[47] In practice, this movement primarily concerns itself with improving the plight of the Kazakh nation, which "suffered greatly from the colonial and Russification politics" of both the Tsarist and the Soviet periods; supporters of the coalition fear that non-Kazakhs will disproportionately benefit from the privatization of national assets.[48] Russian nationalism, as well, has become a pronounced feature of political activity over the last few years; Yedinstvo largely represents Russian reaction to the movement commenced in 1989 to revive the status of the Kazakh language, which resulted in Kazakh being named the state language in the constitution. In addition, there are numerous small Cossack associations which essentially advocate secession of the northern, predominantly Russian-populated territories; their demands have potentially the most explosive implications for Kazakh-Russian relations.[49]

Still, in view of the greater influence of religion manifested in Muslim countries over the last two decades, the reader may ask what would make Islam a stronger, and possibly divisive force among political parties? As a community-oriented philosophy with many social welfare features, Islam often appeals to oppressed or disadvantaged members of society. If, for example, a significant portion of the ethnic Kazakhs begin to perceive that in spite of, or even because of economic reform, they are a disadvantaged population, or if Russian nationalist movements begin highlighting the importance of Christian Orthodoxy for the achievement of their goals, Islamic parties could come to represent more than a fringe of the population.

Legislation, Governing Institutions, and Official Ideology

Given the increased authority of the Kazakhstan muftiate and the appearance of a political party with an Islamic-oriented platform, it is useful to consider how such developments fit in with overall state policy toward religion. The official policies of the independent state of Kazakhstan, while more tolerant of religious activity than those of the Soviet state, clearly limit the political role of religion. First of all, Kazakhstan legislation maintains a separation between the church and state; all governing institutions are to be secular in orientation, and the president and people's deputies are to be freely and regularly elected at all levels. Second, a major goal during Nazarbaev's tenure has been the maintenance of multiethnic, multiconfessional harmony; much of the increased visibility of religion in politics has been used to give the appearance of a harmonious multinational identity.

When we examine legislation and state institutions, we see *no* evidence of preference being given to the Islamic religion, or any religion for that matter. The very first article in the "Principles of Constitutional Structure" states, "The Republic Kazakhstan (Kazakhstan) is a democratic, secular and unitary state."[50] National holidays consist only of the celebration of secular events; Islamic holidays have not acquired the status of official holidays.[51] Kazakhstan legislation asserts equality before law for all citizens, "regardless of the grounds on which citizenship had been acquired, origin, social and property status, race and ethnic background, sex, education, language, religious beliefs, political and other convictions, kind and nature of occupations, place of residence and other circumstances."[52] Moreover, the law on public associations forbids the creation of organizations whose "statutory or program documents proclaim or realize in practice the ideas of racial, national, religious, and social, including class, exclusivity or enmity";[53] this codification of official policy is precisely why Alash has experienced so many difficulties trying to register as a party.

One of the constant themes expounded under the Nazarbaev leadership has been the multiethnic, multiconfessional harmony of the Kazakhstan population. While the focus is mainly on the dangers of ethnicity based conflict, viewed as the potential Achilles heel of Kazakhstan's economic reform process, concern is also expressed about religious sentiments which could lead to conflict. In this light, the president has asserted he "will struggle uncompromisingly against organizations of a clearly directed nationalist, chauvinistic persuasion. Kazakhstan is a multinational republic, and its future and prospects [lie] only in the equality of all people irrespective of nationality, language, religion, and party affiliation."[54] A self-professed atheist, the president consistently rejects the possibility of Islamic or any other "fundamentalism" in Kazakhstan: "We want to build a normal democratic state with an open economy, which is completely incompatible with any religious fundamentalism. . . . One must take into account that in our republic there are various faiths. . . But none of them can become [a] state [religion]."[55] Consequently, the secularism and centrism of the government's domestic policy feed into Alma-Ata's policies toward the outside world; Nazarbaev points out that the complex ethnic and religious composition of the population of Kazakhstan make the country a natural bridge between East and West, Turks and Slavs, and Muslims and Christians.[56]

Yet in view of this secular centrism, what can explain the enhanced status granted to domestic Islamic institutions? Just as the muftiates established by Catherine II and Stalin served state interests, in the first case to reconcile the long-persecuted Muslims of the Russian empire, and in the second, to gain support of Soviet Muslims during the second world war, the increased visibility of the Kazakhstan muftiate does imply greater recognition of local Muslims' needs by the authorities. This development, however, should be seen in light of a general official softening toward all religions, and efforts to enlist spiritual leaders in support of regime goals. Mufti Nysanbai-uly attends all major official celebrations on holidays such as the National Flag Day and Independence Day, and other public functions, but he is usually shadowed by the local representative of the Russian Orthodox Church, Father Aleksei (the Alma Ata and Semipalatinsk archbishop). Other activities range from giving opening speeches at the annual Voice of Asia Music Festival and at the first World Conference of Spiritual Concord to blessing the construction of orphanages and children's medical centers.[57] The spiritual leaders often arrive and sit together at such functions, giving the appearance, at least, of interconfessional cooperation.

Conclusion

The evidence cited above indicates that Kazakhstan's Islamic heritage does have an impact on contemporary politics, as official circles and independent political organizations express an interest in drawing closer to Muslim states and recognizing the rights of Muslim believers. Islam in and of itself, however, does not determine the identity of the Kazakh people, nor the development of political parties. Islam came relatively late to the Kazakh steppe, the Kazakh people incorporated the religion into a highly variegated nomadic culture, and the development of Islam in Kazakhstan was further modified, and highly constrained, by seven decades of communism. The sketchy understanding ethnic Kazakhs often have of the precepts and traditions of Islam underscores the limited influence the religion can have in shaping the national identity of independent Kazakhstan.

In constructing a foreign policy, the leadership of Kazakhstan has responded to overtures by countries of the Islamic world to expand relations, but has used its Islamic heritage as merely a framework within which to pursue national economic interest in a part of the world that happens to share the same religion. The Kazakhstan leadership has skillfully maintained a balance by forging close ties with Western nations and international organizations, and clearly recognizes that it stands to gain more economically from Western industrialized nations and the capitalist East than from Muslim nations, many of whom lack the very infrastructure and trading ties that Kazakhstan hopes to acquire.

On the domestic front, Islam plays a greater role in public affairs than it ever could under the pre-*glasnost'* Soviet regime; both the high visibility of DUMK and the chief mufti and the activities of the Alash party are striking. Yet the present government elicits the support of the Alma Ata-based muftiate to distance the Kazakh community from religious developments in Uzbekistan and other Central Asian republics, and enlists both the Islamic and Orthodox clergy in trying to maintain the balance between all ethnic and religious communities in the state. The development of parties like Alash, or even Azat, provides further evidence that Islam is being tapped in a way not incompatible with the goal of constructing a secular and tolerant state; preference for secular development models and recognition of the need to ensure freedom of worship for all citizens in the republic is encouraging. The fact that the issues which political movements raise often have an ethnic or nationalist tinge, and that the leadership of Kazakhstan expends so much effort on propagating the need to maintain multiethnic harmony, suggests that the historical and linguistic revival of the Kazakh nation and other nationalities of the country will play a larger role than religion in determining the political character of independent Kazakhstan.

Notes

1. In addition to a large grain- and coal-producing capacity, Kazakhstan possesses tremendous petroleum and gas reserves, some 90% of the chrome reserves of the former Soviet Union, and about half the former USSR's reserves of lead, tungsten, copper and zinc. Of the nuclear arsenal of the former Soviet Union, 104 intercontinental ballistic

missiles and 40 strategic bombers are located on Kazakhstan territory. See Kazakhstan, Georgia, Armenia, Azerbaijan, Central Asia: Country Profile 1992-93, (London: The Economist). *Economist Intelligence Unit Country Profile 1992–93,* pp. 62–64.

The 17 million inhabitants of sovereign Kazakhstan belong to over 100 distinct ethnic groups, with the indigenous Kazakhs making up 41.5 percent of the population, Russians 36.7 percent, and Germans and Ukrainians forming the other largest minority populations. See Maqash Tatimov, "Think About it, Kazakhs!" *Leninshil Zhas,* 26 July 1991, pp. 2–3, translated in JPRS [Joint Publications Research Service]-UPA–92–001, 9 January 1992, pp. 41–52.

2. Dimitry Volsky, "After Bishkek—What?" *New Times International,* no. 19 (May) 1992, p. 7; Youssef M. Ibrahim, "To Counter Iran, Saudis Seek Ties with Ex-Soviet Islamic Republics," *The New York Times,* 22 February 1992; Mikhail Konarevski, "The Legacy of Lenin's Empire," *Far Eastern Economic Review,* 26 March 1992, p. 14; Chris Hedges, "Turkey Is to Broadcast to 6 Ex-Soviet Lands," *The New York Times,* 12 April 1992.

3. Susumu Awanohara and Salamat Ali, "Fear of Islam", *Far Eastern Economic Review,* 30 January 1992, pp. 20–22. Both Kazakhstan and Iran repeatedly denied the accusations as "sheer lies" and "a propagandistic move"; see *Moscow INTERFAX in English,* 11 January 1992, in FBIS [Foreign Broadcast and Information Service]-SOV [Soviet Union]–92–008, 13 January 1992, p. 56, *Kazakhstanskaia Pravda,* 29 and 30 January 1992, p. 1, and *Teheran IRNA* in English, 31 January 1992 in FBIS-SOV–92–023, 4 February 1992, p. 67.

4. "Nazarbayev Interviewed on Relations with Arabs," *Sawt al-Kuwait al-Duwali* (London), 7 November 1991, p. 10, translated in FBIS-SOV–91–217, 8 November 1991, p. 75.

5. Peter B. Golden, "The Karakhanids and early Islam," in *The Cambridge History of Early Inner Asia,* edited by Denis Sinor (Cambridge, UK: Cambridge University Press, 1990), pp. 343–346; *Uchebnoe posobiie po istorii Kazakhstana s drevneĭshikh vremen do nashikh dneĭ* (Alma Ata: Ministerstvo narodnogo obrazovaniia Respubliki Kazakhstana, Institut istorii i etnologii imeni Ch. Ch. Valikhanova, Akademii Nauk Respubliki Kazakhstana, 1992), pp. 26–29.

6. Ira Lapidus, *A History of Islamic Societies* (Cambridge, UK: Cambridge University Press, 1988), pp. 414–423; Geoffrey Wheeler, *The Modern History of Soviet Central Asia* (London: Weidenfeld and Nicolson, 1964), pp. 33–35.

7. Azade-Ayse Rorlich, *The Volga Tatars* (Stanford, CA: Hoover Institution Press, 1986), pp. 40–43; see also chapter in present volume by Edward Lazzerini.

8. Chokhan Valikhanov, *Izbrannye proizvedeniia* (Alma Ata: Kazakhskoe gosudarstvennoe izdatel'stvo, 1958), p. 187. The essay "O musulmanstve v stepi" was written no earlier than 1863.

9. Elizabeth Bacon, *Central Asians Under Russian Rule* (Ithaca, NY: Cornell University Press, 1966), pp. 41–43; Wheeler, especially chapter 3; for more about the pre-Islamic and early Islamic history of the Central Asian Turkic peoples, see Vasiliĭ Vasilievich Bartold, "Dvenadtsat' lektsiĭ po istorii turetskikh narodov Sredneĭ Azii," *Sochineniia,* v. 5 (Moscow: Izdatel'stvo Nauka, 1968).

10. For a partial listing of Kazakh social movements, see Zhusipbek Qorghasbekov, "The Supporter, Glasnost, the Helper, Democracy," *Qazaq Adebiyeti,* translated in JPRS-UPA–91–028, 23 May 1991, pp. 30–32.

11. *Dini taqwim* (Alma Ata: Dukhovnoe upravleniie musul'man Kazakhstana, 1991). Sample titles of books and pamphlets: V. Irving, *Zhizn' Magometa,* translated by L. P. Nikiforova (Kazan, fourth printing; original publication, 1849); V. Solov'iov, *Magomet: Zhizn' i religiia* (Alma Ata, 1990; original publication, St. Petersburg, 1896); A. Saghai, *Arapsha-Qazaqsha salystyrmaly Quran Khamim* (Alma Ata: "Baraka" Creative Union of the Kazakhstan Writers' Union, 1991); *Novoe Poslaniie Allakha Miru* (Alma Ata: Izdatel'stvao "Ekspress-pechat"' i "Kaǐnar," 1992).

12. Raushan M. Mustafina, *Predstavleniia, kul'ty, obriady u kazakhov* (Alma Ata: Qazaqstan universiteti, 1992), pp. 159–161.

13. *Ibid,* pp. 34–39. One example is modification of the annual fasting requirement: many people assert that monthly contributions to the mosque can substitute for fasting; others believe the fasting period can be limited to nine days: three days each in the beginning, the middle, and the end of the month.

14. *Ankara Domestic Service* in Turkish, 15 March 1991, in FBIS-SOV-91-052, 18 March 1991, p. 71.

15. *Alma Ata Kazakh Radio Network* in Kazakh, 26 September 1991, in FBIS-SOV-91-189, 30 September 1991, p. 90.

16. *Kazakhstanskaia Pravda,* 5 May 1992, p. 1.

17. *Moscow TASS International Service in Russian,* 11 December 1991, in FBIS-SOV-91-244, 19 December 1991, p. 52.

18. Instead of openly earning interest, Islamic banks today often receive some sort of a commission or service fee from the borrower. A depositor may enter into a *mudarabah,* a limited partership with the bank, and receive, instead of interest, a portion of the earnings from the bank's ventures.

19. *Tehran IRNA,* 31 January 1992, in FBIS-SOV-92-023, 4 February 1992, p. 67.

20. *Islamabad PTV Television Network,* 24 February 1992, in FBIS-NES-92-037, 25 February 1992, p. 55.

21. *Kazakhstanskaia Pravda,* 27 June 1992, p. 1.

22. *Izvestiia,* 30 November 1992, p. 4.

23. *Kazakhstanskaia Pravda,* 21 September 1991, p. 1. See D. J. Peterson, *Troubled Lands: The Legacy of Soviet Environmental Destruction,* (Boulder: Westview Press, 1993), pp. 102–119, for a description of problems associated with the cotton monoculture, pesticide use, and the desiccation of the Aral Sea.

24. *Izvestiia,* 30 November 1992.

25. *Komsomolskaia Pravda,* 24 September 1991, p. 2; *Moscow Mayak Radio Network* in FBIS-SOV-92-170, 1 September 1992, pp. 41–42; "Nazarbayev on Current Issues," Moscow Teleradiokompaniia Ostankino, 6 September 1992, in FBIS-SOV-92-174, pp. 40–46.

26. James Critchlow, "Ties with Turkey: A Lifeline for the Central Asians?,"*Report on the USSR,* v. 3, no. 6, 8 February 1991, pp. 19–21; "Turkey Discovering New Role in Former Soviet Central Asia," *Financial Times,* 11 February 1992, p. 2.

27. *Cumhuriyet,* 16 December 1991, p. 7. See also interview in *Vienna Kurier,* 20 February 1992, p. 5, translated in FBIS-SOV-92-037, 25 February 1992, p. 66.

28. *Cumhuriyet,* 16 December 1991, p. 7.

29. *Moscow International Service in Korean,* 12 December 1990, in FBIS-SOV-90-249, 27 December 1990, p. 74.

30. "Qazaqstan Aziia zholbarysy bola ala ma?" ("Can Kazakhstan become an Asian

tiger?") in *Zaman* (Alma Ata), 5 June 1992, p. 1; see also Nursultan Nazarbaev, *Bez pravykh i levykh* (Moscow: Molodaia Gvardiia, 1991), pp. 60–61, 108–109; Bess Brown, "Central Asia and the East Asian Model," *Report on the USSR*, v. 3, no. 6, 8 February 1991, pp. 18–19.

31. *Moscow INTERFAX in English,*, 10 April 1992, in FBIS-SOV–92–072, 14 April 1992, p. 56; *Alma Ata Kazakh Radio Network in Russian*, 8 September 1992, in FBIS-SOV–92–175, 9 September 1992, p. 42; *Kazakhstanskaia Pravda*, 31 October 1992, p. 6.

32. Of Kazakhstan's exports, 55% go to Western industrialized countries, 36% more to the former socialist world. Moreover, Kazakhstan is dependent on the former USSR and China for 69% of its imports. See *INTERFAX in English*, 18 September 1992, in FBIS-SOV–92–184, 22 September 1992, pp. 52–53.

33. "Vse my brat'ia" [interview with Kazakh Chief Mufti Hajji Ratbek Nysanbai-uly], *Ekonomika i zhizn'*, no. 4, January 1991, p. 13.

34. Article 6 of "the Law on Freedom of Religion", *Kazakhstanskaia Pravda*, 7 February 1992, p. 3. Selection and dismissal of the Chief Mufti and other religious officials takes place at DUMK's annual congress.

35. Author's interview with Mufti Nysanbai-uly in Alma Ata, 5 August 1992.

36. *Ibid.*.

37. "Worship Heaven" [interview with Hajji Muhammad Husayn Usman-uly, Deputy Mufti of DUMK], *Leninshil Zhas*, 15 September 1990, p. 4, translated in JPRS-UPA–91–008, 12 February 1991, pp. 93–94. Mufti Nysanbai-uly also noted that among the first group of students were representatives from all *oblast's* of Kazakhstan, as well as from Mongolia, Turkmenistan, and the Altai, Tomsk, and Astrakhan oblasts of Russia.

38. "Almatyda otken Qazaqstan musylmandarynyng II-kuryltai turali," *Iman* ("Faith," the newspaper published by DUMK), 2 June 1992, p. 1. While representatives from the other Central Asian republics did not attend, or their participation was not deemed important enough to enumerate, attending the conference *were* representatives from the Chechen republic, North Caucasus, and Orenburg (Tatar) Islamic establishments.

39. Alash held its founding congress on 14–15 April 1990. For further details, see P. Verkhovskiĭ, *Politicheskiie partii i dvizheniia Sredneĭ Azii* (Moscow: Panorama, 1992), p. 20.

40. Guy Dinmore, "Soviet Collapse Revives Islam in Central Asia," *Reuter Library Report*, 13 April 1992; Andrew Higgins, "Kazakhs in Thrall to a Colonial Past," *The Independent*, 14 April 1992.

41. Program of the "Alash" Party of National Liberation, published in *Haqq* (Moscow), no. 2, 1992, p. 2.

42. "Report Notes Trends Among Country's Youth," *INTERFAX* in English, FBIS-SOV–92–175, 9 September 1992, p. 45.

43. *Kazakhstanskaia Pravda*, 17 December 1991, p. 1; *Haqq*, no. 2, 1992. Naturally, there is a wide discrepancy between official accounts of what occurred and those of the activists; *Alash* asserts that in response to demands made by the crowd, Mufti Nysanbai-uly agreed to retire from his post and drove away unharmed.

44. *Programma partii Narodnyĭ Kongress Kazakhstana na perekhodnyĭ period do 2000 goda (proekt dlia vnutripartiĭnoĭ diskussii* (Taldy-Kurgan: 1992), pp. 23–24.

45. Conversations with members of the movement in fall 1992; also *Kazakhstanskaia Pravda*, 13 January 1993, p. 3.

46. Author's interviews with Saltanat Yermekova, member and spokeswoman of the Alash party bureau, in Alma Ata, 12 and 13 June 1992.

47. "Deklaratsiia osnovnykh tseleĭ i printsipov GDK Azat," *Azat* in Russian, January 1991, p. 4.

48. "Obrashcheniie k russkomu naseleniiu Kazakhstana," a flyer disseminated by the Coordinative Council of Civil Democratic Movement "Azat," in May 1992, calling on the Russian population to recognize the suffering of the Kazakh nation; *Nezavisimaia Gazeta,* 11 April 1992, p. 3.

49. *Alma Ata Kazakh Radio Network,* 16 September 1991, translated in FBIS-SOV, 18 September 1991, and *Pravda,* 20 November 1991; see also the description of these events in Martha Olcott, "Kazakhstan: a republic of minorities," in *Nations and Politics in the Soviet Successor States,* edited by Ian Bremmer and Ray Taras (Cambridge, UK: Cambridge University Press, 1993), pp. 322–326.

50. Full text of constitution appears in Russian in *Kazakhstanskaia Pravda,* 2 February 1993, pp. 3–4.

51. *Kazakhstanskaia Pravda,* 4 February 1992, p. 1. National holidays observed are Independence (or Republic) Day (16 December), New Year's Day, International Women's Day, Naw Ruz Meyram (the new year/spring solstice holiday of pre-Islamic origin celebrated in many lands which came under Persian influence), International Labor Solidarity Day, and Victory Day.

52. *Kazakhstanskaia Pravda,* 14 January 1992, p. 3.

53. *Kazakhstanskaia Pravda,* 25 April 1991, pp. 1.

54. *Komsomolskaia Pravda,* 13 April 1991, p. 2.

55. *Kazakhstanskaia Pravda,* 14 May 1992, p. 2.

56. *Komsomolskaia Pravda,* 9 September 1992, p. 1; *Kazakhstanskaia Pravda* 24 October 1992, p. 2.

57. *Kazakhstanskaia Pravda,* 20 October 1992, p. 1, and 27 October 1992, p. 1.

PART THREE

CENTRAL ASIA AND RUSSIA

CHAPTER 9

Commensals or Parasites? Russians, Kazakhs, Uzbeks, and Others in Central Asia

Edward Allworth

Before the Soviet national republics started independently disassembling in 1991, fervent partisans in the USSR had argued impolitely over who supported whom. In an enforced multi-ethnic union such as the former Russia-dominated Soviet Union, one ethnic group appeared to feed on another. How much did a certain group or region owe the remainder? In what way could parity be achieved between nationalities that lived in conditions of mutual disrespect and discomfort? In other words, were Russians and Central Asians eating at a communal table, or were Russian supremacists entirely accurate when they claimed they supported the welfare of Uzbeks and fellow nationalities?[1] Though the definition for parasite today specifies a one-sided gain or loss by one of two parties to the arrangement, in the old Greek meaning for *parâsitos* the guest sang or conversed wittily for his supper, presumably pleasing his host as well as himself. No evidence has emerged in the sources that makes it sensible to envision that amiable concept as an image for any relations, present or future, between the very unamused principals, Central Asia and Russia.

How can scholars determine where the responsibilities of the most powerful group begin and end? In that arrangement, to what extent did Russians desire and work for the good of non-Russians, especially Central Asians? The range of such attitudes diagrams not only territorial relations but ethnic viewpoints in the interplay between the effect one group exerts upon the other. And dominating it all has been the huge presence of Russia, with its propensity to consume the resources, natural and human, of Central Asia, like all the former Union.

Central Asians and others regard the non-Russian nationalities of central Russia and Siberia virtually as agents of Russification. Especially the Finnic and Turkic ones have undergone centuries of cultural and linguistic assimilation. This presents a strange paradox, for it was precisely the Russians who insisted that Central Asian Karakalpaks, Kirghiz, Tajiks, Uzbeks, and the like

---

This chapter is dedicated to Frederick C. Barghoorn (1911–1991), colleague and friend.

adopt Russian-style monoethnicity in place of their traditional supraethnic heterogeneity. In this respect, Russia may have made a lasting impact upon the thinking of generations of Central Asians.

Kinds of Direct and Indirect Russian Influence

This possibility gives a reminder that an inquiry into Russian influence in Central Asia can consider the extent of the effect, the permanence of the influence, and/or the nature of such impact. At least two of those dimensions of the question help to frame the main proposition: under the new conditions of declaratory independence, Central Asians may very likely abandon superficial Russianisms. Irrelevant now are the tense public debates that as recently as 1985 arose around the substitution of a local term (*torwä* bag, shopping bag) in place of a common loan word from Russian, (*sumka*).[2] Central Asians no longer indifferently tolerate naming their streets or institutions for Maxim Gorky or dutifully attaching the Slavic patronymic *-ov/-ovna/-evich* to young children's names. Not nearly so easily, though, can they cast out the less visible, more manipulative and deeper intrusions of Russian influence into the Central Asian way of urban life and manner of thought.

The changed situation today will force Central Asians and scholars studying their civilization to think very differently from the way they did earlier about the best ways to understand the present relationships between old partners (persons associated with another in some endeavor) such as Russia and Central Asia, large conglomerates associated whether they like it or not, for better or for worse. Qualitatively, what is the nature of that association now and what might it become?

It appears that urban dwellers, notably the town intelligentsia, experienced the strongest impact of planned Russian influence, for the Russian authorities meant to shape the new men and women in their image. This suggests that such influence may have exerted its effect selectively in different degrees according to variations in social identity among the population of Central Asia.

Another argument that seems to support the proposition regarding durable Russian impact indicates that negative, disruptive and therefore insidious influence evidently has had a more persistent effect than constructive influence on countryside as well as town. Central Asian dissenters and independent thinkers among the local population probably rightly judge certain seemingly positive measures taken in the area by Russian authorities to be detrimental to indigenous cultural identity.

Among other factors, the amount and frequency of contact between Russian residents and Central Asian inhabitants made a difference in attitudes toward Russia and its cultural and political loans to the region. Official statistics showed that nearly 24 million Russians resided in the USSR outside the Russian Republic in 1979, and 25.3 million in 1989, but in some republics Russian numbers had begun to decrease. In Uzbekistan between 1979 and 1989 the Russian population dropped slightly from 1,666,000 to 1,653,000, reversing long-term trends. Tajikistan also seemed to grow less hospitable to Russians. Some 6,600 fewer lived there in 1989 than had claimed residence in 1979. Though Turkmenistan, too, saw a small drop in numbers of Russians for the same decade, both Kirgizia and Kazakhstan experienced a continued growth in their Russian population.[3] Notwithstanding the persistence of large numbers of Russians in Central Asia, including Kazakhstan, (9,519,958 in 1989), the nature of Russian influence within those non-Russian republics seems likely to alter and the amount of it to decline in certain ways under the new circumstances. To assess that possibility, it helps to identify the influence and the channels communicating influence as a prelude to comparing the past with Russian survivals in the present.

If influence is the capacity or power of someone or something to affect the acts or minds of others without using direct or tangible means, what is "Russian influence?" Conventionally, the definition excludes from this study measures of a physical sort—coercion or force—exerted by the military, the police and government officials. Nor will this interpretation of influence admit "structural violence," a term used in peace studies to describe impersonal, less visible harm inflicted indirectly through measures such as economic confiscation, organized deprivation or careless neglect and comparable policies applied or measures taken against certain categories of people.[4]

Nevertheless, the legacy of suasion under the Russians leaves lingering effects in the memory of Central Asians. A balanced study cannot ignore these memories, though force and violence generated them, as motivations for residual Central Asian attitudes about Russia.

After Amir Temür (Tamerlane) and time put an end to Mongol rule around 1370, Central Asian people experienced independence for many centuries, with very few interruptions. They repeatedly drove off outside enemies or assimilated invaders. Often beset by internal strife, nonetheless, they remained politically self-reliant until conquered by Russians between approximately 1830 and 1885.

After the Russian conquest of Central Asia, traditional Muslims, although formally excluded from politics in Russia, in principle rejected almost everything Russian. In general, the testimony now available for the pre-Soviet period seems to show that while Central Asian reformists in the twentieth century accepted the expedient of learning about Europe's advances primarily through Russian sources, the reformists, too, generally kept aloof from Russian beliefs and values. This response limited and conditioned the nature and the degree of influence exerted at the time by Russia upon Central Asians and their culture. Briefly, between 1917 and 1924, after the collapse of Tsarism in spring 1917, Central Asians renewed that push for independence.

The Soviet period, however, brought a major change. Russians comprised

58.2 percent of membership but nearly 100 percent of the top leadership of the Communist Party as late as 1990. That equation between Communist Party and Russia began to weaken when First Secretary Mikhail Gorbachev officially suspended activity of the CPSU and resigned from the party on August 24, 1991.[5]

Besides the numerous Russian Party members, in 1990, more than 1.2 million Central Asians belonged to the CP.[6] Some observers may regard indigenous, non-Russian Communists in Central Asia more as representatives of Moscow and the Russians than as Communist nationalists primarily affiliated with their homeland. In that case, a study of Russian influence on Central Asia becomes even more complicated than before. An analysis of the relations between local Central Asian Communists and the remaining indigenous population of the region might then necessarily need to include a factor of indirect influence (from Russian CP leaders and members through Central Asian CP chiefs and followers) in assessing the nature and extent of Russian influence exerted upon Kazakhs, Kirghiz, Uzbeks and others. Undoubtedly, some such indirect influence reflects the durability of the Russian impact in Central Asia, though it will be nearly impossible to measure its degree. But, while some local political structures resemble the pre-1991 constellation, two aspects of the present configuration radically differ from the pattern of the past.

The Russian Republic presently acts independently of the former center but rather paternalistically toward some non-Russian republics such as Armenia and Kazakhstan. And, non-Russian republics of the former Soviet Union are seeking and getting responsibility for their domestic affairs to a large extent.

This history raises a puzzling question about the depth of Russian influence in the 1990s. Why did the leaders of the present five Central Asian republics (including Kazakhstan) cling to Moscow now? On October 18, 1991, the five signed President Mikhail Gorbachev's economic accord, affirmed again in November when they joined seven other leaders to sign another version of such an agreement. During his visit to the USA in October, 1991, Dr. Askar Akaev, President of Kyrgyzstan, known to embrace democracy and treasure independence, declared that it was the only sensible thing for his republic and others to join with Russia in an economic union.[7]

A fear of economic inadequacy seems to combine with habitual conservatism among many southern Central Asians to overpower the old memory of independence and dampen the desire for freedom. How strongly they recall very recent Communist Party retaliation against dissent cannot be forgotten. Nor is it clear how important a role the motives of power and privilege among some Central Asian leaders (in Tajikistan and Uzbekistan, for example) now plays in this reluctance to leap at the chance for true self-reliance.

One tentative explanation for the Central Asian refusal to throw off the ties that bind them to the old constellation of Soviet republics may be stated in the following proposition: Although many decades of Soviet Russian indoctrination have not entirely erased a collective memory of independence, the most profound Russian influence, conscious or unconscious, seems to be the successful transmission to Central Asia of a sense of inferiority amounting to dependence. This influence is conveyed either by analogy (through sharing Russia's persistent sense of pusillanimity before Western Europe's culture and economy) and/or as a consequence of Marxist-Leninist ideology. The relentless propaganda and daily practice transmitted to Central Asian society and leadership a sense of incompetence to manage the region's affairs under Communism without Russian direction. That capacity of Russian influence to demoralize non-Russian society also appears to have destroyed Central Asians' ideas of community that once gave a greater sense of coherence than at present to the populace of the region.

Under the changing conditions of the 1980s and 1990s in Central Asia, the extent of the evolution to a modern group identity will determine the nature of answers to questions about dependence or self-reliance in the region. How far Central Asia's evolution to a modern identity can go under the changing conditions of the 1990s depends in good part upon how effectively people of the region understand, confront and deal with the pervasive Russian influences of the past and present. If they reject entirely the Communist system and ideology that they associate with the Russians, Central Asians will have to decide what aspects of the Russian ways that they have been trained to accept for over 120 years they can safely, logically retain.

Russian Attitudes Toward Central Asians

Russian chauvinism, like the doctrine of white supremacy articulated during the 1950s–1960s in the southern U.S., has poisoned the ground on which non-Russians live in many parts of the Empire—Tsarist, Soviet or post-Soviet. At the same time, the frequent expression of notions about Russian supremacy commonly carried with them one central conviction. People on either side of the Russian/Central Asian cultural divide seemed sure that the others—non-white or white, Asian or Slavic—benefited more than they did from either voluntary or enforced association in the shared society.

This conviction typically reinforced several crippling attitudes among its partisans. The dependent ethnic group often felt itself inferior and behaved accordingly, thus prolonging the inequality. In turn, resentment arose in the dominant group if members of the dependant group appeared to make even small economic or social advances. Frequently, Central Asian people blamed neighboring non-Russians for their own distress. Russians despised Central Asians.

Soviet Russians inherited from their Tsarist predecessors several assumptions that contribute to the complexity of the relations between them and Central Asians on the territory of the former Soviet Union. These opinions hold that the Russian culture, political system, character and, ideology are innately superior to those of Central Asia.

Culture. At least as early as the eighteenth century, Russian aristocrats assumed that they possessed a superior culture and language that non-Russians in or around the Empire should accept and prefer to any other.

Political System. After the nineteenth-century Russian invasion of Central Asia, Russians in St. Petersburg and at the colonial headquarters in Tashkent believed that they owned the people and lands of the Central Asian region and that an authoritarian colonial system best conveyed the alleged benefits of Russian civilization to non-Russians in the state. Even before Tsarist troops completed the conquest, one Russian spokesman summed it up when he advocated "the inculcation of a Russian way of life (*nachala zhizn'*) among the native population [of Turkistan]."[8]

Character. The ordinary Russian, sure that he could identify Asians by physical appearance, customs or speech, considered them dangerous and tricky. In the nineteenth and early twentieth centuries, when he regarded Asians as human, he called them *zver'*—"beast" and rated them humanly inferior to everyday Russians.[9] Late in the twentieth century, such Russians continued their denigration of Central Asians. A story circulated among ordinary Russians in the USSR in the 1970s illustrates the attitude:

> A Russian lieutenant passing before a row of new conscripts goes up to one of them and asks: "Just who are you?" "Private Ivanov," answers the soldier. The lieutenant approaches another and puts the very same question: "Private Petrov," answers the soldier. "Good man," says the lieutenant and moves on. He approaches yet another soldier and asks: "Who are you?" That one answers, "An Uzbek."
>
> "Look," says the lieutenant, "you're in the Army, now; they gave you a uniform and shaved your head, who are you at present?" "An Uzbek," answers the soldier. "Sergeant," says the lieutenant, "please explain to the soldier who he is." The Ukrainian sergeant and the Uzbek move out of the ranks. In five minutes they return, the sergeant rubbing his knuckles, the Uzbek battered and bruised. "Now do you know who you are?" the lieutenant asks the Uzbek. "Yes sir, comrade lieutenant," responds the Uzbek. "A fucking *churka* (*yabannaia churka*)."

A young emigrant from the Soviet Union related this "joke" to the author of this chapter to illustrate the Russian view of Central Asians prevalent in the second half of the twentieth century. Other sources confirm this attitude.[10] His story demonstrates that outlook well enough, and its language also shows that the soldiers bearing the common Russian names Ivanov and Petrov felt themselves at home in the Soviet military. Asked to identify himself, the third draftee specified his nationality instead of his name, for he knew himself an alien in the Soviet system. His experience paralleled that of countless Central Asians placed in Soviet organizations, universities, and institutions inside and outside Central Asia before the late 1980s.

Ideology. Both before and after 1917, Russians generally convinced themselves that Central Asia was and is a backward region requiring their ideological guidance, both religious and political. Russian intellectuals and other observers have not always agreed that the Russian model justified such faith. An author visiting Central Asia in 1901 wrote of the plentiful use of alcohol: "At festive times, beer and brandy sends Muslims reeling and shouting through the streets, visiting houses of ill repute, misbehaving themselves in every way and rounding out the festival with a day or two in the police station. . . . With the advent of the Russians, prostitution has entered and has spread rapidly, even in the family circle."[11]

Almost a decade later, a Russian observer offered an interesting thesis concerning the lamentable effects of imposing one culture upon another. Using Central Asia as his example, he proposed that, "The negative side of any civilization is always adopted faster and more readily [than the positive aspects] by the ordinary people and produces the most melancholy results." He cites what he calls mass "Russian" drunkenness on bazaar days, a borrowed vice unknown before Russians arrived, if people disregard the use of *kumys* and *buza* (slightly alchoholic drinks of fermented mare's milk and of millet). "The main cause of the spread of drunkenness among the Sarts," he writes, "of course must be seen in the *urus mardzha* (the Russian hussy), who is the main attraction in all the disreputable drinking places." He adds that open prostitution came to Turkistan after the Russian invasion.[12]

Much more recently, Russians at lower and higher levels of society have expressed great contempt toward non-Russians. The Russian patriotic organizations Pamiat' and Otechestvo frequently focused conservative opinion in the late 1980s and later. The "Manifesto" of Pamiat' that appeared in Moscow in January 1989 included several articles demanding what it considers the restoration of Russian hegemony in one great power.[13] The individuals assembled in such organizations have another pointed grievance. They insist that through a kind of affirmative action the Soviet state subordinated Russians to the nationalities in the USSR and, by pursuing this policy, curried favor with the non-Russian republics and their people. At the same time, Pamiat', for example, appears to favor segregation and banning miscegenation between ethnic groups in order to preserve what it imagines to be a racial purity of real Russia.[14]

While those threatened by genuine or fancied accomplishments among non-Russians of the Soviet Union focused upon recovering what they described as equality, some more erudite Russians harbored a surprisingly patronising attitude toward nationalities. Academician Dmitriĭ S. Likhachev, speaking to Columbia University's W. Averell Harriman Institute for Advanced Study of the Soviet Union in November 1990, surprised some listeners by restating old ideas about Russia's "white man's" burden to enlighten the state's non-Russians. Academician Likhachev said

> Russia's mission has been determined by her position among other nations, small and great—some three hundred of them—that have required protection. Russia served as a vast 'bridge', chiefly cultural, for these peoples. . . . Although the Russian people's culture and mentality seem alien to such acts of aggression as the partitioning of Poland and the annexation of Central Asia, these acts were undertaken by the state on the people's behalf. . . .[15]

To western ears that traditional Russian interpretation of and attitude toward Russia's role in regard to non-Russians of the Empire sounded out-dated. Yet the persistence of such views is truly relevant to any attempt to understand the nature of Russian influence in Central Asia.

Response to Russian Influence and Attitudes

Evidence for Central Asians' assessments of Russia and Russians generally remains more diffuse and elusive than these accounts. In the nineteenth century, diplomats, merchants and their retinues traveling from Bukhara or Khiva to Russia admired St. Petersburg's or Moscow's streets, facilities, and other institutions, apparel, and additional signs of the standard of living enjoyed by the well-to-do. Some Central Asians also marveled at what they observed in the new (Russian) city constructed in part of Tashkent.[16] The attitudes of people less impressed by the material side of Russian life for the most part evidently remain unpublished. Before the conquest of Central Asia by Tsarist troops, officials and religious leaders in the Bukharan Emirate and Kokand Khanate denounced Russians as unbelievers and enemies. After the Russian occupation began, however, panegyrics to Russian princes came promptly from the pens of Central Asian poets accustomed to living under tyrants. But those eulogies (*qasidas*) probably reflected traditional reactions more than contemporary attitudes.[17] Thus, it would be inaccurate to say that Central Asian Communist politicians learned the function and art of issuing eulogies to rulers from Russians. This then developed into the practice of dedicating panegyrics to political party officials during the regime of the Russian-dominated Communist Party of the Soviet Union (CPSU).[18]

Some Jadids (reformists) of the early twentieth century, after the first 50 years of Russian colonial government over southern Central Asia, complimented Russia's university system and advocated learning the Russian language as a route to economic progress.[19] Most reformists refrained from praising the values or the thinking of the Christian Russians.

Until the 1980s, Russian-backed nationality policies affecting Central Asians and other non-Russians of the Soviet Union seemed well on the way to producing among the nationalities a new indigenous intelligentsia devoid of original thinking. Independent thinkers, carefully monitored, could transmit their insights regarding the Central Asian condition only privately by word of mouth, if at all. Following the opening of the press and broadcast media to a variety of viewpoints beginning around 1985, the individualism of some intellectuals soon attracted notice.

This Central Asian alternative to the plentiful Russian-molded CP drones made a difference in public opinion. For the first time since the 1920s some independent thinkers moved discussion away from the prescriptive adulation of everything Russian and turned to the harmful effects of the long Russian domination in the region. Government reforms made under "openness" only partially explain why these Central Asians started to speak out more loudly in the mid-1980s. An articulate minority, born no earlier than the late 1930s, had matured after World War II and the death of Joseph V. Stalin, CPSU First Secretary. This cohort of Central Asians grew up mostly aloof from the psychological damage of communist police terror. As a result, it possessed an outlook quite different from that of its parents' generation.

Nonconforming Central Asian intellectuals of the 1980s seemed to sense the coming collapse of Soviet Russian authority over them. In addition to benefitting from that accident of birth and possibly partly because of it, these rising intellectuals intuitively seemed to foresee a change impending in their social and political environment. Some used the unexpected opportunity to advance professional careers. A very few others turned to renewal, through cultural/social introspection, vital for their countrymen. These undertook group self-analysis that entailed publicly interpreting the evidence and the myths concerning the Central Asian experience under the Russians. The late twentieth-century writers looked pointedly at the humiliation and disabilities suffered by Central Asia through long subjugation to the attitudes shown by Russian leaders.

Almost inevitably, as in the Jadid circles of 1900–1920, writers and poets made up these new "reformists." Abduqahhar Ibrahimov (b.1939), Jamal Kamal (b.1938), Halima Khudayberdieva (b.1948), Muhammad Salih (b.ca.1949), Olzhas Suleimenov (b.19??), Erkin Wahidov (b.1936), and others initially earned respect among the readers of present-day Central Asia for offering audiences expressive poetry and fiction. The reformists of much earlier decades had composed lessons in the forms of stories and plays to be performed for a community that could not read. Unlike the Jadids of old, the new intellectuals endeavored to reach out to a more schooled population painfully illiterate in the language of non-conformity and self expression.

Reformist Jamal Kamal, writing about the great artistic legacy left to the Shaybanid Uzbeks and subsequent Central Asians by Temür descendants, reminded readers in 1991 that Tsarist Russia's orientalists sometimes arrived in Central Asia with more than a scholary agenda. After several visits to Turkistan, Professor Vasiliĭ V. Barthold reported to his colleagues in St. Petersburg: "The Turkistanians have all yielded to our military superiority, but have in no way submitted to our spiritual/moral superiority. The task [we face] consists of bringing about acknowledgement of that very thing. . . .We would be unable to say that we decisively earned a victory so long as they did not accept that superiority."[20] Reformist Kamal commented that for 100 years Central Asians have remained subject to that slogan about their spiritual inferiority to Russia.

Consistent with the complaint about historical abuses are the more recent charges advanced by Abduqahhar Ibrahimov, noted first as an important dramatist. If Uzbekistan requires specialists to aid its rebuilding, attract them from the Arab Middle East, he advocates. One should not allow migration into Uzbekistan by people who come only for their own gain. During the years of the Russian revolution, regrets the author, mainly troops for Mikhail Frunze and police for Felix Dzerzhinskiĭ came to the area. Even the "learned echelon" that opened a university arrived not to help Central Asia. Citing registration figures, he notes that out of 1,467 students enrolled in the Turkistan State University in 1920, 38 were Central Asians. And as soon as this "echelon" arrived, authorities closed the Turkistan State Darilfunun established by Munavvar Qari in 1918 for Central Asians.

Turning to abuses in more recent decades, Mr. Ibrahimov reported an interview with an Uzbek medical official who testified that the laborers from elsewhere in the USSR who poured into Tashkent after the earthquake of 1966 imported with them venereal diseases that started an epidemic in Central Asia. But such carriers of disease could not be deported, for that would have harmed the "friendship between ethnic groups" so persistently sloganized by ideologists. He urged non-Central Asians to leave Central Asia and re-emigrate to their homelands. Though he pointedly avoided mentioning the Russians, he listed groups often seen by Central Asians as their proxies, the Tatars in Uzbekistan (467,800 in the 1989 Soviet census reports), Koreans (183,000 in 1989), and Ukrainians (153,000 in 1989).[21] Finally, Mr. Ibrahimov observed that Russian-language newspapers and journals, being published in Moscow as outlets of Union-wide organizations or agencies, almost never publicized the life of Uzbekistan, or if they did, only from a one-sided or erroneous standpoint.

When Central Asia's new reformists aired a grievance, they departed from the behavior so long part of the etiquette expected among the non-Russians. That change evidences a slackening of fear of repercussions. It also shows that the intellectuals ceased to respect the authority of Russian ideas, not only of political and social decorum in public opinion, but of the ideas that for decades greatly influenced Central Asian behavior. The contemporary Tashkent poet and political activist, Muhammad Salih, announced as a candidate for the presidency of Uzbekistan opposing the Communist Party holdover Islam A. Karimov in 1991.[22] As a People's Representative of Uzbekistan in December 1990, Mr. Salih had openly discussed the danger of prolonging the seventy years of Central Asia's subservience for another 70 years if Uzbeks and their kinsmen failed to strike out on a new path, away from the habitual dependence.[23]

One bone of contention between the Russian center and Central Asians in the late Soviet period was the proposal to control births in Central Asia and other non-Slavic areas. The eponymous nationalities of Tajikistan, Uzbekistan and other republics are known to prize large families. As early as 1982, Uzbeks had recognized by far the most families (65,000 mothers) with ten or more living offspring apiece under the age of 20 on the territory of the Soviet Union.

The USSR program to encourage childbirths began officially on July 8, 1944 in a move to replenish the manpower and womanpower of the Soviet West, drastically depleted by losses in World War II. Statisticians recorded these numbers carefully, because government authorities decorated such women with medals, granted them financial support according to the number of living children, entitled many to pensions by the age of 50, and the like. During a nine-week period from May 2 to July 11, 1973, for example, the Supreme Council of the USSR awarded the title of "Heroine Mother" to 3,483 women. Central Asian mothers made up 2,549 (73.18 percent) of the total, though the population of Central Asia, including outsiders, in 1970 represented but 32,799,442 (13.56 percent) of the Soviet Union's 241,720,134 people.[24] The pattern continued. The last two weeks in May 1989, the Supreme Council of the USSR recognized 758 women for their many living children. Mothers in Central Asian republics bore 631 (83.2 percent) of them.[25]

Thus, policies limiting births would have curtailed family economic allowances and, from a non-Russian's point of view, might have restricted the growth of the relatively small Central Asian nationalities.

Mr. Salih carried on a polemic against the Russian policy of limiting fertility in Central Asia by challenging the remarks of an Uzbek economist and social commentator, Dr. Rano Ubaydullaeva. Consonant with the Russian policy, she advocated a substantial reduction in the child-woman ratio through spacing out each Central Asian woman's pregnancies to no more than one in each five to seven years. If applied, that formula would have strikingly limited the numbers of children in a great many families. Mr. Salih apparently regarded this proposed Russian-sponsored policy toward natality as an undesirable form of influence, perhaps one that reached beyond persuasion and, in his mind, amounted to "structural violence."[26]

If all reform-minded Central Asians spoke up about specific actions and attitudes influencing their lives owing to the overlordship of Russia, they could undoubtedly cite many more instances of it than the few mentioned here. These examples have a purpose different from providing an inventory of complaints. Instead, they testify to the underlying assumptions and policies of Russians and of certain Central Asian responses to them. One important effect, in addition to those already discussed, becomes apparent only now, when a new outspokenness allows reformists to reveal their real feelings about the tutelage they have endured for decades.

A younger, well-educated Central Asian has since 1990 assessed Russian influence in relation to the social stratification of his countrymen in the following terms:

1. Russian influence is diminishing generally among the urban intelligentsia;
2. even before the introduction of President Mikhail S. Gorbachev's policies called restructuring and openness, such influence was virtually non-existent in the Central Asian countryside: "country people don't want to be around Russians";
3. ordinary citizens (*fuqara*) in town and country lack any inclination toward the Russians;
4. if the ordinary citizen thinks about the Communist Party (in Uzbekistan in 1991 renamed the *Khälq Demokrätiyä Pätriyäsi*) at all, he identifies it with the Russians.[27]

On the other hand, another Central Asian intellectual pointed out in late 1991 that the upbringing of young Central Asians who proceeded through the levels of the schooling system and on to university training corresponded everywhere in the region to the Russian practice and organization of education. Russian methods, vocabulary and values pervaded his entire cultural life. He felt that it would take decades to discard such influence from the Central Asian society. In other words, such Russian influence would persist until the rise of new generations in Kyrgyzstan, Tajikistan and everywhere in Central Asia supplied a population without the imprint of Russian influence, direct or indirect.[28]

The imposition of the Russian language in Central Asia and its influence on local language has been the subject of much discussion. A series of laws put through by individual republics at the end of the Soviet period replaced Russian with local languages in the administration of essentially all the Central Asian republics. Nonetheless, reaction to this legislation varies from one place to another. In Kirgizia the Supreme Council legally made Kirghiz the state language on September 23, 1989.[29] Nevertheless, Russian continues to play a role in the Republic. During a visit in fall 1991 to the United States of America, the young President of Kyrgyzstan, Dr. Askar Akaev, and his Foreign Minister, Dr. Muradbek Imanaliev, asked one academic group what language they would prefer to use on the occasion, agreeing with the Americans that Russian might serve best. Each visitor, fluent in Kirghiz and other languages, then chose to speak to Americans in perfectly unaccented Russian.[30] Thirty-five-year-old Minister Imanaliev described to this author a regimen of schooling and higher education entirely in the Russian language lasting from early boyhood to professional training and work. In his view, such a pattern was typical of his generation in Kirgizia and Kazakhstan.[31]

Senior professors visiting the United States of America at different times during 1991 from Alma Ata's Institute for Language and Arts of Kazakhstan, on the other hand, never raised the possibility of using Russian. In fact, they also declined to employ Russian in individual conversations. Although capable of speaking Russian fluently, they always addressed their various audiences in Kazakh. Kazakhstan, too, in fall 1989, had designated its eponymous language the state language of the Republic.[32]

Evidently, this Central Asian nationality regards as especially appropriate and important the public assertion of linguistic identity. Professors Baghïbek Qundaqbaev in March 1991 and Rahmanqul Berdibaev in August 1991 made contact with a number of scholars and students in New York City. Not once did the author of this chapter hear either of them resort to Russian in communication, although they often encountered individuals who could not understand the Kazakh language. According to a graduate student, Mr. Orhan Söylemez, who met Professor Berdibaev on his arrival at the international airport, the Professor refused to speak Russian, though the student had great difficulty communicating with him in Kazakh, which he did not know at that time. At the University of Washington, Professor Berdibaev once lectured in Russian, only, as he said, "because I am speaking in 'Russia House' (a facility on the Seattle campus devoted to Russian culture)."[33]

These reactions point not only to group influence, but to the noticeable disconnection between Russians and certain indigenous groupings and communities in the region. It may be ventured that the regime headquartered in Moscow after 1917 squandered a splendid opportunity to win the hearts of this major Asian segment of the former Russian Empire. Overbearing Russian influence has proved counterproductive by generating antagonistic opposition in place of ready acceptance among Central Asia's rising cultural leaders. Nevertheless, a mature generation of bureaucrats, political figures, officials and administrators of the Academy of Sciences, Ministry of Culture and other ministries remain partial to the old system. They committed themselves to it despite the fact that the Russian ideas guiding them largely undermined the urge for separate Central Asian identity and independence from Russia. Now, under drastically altered circumstances of independence for the five republics, both those who cooperated zealously with the Soviet system and those who did not must face the presence of Russians and the heritage of Russian influence in a new way.

Motives and Feelings that Color Group Relations

Not all influential men and women slavishly adhered to the old system. Perhaps Central Asian intellectuals now recognize Russia's real feelings toward them as the irrational attitude it is—all racism or ethnocentrism being emotional rather than reasoned. The First Secretary, Leonid I. Brezhnev, revealed this clearly while talking in Russia with visiting British Prime Minister Margaret Thatcher in the 1970s. To her comment (made before Russian and Central Asian troops invaded Afghanistan in 1979) that it was gratifying to find no serious difficulties putting their two countries at odds, the First Secretary answered: "Madam, there is only one important question facing us, and that is the question [of] whether the white race will survive." In a sentence, the Russian leader confirmed directly what many other sources hint at. Russians fear the Asians within and without the old Empire and categorize them as dangerous to the survival of fair Slavdom.[34]

It is unimaginable that the ethnic groups comprising the two mutually suspicious sides of this pairing can find the trust needed to accept what might be beneficial exchanges between them. Yet, rationality usually prevails in some spheres, and it will reveal that goodness, talent, and positive attributes reside somewhere in Russia and in Central Asia.

When the indigenous peoples of Central Asia succeed during the 1990s in reestablishing themselves as an independent country or countries separate from Russia, previous arguments couched in terms of inequality and affirmative action within one state will cease to apply. As populations of sovereign states, Central Asia's peoples can to some extent determine how much they will share with Russia in developments ahead and how much they will stand alone.

Should Central Asians decide to remain within some kind of symbiosis (mutualism) with Russia, they would face a choice between two sorts of possibilities, with variants: commensalism or parasitism. In the Commonwealth of Independent States, should it survive, commensalism will imply living with, on, or in another organism, without injury to either, or, for instance, merely sharing the same table at eating time.

The parasitism harshly stigmatized among the Soviet people, and criminalized during a campaign against dissident intellectuals beginning in the 1960s, differs from the generally accepted definition.[35] The customary meaning of parasitism entails one partner's living at another's expense, receiving an advantage without equal or proper return. But there is another meaning which may relate to the interactions within the former USSR that implies a kind of mutually acceptable collusion between those involved in relations as disjunctive symbionts. Central Asians' capacity to make the best of either arrangement will demand much more than an ability to manage their economy efficiently. Success in commensalism will depend upon their willingness to discard their former passivity or embrace any degree of parasitism. They will need to reject the debilitating ideas, attitudes and effects of living more than six generations under Russian tutelage.

As commensals, Central Asians will have to chart a very new course for themselves, though they may retain close connections with Russia. If Central Asians decide to stand entirely aloof from a Russian-dominated Commonwealth, they will require especially cultural, intellectual and political self-reliance. In that case, the degree of Russian influence may be allowed to exceed the amount a dependent would permit itself, because the independent nationality would not fear such a threat to its separate group identity. If independence did not open the way for a repetition of the subordination and the sense of inferiority stimulated by much Russian influence in the past, this course of action could permit Central Asians to behave less defensively. They might reasonably admit the foreign influence beneficial to their culture and society, such as, for instance, a knowledge of the art and literature of the Slavs, the usefulness of having an internationally-functional foreign language of communication, and of adopting some aspects of Russian organization and experience.

In the end, the earlier tension over obligatory support/dependence in the Soviet situation should now give way to a kind of new cultural and political dialectic based upon voluntary mutual—and self—interest between Russia and Central Asia, as at least three out of five existing republics seem in 1991–1992 to be doing. Political independence alone cannot cancel out the tension that has existed between dominance and submission in that relationship. When that tension abates, the times will allow the flowering of the true condition of the commensals. But so long as Central Asians permit the men of the old (Communist) regime to control them, it will be unlikely that many negative aspects of Russian influence will disappear in Ashkhabad, Dushanbe, Tashkent or other major centers of the region.

Notes

1. I. M. Ambartsumova and V. K. Proskurin, "Razvitie form sobstvennosti i sblizhenie uslovii agrarnogo i industrial'nogo truda," *Obshchestvennye nauki v Uzbekistane* No. 4 (1990), p. 15, cited also in Andrew Weiss, *Between Sovereignty and Dependence* (New York: unpublished essay, 1991), p. 3; Boris Z. Rumer, *Soviet Central Asia. "A Tragic Experiment"* (Boston: Unwin Hyman, 1990), pp. 177–182.

2. Karim Nazaraw, "'Torwä' mi yaki 'sumkä'?" *Shärq yulduzi* No. 11 (1985), pp. 171–173.

3. *Naselenie SSSR. Po dannym vsesoiuznoǐ perepisi naseleniia 1979 goda* (Moscow: Izdatel'stvo Politicheskoǐ Literatury, 1980), pp. 27–30; "Vsesoiuznaia perepis' naseleniia. Natsional'nyǐ sostav naseleniia SSSR," *Vestnik statistiki* No. 7 (1980), pp. 41–44; *ibid.*, No. 8 (1980), pp. 64–70; *ibid.*, No. 9 (1980), pp. 60–70; *ibid.*, No. 10 (1980), pp. 70–73; *ibid.*, No. 11 (1980), pp. 60–63; *ibid.*, No. 11 (1990), p. 77; "Vsesoiuznaia perepis' naseleniia," *Vestnik statistiki* No. 10 (1990), pp. 69, 72; *ibid.*, No. 12 (1990), p. 70; *ibid.*, No. 4 (1991), p. 76; *ibid.*, No. 5 (1991), p. 74; *ibid.*, No. 6 (1991), p. 72.

4. Johan Galtung, "Violence and Peace," in Paul Smoker, Ruth Davies, Barbara Munske, eds. *A Reader in Peace Studies* (Oxford: Pergamon Press, 1990), pp. 10–11; also, Kenneth E. Boulding, "Peace Theory," ibid., p. 4. Martha Merrill very kindly brought this term and reference to the author's attention.

5. "Statisticheskie dannye po KPSS na 1 ianvaria 1990 g.," *Izvestiia TsK KPSS* No. 4 (April 1990), pp. 113–114; Serge Schmemann, "Gorbachev Quits As Party Head; Ends Communism's 74-year Reign," *New York Times* (25 Aug. 1991), p. 1.

6. "Statisticheskie dannye po KPSS na 1 ianvaria 1990 g.," *ibid.*, pp. 113–114.

7. Francis X. Clines, "8 Soviet Republics Sign Economic Pact," *New York Times* (19 Oct. 1991), p. 3; Celestine Bohlen, "Warning of 'Abyss', Gorbachev Demands Republic Cooperate," *New York Times* (5 November 1991), pp. A1, A15.

8. M. Veniukov, "O novom razdielenii aziatskoǐ Rossii," *Izviestiia IRGO*, vol. VIII, second section (1872), p. 325.

9. Edward Allworth, *The Modern Uzbeks* . . . (Stanford: Hoover Institution Press, 1990), p. 179.

10. S. Enders Wimbush and Alex Alexiev, *The Ethnic Factor in the Soviet Armed Forces* (Santa Monica, Calif, The Rand Corporation, March 1982), p. vii, xiii, 40–43.

11. Friedrich Duckmeyer, in *Allgemeine Zeitung* no. 250 (1901), cited by Arminius Vambery, *Western Culture in Eastern Lands* (New York: E. P. Dutton, 1906), p. 56.

12. Gr. Andreev, "Zakulisnyia storony sartskago byta," *Sredniaia Aziia* No. 5 (1910), p. 114–115.

13. John Garrard, "A Pamyat Manifesto: Introductory Note and Translation," *Nationalities Papers. Pamyat* (Special Issue), No. 2 (Fall 1991), pp. 134–140; especially, p. 138, articles 42–48.

14. Paul Midford, "Pamyat's Political Platform: Myth and Reality," *Nationalities Papers* No. 2 (Fall 1991), pp. 202, 204.

15. Dmitriĭ Sergeyevich Likhachev, *The National Nature of Russian History* (Columbia University: The W. Averell Harriman Institute for Advanced Study of the Soviet Union, 1990), p. 12–13.

16. Zakirjan Furqat, "Qilib täklif bir zati kirami, / Kirib gimnäziyä kordik tämami . . . ," *Ozbek ädäbiyati* (Tashkent: OzSSR Däwlät Bädiiy Ädäbiyat Näshriyati, 1960), vol. 4, pp. 113–115; [Ahmad Donish], *Risolai ahmadi donish 'Ta'rikhi saltanati manghitiya'. Traktat Akhmada Donisha 'Istoriia mangitskoĭ dinastii'* trans. I. A. Najafova (Dushanbe: Izdatel'stvo "Donish," 1967), pp. 103–106.

17. Edward Allworth, *Uzbek Literary Politics*, p. 26–29; Edward Allworth, ed., *Central Asia: 120 Years of Russian Rule* (Durham and London; Duke University Press, Central Asia Book Series, 1989, rev. 2d ed.), p. 172–173, 354.

18. Edward Allworth, *Uzbek Literary Politics* (The Hague: Mouton & Co., 1964), pp. 211–212; Edward A. Allworth, *The Modern Uzbeks . . . A Cultural History* (Stanford: Hoover Institution Press, 1990) p. 327–328.

19. Mahmud Khoja, "Munazärä häqidä," in Fitrat, *Hindistandä bir färanqi ilä bukharali bir mudärrisning bir nichä mäs'älälär häm usul-i jadidä khususidä qilgan munazäräsi* (Tashkent: Tipo-Litografiia V. M. Il'ina, 1913), p. 37–38.

20. Jamal Kamal, "Quyashdek räwshän häqiqät," *Ozbekistan awazi* (27 September 1991), p. 4.

21. Äbduqähhar Ibrahimov, "Aldingdä oqqän suw," *Ozbekistan ädäbiyati wä sän'äti* (1 February 1991), p. 2; "Raspredelenie naseleniia Uzbekskoĭ SSR po national'nosti i iazyku," *Vestnik statistiki* No. 11 (1990), p. 77.

22. *RFE/RL Daily Report no. 224* (November 26, 1991), p. 4.

23. Muhammad Salih, "Milliy huquq—sawghä emäs," *Ozbekistan ädäbiyati wä sän'äti* (21 December 1990), p. 1.

24. Rafail Kh. Avanesov, *Soviet Uzbekistan, Facts, Figures* (Tashkent: "Uzbekistan" Publishers, 1983), pp. 42–45; *Vedomosti Verkhovnogo Soveta SSSR* Nos. 18, 20, 24, 28, (May 2, May 16, June 20, July 11, 1973), respectively, pp. 277; 307; 382–383; 438; "Mat'-Geroinia," *Bol'shaia sovetskaia entsiklopediia* (n.p.: Gosudarstvennoe Nauchnoe Izdatel'stvo *Bol'shaia sovetskaia entsiklopediia,* 1954), vol. 26, pp. 537–538; *Itogi vsesoiuznoĭ perepisi naseleniia 1970 goda* (Moscow: "Statistika," 1973), vol. IV, pp. 12–15.

25. *Vedomosti Verkhovnogo Soveta SSSR* No. 21 (24 May 1989), p. 253; ibid., No. 22 (31 May 1989), p. 267.

26. Rano Ubaidullaeva, (Zam direktora Instituta Ekonomiki AN UzSSR, Doktor ekonomicheskikh nauk, professor), "Planirovat' razvitie sem'i," *Pravda Vostoka* (9 February 1988), p. 3; ibid., "Legko byt' zhenshchinoĭ?" *Pravda Vostoka* (19 March 1989), p. 2; Muhammad Salih, "Daite zhenshchinam zdorov'e!" *Pravda Vostoka* (12 March 1988), p. 2.

27. An interview of the author with Dr. Abdujabbar Abduwakhitov, November 15, 1991, in New York City.

28. Conversations with Professors Parvano Jamshidi and Narinbek Davletov in New York City, December 1991.

29. "Kïrgïz SSRinin mamlekettik tili jönündö. Kïrgïz Sovettik Sotsialisttik Respublikasïnïn Zakonu," *Kïrgïzstan madaniyatï* 5 October 1989, pp. 2–3.

30. President Akaev gave an address, in Russian, to an academic gathering during his appearance at Columbia University on October 22, 1991. Kirgizia announced its decision to make Kirghiz its state language in *Kirghizstan madaniyati* No. 40 (5 October 1989).

31. Interview of the author with Foreign Minister of Kyrgyzstan, Muradbek Imanaliev, on November 18, 1991, Columbia University, New York City.

32. *Qazaqstandaghï til sayasatï zhäne onï zhüzege asïru zholdarï. Respublikalïq ghïlïmi-praktikalïq konferentsiyasïnïng tezisteri* (Alma Ata Qazaq SSR Ghïlïm Akademiyasï . . . Akhmet Baytursïnov atïndaghï Til Bilimi Institutï, 1990), p. 3.

33. The Supreme Council of the Uzbekistan Conciliar Socialist Republic adopted the law concerning Uzbek as the state language on October 21, 1989. See *Ozbekistan Sawet Satsiälistik Respublikäsining qanuni Ozbekistan SSRning däwlät tili häqidä.* Tashkent: "Ozbekistan."

34. Cited in Freeman Dyson, "Russians," *The New Yorker* (20 February 1984), p. 86.

35. Frederick C. Barghoorn and Thomas F. Remington, *Politics in the USSR* (Boston: Little, Brown and Company, 1986, 3d ed.), p. 381–384.

CHAPTER 10

Post-Soviet Central Asia and the Commonwealth of Independent States: The Economic Background of Interdependence

Bakhtior A. Islamov

In the course of 1991 it became clear that the Soviet Union could not survive the growing tensions between the republics and the center. The Moscow coup of August 19–21, 1991, which attempted to restore the pre-*perestroika* administrative command system failed. All the former Union republics obtained the chance to become fully independent. Nonetheless eleven of them chose to become part of the Commonwealth of Independent States (CIS).

In this chapter I shall examine the *underlying reasons* why the Central Asian leaders in their summit meeting on December 13, 1991 decided to join CIS in Alma Ata on December 21, 1991 and signed an agreement as co-founders of this loose and hastily formed institution. Despite the desire of the former Soviet republics to build their independent national statehood and the centrifugal forces demonstrated at the beginning of 1992, in the second half of 1992, between the May 15 CIS summit in Tashkent and the October 8–9 summit in Bishkek, the centripetal forces in the CIS and the desire for bilateral relations of Central Asian Republics with Russia started to prevail.

We also need to explain the decision both of the Central Asian Republics (Kazakhstan, Kyrgyzstan and since May 1992, Uzbekistan) and also Russia, Belorussia, and Armenia to revitalize some Union institutions, to keep the ruble zone, organize an economic arbitration court and to take other steps towards inter-republican trade and economic integration.

Of course there are some political considerations: the need to keep a common security and military zone, and to form peace-keeping forces, to deal for example with the civil war in Tajikistan. The danger of the escalation of ethnic conflicts in this and other regions of the former Soviet Union is considerable. However the primary motive is economic. The biggest issue affecting the people of all independent states has been the worsening of the standard of living. And one of the obvious factors contributing to this is the disruption of existing inter-republican economic ties.

To understand this fundamental factor and its influence on the Central Asian republics it is necessary to make a thorough analysis of the mechanism of administrative command integration set up in the Soviet period. Inter-republican integration, based on overspecialization and centralization, functioned through an active strategy of distributional and redistributional instruments. The author of this chapter has used recent statistics (including data of IMF and World Bank publications) to give a new economic evaluation of the distortions in trade and national income balances caused by Soviet economic practices, including prices established on a non-economic basis, the use of turnover taxes, and subsidies.

This analysis can provide a fuller understanding of the economic relations of Central Asian republics with Moscow during the later *perestroika* years, which produced a strong inter-republican trade dependence and considerable distortion of economic relations. More importantly, it will counter the widespread misinterpretation of the Central Asians' economic role, which casts them as "net recipients" in economic redistribution mechanisms. This will help us to understand the present comparative advantage of Central Asia within CIS and to forecast its economic future in the long run as favorable for independent development in contrast to other studies which have given gloomy projections for the area. The analysis of the economic interdependence of Central Asians with other republics of the former Soviet Union also explains why the Commonwealth of Independent States is necessary and viable not only as a transitional framework for the dissolution of artificial ties and the resolution of property issues, but also as a vehicle for the conversion of administratively regulated inter-republican ties to market-based relations and the gradual reorientation of the economy towards integration into the world market.

Administrative-Command Integration and the Central Asian Republics: General Characteristics

The seventy-odd years of Soviet government formed a single all-union economic complex, which was based on administrative-command integration of Soviet republics and the division of labor among them. Economic goals and policies were set by the central government and implemented through central, sectoral and republic ministries.[1] The main characteristics of this were as follows:

- a bureaucratic and over-centralized planning and financial system;
- the predominance of departmental organizations over regional management;
- artificially and unreasonably high specialization and the concentration or monopoly of production;
- indirect inter-republican economic relations based on strong vertical ties to the center, rather than direct horizontal ties among republics;

- a distorted system of prices, taxes, subsidies, grants, etc. used as instruments of a market formed by the central government through interference in trade, financial flow, income distribution and redistribution between the center and republics, and among the latter.

Institutionally the all-Union government created and leaned upon the State Planning Committee *Gosplan,* the Ministry of Finance, and dozens of ministries with administrative power in almost all branches of the economy running inefficient, giant monopolist enterprises in each republic; these became the main tools of integration. The predominant principle of Soviet bureaucratic planning, financial and managerial systems was a sectoral approach, despite the often proclaimed need to combine it with a regional one. In conformity with this approach, plans were concentrated on branches or sectors of the economy, and allocations of financial and material resources were made not by regions or republics but by ministries. Central institutions, especially all-Union ministries, ignored the alternative principle, namely an organic combination of product specialization in Soviet regions and republics with diversification of their economies. The central government also ignored in practice the goal of equalizing the socio-economic levels of development in different republics, which had been widely advertised for propaganda purposes.

As a result, by 1989 about 95% of the industry of the USSR was supervised by the center. The share of different republics varied slightly but did not exceed 10%.[2] Decades of central planning left just one or two factories supplying the entire Soviet market with anything from rails to sewing machines. Economists at the Central Economics-Mathematics Institute have calculated that, of 5,884 product lines, 77 percent were supplied by just one producer. One-third of the value of Soviet goods in 1990 was produced on single sites,[3] resulting in strong dependence of the economy on these monopolist enterprises.

Product specialization was carried to absurd proportions in agriculture as well. The monoculture of cotton in the Central Asian republics, which produced 92% of Soviet cotton fibre in 1990 (62% in in Uzbekistan alone), became a symbol of this policy. The advantages of economies of scale and the exploitation of comparative natural advantages (climate, soil, water, traditional skills in irrigation and agriculture) were vitiated by huge ecological and socio-economic problems caused by distortions in the structure of production. Kazakhstan's grain specialization, notably the famous "Virgin Lands" campaign in the 1950s, the ecological and social consequences of which have not yet been overcome, is another example. Product specialization in natural resources was also organized exclusively by the center and at the expense of the complex development of Central Asian republics. The government pumped raw materials out to other regions as intermediary products at cheap prices, barely above the cost of production, and had them manufactured outside of the area.

Moreover, because of the sectoral structuring of the economy supervised by

Moscow, enterprises in the same republic were subordinated to different central ministries and often had to import raw materials from outside republics which were available at home. For example, in 1990 raw materials to the value of 700 million rubles were imported to Uzbekistan, more than half of which could have been replaced by the products of mining enterprises situated within the republic. It is noteworthy that the cost of transportation alone was about 100 million rubles. The program of import substitution of raw and construction materials and fertilizers adopted in the republic since independence should produce a gain of 250 million rubles within 2 years, and 500 million rubles by 1995.[4]

Trade Balances

The problem of "net" balances of inter-republican and foreign trade emerging from discussions on the "economic accountability" of the republics and regions had by the end of the 1980s become a key issue and had prepared the ground for the concepts of economic independence and sovereignty. Soviet statistics published in 1990 have given much fuller information about the state of affairs in this field, permitting us to make a more satisfactory analysis on the basis of reassessments and adjustments. Although even now the issue of "loser-winner" republics is to a large extent disputable, one can better see the distortions caused by the center and the mechanism of administrative-command integration in the distributional sphere.

According to *Goskomstat's* (Soviet State Statistical Commission) data published in its magazine *Vestnik Statistiki* no. 3 and no. 4 (1990), almost all republics except for Belorussia and Azerbaijan had in 1988 a deficit of trade balances in terms of inter-republican and foreign trade computed together in domestic prices. The lion's share of the trade balance deficit belonged to Russia: 33.3 bln rubles out of a total sum of 50.4 bln rubles. The second largest deficit was in Kazakhstan—7.3 bln rubles. The other Central Asian republics had smaller deficits—4.5 bln rubles total, broken down as follows: Uzbekistan—1.8 bln rubles, Kirgizia—1.2, Tajikistan—1.2, Turkmenistan—0.3 bln rubles. This compares to a deficit in other republics ranging from 0.7 bln rubles in Estonia to 2.9 bln rubles in the Ukraine in absolute terms.

In inter-republican trade exchange five republics had positive balances (in bln of rubles): Russia—0.26, Ukraine—3.62, Belorussia—4.05, Georgia—.029, Azerbaijan—2.10. Ten other republics, such as the Baltics, Moldavia and Armenia, and all of Central Asia, had a deficit, for example (in bln rubles): Kazakhstan—5.4, Uzbekistan—1.7, Kirgizia—0.5, Tajikistan—1.0, Turkmenistan—0.1. These data suggest that the prices in inter-republican trade were least favorable to Central Asians, and largely contributed to the total trade deficit in Uzbekistan and Tajikistan in relative terms and Kazakhstan in absolute figures. Azerbaijan and Belorussia were gainers—getting 19 and 15 percent of their net material product (NMP) respectively from intra-union trade. The Ukraine ran in absolute terms the second largest surplus; the RSFSR was approximately in balance.

Foreign trade in domestic prices caused more distortions, contributing to the deficit of all republics, with the largest one for Russia—33.6 bln rubles, then Ukraine—6.6, and Belorussia and Kazakhstan, with approximately 2.0 bln rubles each. Those four republics accounted for about 82% of the total Soviet trade deficit. Uzbekistan (−0.17 bln rubles), Tajikistan (−0.13), Turkmenistan (−0.18) had the smallest trade deficit with foreign countries both in absolute and relative terms (1 to 4 percent NMP respectively). After Russia—32.5% and Ukraine—14.7%, they had the largest ratio of foreign exports to total external (foreign plus inter-republican) sales: Uzbekistan—14.6%, Tajikistan—14.1, Turkmenistan—9.3%. It is noteworthy that Uzbekistan and Tajikistan were the only republics in the Soviet Union which had a higher ratio of foreign export to total external sales than of foreign imports to total external purchases (13.8 and 13.5% respectively). In all other Central Asian republics the share of foreign import within total import exceeded the ratio of foreign export relative to the whole export; for example in Kazakhstan (16.7 and 9.0%), Turkmenistan (14.8 and 9.3%), with the largest disproportion in Kirgizia (20.6 and 2.3%). The reason for these figures is that imported goods were artificially expensive in domestic prices. If one recalculates Soviet foreign trade in world prices one finds a deficit of only 2 bln so-called *invaluta* rubles, instead of the 50 bln rubles in calculated domestic prices.[5]

In an effort to correct for distortions arising from set domestic prices *Goskomstat* recalculated the export-import balances of the republics. When trade was reassessed at world market prices, both the inter-republican and foreign trade balances of the Russian Republic improved sharply, moving from a deficit of −28.8 billion rubles to a surplus of 41.3 bln rubles in 1987. This is explained by artificially low domestic prices for fuels, of which Russia is the biggest exporter internally and internationally, relative to the high domestic prices of food and consumer goods, which are Russia's principle imports. According to the 1987 data, Uzbekistan and Tajikistan achieved a surplus of 0.1 billion rubles each in foreign trade at world prices. However, at the same time in inter-republican trade their balances deteriorated, as did those of the majority of republics. Aside from the RSFSR, only Azerbaijan had a positive balance in inter-republican trade at world prices, while Turkmenistan showed a zero balance. In Kazakhstan and Kirgizia world prices slightly improved the foreign trade balance, while they worsened the balance on inter-republican trade and affected the total balance (see Table A.2).

The *Goskomstat* 1988 data gave almost the same picture: the results were better only for the RSFSR, which moved from a deficit of −33.32 rubles at domestic prices to a surplus of 30.8 bln rubles at world prices; all other republics (excluding Turkmenistan's zero balance), somewhat improving or worsening their balances, had a negative total balance.

Does this mean, as the *Economist* stated in 1990, that "The net result is that the Russian republic subsidizes the rest of the country to the tune of 70 bln rubles a year?"[6] The difference in Russia's figures in 1987—between a deficit of 28.8 billion rubles at domestic prices and a surplus of 41.3 billion at world prices, and between (−33,32) and (+33.8) billion rubles in 1988, as well as between (−34.7) and (+32.1) billion rubles in 1989—covered all the export and import of the republic, including foreign exchange. This fact is very important because most gains were connected with the correction of distorted domestic prices for foreign import.[7] In this respect more realistic data was given by the Prime Minister of RSFSR, I. Silaev, in his article published by *Pravda,* in which he stated that "the equivalent of trade should give to Russia additionally 24 bln. rubles annually."[8]

Speaking about the quality of these reassessments it is necessary to emphasize that they have some limitations:

1. Technically the two balances of trade at domestic and at world prices cannot be summed up directly because they are calculated in different currencies: the real inflated ruble and an artificial *invaluta* ruble equivalent to hard currency introduced for calculations of foreign export and import;
2. Conversion coefficients (ratios of domestic to foreign prices) are used for highly aggregated commodity groups;[9]
3. Principally, in this author's opinion, recalculations concerning goods which had real buyers in the world markets should be figured in real export prices, and therefore real and not hypothetical foreign prices. Such goods in trade between independent republics could and should be bought for real money (hard currency) at world prices.

As for other goods, which were subject to inter-republican trade and have no real market of foreign buyers, the world prices cannot and should not be used. But in these cases it is necessary to use domestic prices free from the distortions created by turnover taxes and subsidies.[10]

Turnover Taxes and Subsidies

The turnover tax was introduced into the Soviet administrative-command economic mechanism at the beginning of 1930. From then on it was a cornerstone of the centrally fixed system of prices and a major source of Soviet state budget revenues. The system of turnover tax consisted of the difference between retail and wholesale prices, minus a national trade (wholesale and retail) margin. This method of calculation was applied to goods which generated more than four-fifths of the turnover tax. For goods such as petroleum derivatives, tobacco products, matches, bread and other wheat products, the turnover tax was calculated at a fixed amount per unit. For a few goods subject to local price regulations the rates were ad valorem, ranging from 5 to 50 percent of the retail price net of the trade margin. It excluded only a small share of products. The Soviet turnover tax was not comparable to any conventional turnover tax used in market-oriented economies because it lacked explicit fixed rates.

In 1989, almost two-thirds of the revenue from turnover tax came from the food and beverages industry and light industry. It consisted of 71.8 billion rubles out of a total of 11.1 billion rubles of turnover tax revenues (see Table A.4). A large share of turnover taxes were connected with the sales of alcoholic beverages, mainly vodka (27.5 percent). Estimates for 1989 also indicated that on average the turnover tax amounted to 27.5 percent of gross retail commodity sales for alcoholic beverages; the tax revenue was equivalent to 82.4 percent of recorded consumption.[11] (see Table A.4).

Let us consider why the problem of taxation, and turnover tax specifically, is so critical for understanding center-republic tensions in economic power-sharing, and what its implications are for inter-republican trade and national income balances. The turnover tax was one of the biggest sources of redistribution of value-added between the center and the republics. In 1989 it contributed almost one third of Soviet state budget revenues and republic revenues through the mechanism of retail and wholesale prices.[12]

The republics which produce more final commodities, which are subject to retail sale, accumulated more turnover tax and gained more share of value added, including value added created in previous stages of production. Conversely, the republics producing more intermediate products (raw materials, semi-finished components) which were shipped to final manufacturers at wholesale prices, lost value-added. Thus republics which have only primary manufacturing enterprises got a smaller part of the value-added created by them than did the final manufacturers who used their product for further processing.

For example, more than 90 percent of the cotton fiber produced in Uzbekistan was shipped out for manufacturing to other republics and foreign countries. The rate of turnover tax imposed on the stage of primary processing of raw cotton was 410 to 600 rubles per ton of raw cotton, whereas products from industrial manufacturing of each ton of the same raw cotton obtained 1,260 to 1,700 rubles.[13]

There are two issues important to our analysis:

1. The allocation of turnover taxes between center and republics;
2. the adjustment of trade and national income balances in consideration of the contribution of each republic in value added.

Up to now analyses of turnover taxes and redistribution of revenues between Soviet republics and the center have focused on the first issue. The conclusion drawn by Soviet and Western economists was that allocation served "as a major device for redistributing revenues and financing economic development in less advanced regions." This conclusion was supported by available statistics and stated for example in the following way: "the Central Asian republics keep almost 100 percent of the turnover tax revenues they collect, while more industrialized regions such as the RSFSR, the Ukraine, and Latvia hand over roughly half of their turnover tax receipts to the all-union budget."[14] Thus turnover tax was considered as an instrument for the advancement of the less developed republics at the expense of the more developed ones.

The above example of turnover tax for cotton fiber and cotton textile shows that in absolute measures, 50 percent of the turnover tax of manufactured cotton, namely 630–850 rubles, was a greater sum than 100 percent of turnover tax for the primary production of cotton fiber, only 410 to 600 rubles. Furthermore, the main cotton producer, Uzbekistan, retained 100 percent of the total turnover tax for only 10 percent of cotton fiber production, 90 percent of which was manufactured outside the republic. A major part of the value added originally created in Uzbekistan was thus shared between the center and other republics.

In absolute and relative terms then, the allocation of 100 percent of turnover taxes would not mean at all that Central Asians were privileged to keep 100 percent of value added on products produced in their republics. On the contrary, the example given shows that a major part of value added created in Central Asia was shared among other republics and the center. Just before the fall of the Union, when some of the most developed Union republics objected to sharing turnover tax revenues, the center had to reveal the second hidden part of this important source of USSR state revenues. In 1990 *Goscomstat* published data which gave the specific size of the distortions which turnover taxes introduced into the inter-republican trade balance and the national income balance of the USSR. Column 2 of Table A.3 (see appendix) shows these adjustments (positive or negative) and how much in quantitative terms is needed for each republic to restore their real contribution in value added.

The analysis of these important data shows:

1. The sum of distortions created by turnover taxes alone in 1988 was 6.4 bln. rubles. This means that value added created by raw-material producing republics was owned by enterprises using them in the production of manufactured consumer goods.

   Uzbekistan was a major loser through the turnover tax mechanism. In 1988 the nine republics lost 1.5 bln rubles, Turkmenistan—0.5, Tajikistan—0.4, Kirgizia—0.3, Kazakhstan—0.2 bln rubles. All in all, Central Asia lost in a single year about 3.0 bln rubles, more than any other region of the Soviet Union. At the same time almost 90 percent of turnover tax gains were accumulated in Russia (3.4 bln), Ukraine (1.2 bln) and Belorussia (1.1 bln) rubles. The remaining 10 percent benefitted the Baltics: Lithuania (0.4 bln), Latvia (0.2 bln) and Estonia (0.1 bln) rubles. Thus, for many years the mechanism of turnover taxes provided a hidden instrument for pumping out big sums of value added from the less developed to the more developed republics and increased the gap between them, creating huge economic, social and ecological problems in Central Asia because of the monoculture of cotton and forced specialization in raw-material production.

2. According to *Goskomstat* data for 1988, state subsidies were the second largest factor in creating distortions in trade and national income balances. Moreover in 1990, for the first time, domestic budgetary subsidies were greater than turnover tax revenues.[15]

What is the essence of subsidies? These were money transfers from the government to enterprises or consumers. Over four-fifths of budgetary subsidies went to agriculture. Nearly two thirds of agricultural subsidies were used to support basic food prices, with most of the remainder provided directly to farmers. Subsidies for milk and meat products alone accounted for almost two fifths of budgetary subsidies (see Table 10.1). The average subsidy rate (with respect to retail price) was estimated at around 65 percent, but, as of 1988, meat was subsidized at 233 percent, butter at 247 percent, and milk at 171 percent.[16]

Only 7 percent of budgetary subsidies were given to heavy industry, four fifths of which went to the coal industry (the share of the latter rose markedly under the pressure of miners' strikes). Other domestic subsidies for services, mainly housing, culture and foreign tourism, remained relatively small and began to fall.

With this outline of Soviet state subsidies, more fully described in the IMF report, let us clarify some of the less examined issues connected with their role in inter-republican trade and the redistribution of national income. In 1988 state subsidies alone created distortions in intra-Union trade of up to 6.2 bln rubles (see Table A.3, column 3). Almost 85 percent of these sums benefitted Russia, which gained 5.1 bln rubles from the production and consumption of state subsidized goods (meat, milk, butter, etc.).

Central Asia was in an unfavorable position in respect to the distribution of subsidies among the republics. Kazakhstan lost 1 bln rubles, Turkmenistan and Kirgizia 0.1; Uzbekistan neither gained nor lost; only Tajikistan slightly benefitted—0.1 bln rubles. All in all the Central Asian republics, including Kazakhstan, lost in 1988 about 4.0 bln rubles through the system of turnover taxes and subsidies, which comprised a significant share of their value added, ranging from 12.7 percent NMP in Turkmenia, 7.2—Uzbekistan, 8.0—Kirgizia, 6.3—Tajikistan, to 4.4 percent in Kazakhstan (see Table A.3).

Table 10.1 State Subsidies on Meat, Butter, and Milk in 1988 (in rubles)

	Producer Price	*Retail Price*	*Subsidy*
Meat (kg)	6.0	1.8	4.2
Butter (kg)	11.8	3.4	8.4
Milk (liter)	0.65	0.24	0.41

Source: Structural fiscal Issues (December 1990), *World Bank Report on USSR,* Vol. 1, p. 78.

The trade balance of these republics, especially Turkmenistan and Uzbekistan, looks much better after adjustments for subsidies and taxes—changing from a deficit to a surplus in the first case and diminishing the passive balance from 8.9 percent to 1.7 percent of NMP in the second one, improving the situation in three other Central Asian republics, though they still have the largest deficit in relative terms, 15.1–22.6 percent of NMP. After Russia's the second biggest deficit in absolute terms is Kazakhstan's.

Thus, these newly available statistics give us evidence that economic relations were shaped by direct interference from the center through commodity-financial instruments of redistribution. This mechanism was based on turnover taxes and subsidies, and as we see from our statistical analysis, this worked not in favor of, as was up to now presupposed, but against the less developed republics.

National Income Balances and the Grants System

There were some more hidden, but no less important mechanisms which provided distribution and redistribution of national income (NMP) among republics. Almost all republics considered themselves losers in economic transfers because of the absence of a transparent picture of the multiple cross-budgetary transfers and price distortions. This process had two sides; the first can be estimated on statistics measured; the second is hidden and very resistant to quantitative evaluation. To understand this we should look first at national income balances, known in the West as net material product (NMP), which is the main macroeconomic indicator at the republic level and is a key category for understanding the Soviet redistributional mechanism.

According to methodology used in the USSR, two separate forms of net material product were identified.

1. National income produced, which was the sum of value added minus depreciation in the productive sphere (industry, agriculture, construction, trade and some related transport services);
2. National income used, which was the sum of the consumption and accumulation funds and the increase in reserves.

Respectively each year, Soviet statistics gave two figures: national income produced and national income used, which characterized respectively the production and distribution of net material product within a certain republic. The difference between national income produced and national income used constituted the final results of the all-Union and republican intergovernmental budgetary transfers through different channels (taxation, subsidies, grants, profit transfers).

National income balances were a broader indicator than the trade balances among the republics and reflected inter-republican value-added transfers through a centrally administered budgetary system. In conformity with "deficit or surplus," the national income balances of all republics were divided into two groups:

1. donors (NMP produced > NMP used)
2. recipients (NMP produced < NMP used)

According to Soviet statistics and available Western assessments,[17] all Central Asian republics were in the group of long-term recipients.

From 1970 to 1989 Kazakhstan was in absolute and relative terms the largest recipient in the USSR with a sum of national income balance of more than 73.2 bln rubles (having 13–18 percent negative balance as a share of national income). Uzbekistan for almost all of these 20 years was the second largest republic in the recipient group with a total deficit in its balances of 20.1 bln rubles. However, in relative terms the second place was contested by another Central Asian republic, Tajikistan, with these indices varying from 6 to 10 percent, while in Uzbekistan they were 1–7 percent. In absolute terms Tajikistan, with a total sum of 7 bln rubles for the whole period, had a smaller deficit than Kirgizia whose balances for that period accumulated a 8.5 bln negative sum. In Central Asia only Turkmenistan achieved a positive sum of about 0.8 bln rubles for 20 years, although for 1984–1988 it also was a net recipient and held a 0.6 bln ruble negative balance.

Judging from these data, Soviet and Western economists concluded that, "geographically, donor republics are mainly the more developed northern Slavic republics and the recipients are mainly the less developed republics in Central Asia."[18]

We must then ask why, despite the increasing redistribution of national income through state budget mechanisms, especially in the last five-year period (see Table A.7), the gap in all principal economic measurements between the two groups worsened not only in relative but also in absolute terms.

The per capita aspect of socio-economic underdevelopment could be explained by the much more rapid growth of the Central Asian population, and the less favorable age structure of labor in this area than in western and northern republics. However, the demographic situation does not fully explain our data. For example, we must consider Azerbaijan, another Turkish speaking and Muslim republic of the USSR, situated in Transcaucasia, and the least developed in the area. Its socio-economic parameters are very close to those of Central Asia and are characterized by almost the same demographic profile: high fertility rates, a low level of urbanization and little involvement of women in production. However, according to the estimates of M. Belkinda and M. Sagers, for the years 1978–1987 this was the third largest donor after Russia and the Ukraine, and the largest one in relative terms, yielding as much as one fourth of national income produced.[19] This example shows that the division between net donors and net recipients in the USSR cannot be correlated with the level of development in the republics, or their real production and consumption.

Thus we cannot draw satisfactory conclusions using only statistics on national income produced by each republic and national income used by its population. A somewhat clearer picture can be drawn from Table A.3, column 7, which gives national income balances for 1988. The adjustments made by considering turnover taxes and subsidies improved the balances of Central Asian republics by 4 bln rubles, reducing deficits by almost 20 percent in Kazakhstan, 40–45 percent in Uzbekistan, Tajikistan, and Kirgizia, and changing the status of Turkmenistan from recipient to donor, while the surplus in Russia was reduced by 8.5 bln rubles, decreasing from 9.5 to 1 bln rubles. However, the example of Azerbaijan, one of the biggest "donors," which in 1988 lost 1.4 bln rubles in the form of turnover taxes and subsidies, suggests that adjustments considering only these two factors are not sufficient to correct distortions.

For Central Asian republics there were direct correlations between the trade deficit and the size of adjustment required because of losses created by turnover taxes and subsidies. To a certain extent these distortions could explain the origin of the deficits in national income balances. But to know the real situation it is necessary to consider the system of grants and profit transfers. In December 1990, the latest data on grants appeared in two tables presented in the *Commission of the European Communities' Report.* In 1989 all Central Asian republics received from the Union about 5.9 bln rubles in grants. Kazakhstan received 2.7 bln, (18.9 percent of its budget), Uzbekistan—1.9 (19.6 percent), Kirgizia 0.5 (19 percent), Turkmenistan 0.4 (20.8 percent) and Tajikistan 0.3 (13.6 percent). This represents a 2–4 fold increase depending on the republic and about 3–5 fold for the whole of Central Asia since 1985. Table A.8 on Union grants to Central Asian republics in the 1990 state budget gives a detailed breakdown. The major grants were as follows: income compensation for regional differences, 2.6 bln rubles, development of social infrastructure about 3.0 bln rubles, and subsidies to Kazakhstan on agricultural prices 2.2 bln rubles. Data on the breakdown of the state budget's plan for 1990, given in the IMF Report, indicates the increased role of regional grants in the revenues of Central Asian republics, totalling up to 26.7 percent in Uzbekistan, 25.0 percent in Kazakhstan, 18.3 percent in Kirgizia, and 30.9 percent in Turkmenistan.

In Soviet and Western literature, the system of grants was usually understood as a help to the Central Asian republics, which had the lowest income per capita and needed aid from the Union at the expense of the other more developed republics. However, newly published statistics and officially recognized data on which republics were gaining and which republics were losing in the distributional process are helpful in this case also. Having these data which partially reveal the second hidden part of budgetary transfers we can compare the losses of Central Asian republics though turnover taxes and subsides with the sizes of the grants they received from the center (see Table 10.2).

In 1989 the sizes of grants to the Central Asian republics more or less correlate with the size of their losses in 1988 though the turnover tax and subsidy mechanism alone. Grants balanced the subsidy on agricultural prices (which in

Table 10.2 Regional Grants Compared with Losses of Central Asian Republics on Turnover Taxes and Subsidies (in bln rubles)

Republics	*Losses in 1988 Because of Turnover Taxes*	*Grants in 1989*
Uzbekistan	1.5	1.9
Kazakhstan	1.2	2.7
Kirghizistan	0.4	0.5
Tajikistan	0.3	0.3
Turkmenistan	0.6	0.4
TOTAL	4.0	5.8

Source: Tables A.3 and A.8.

1990 was more than 2 bln rubles), and were smaller than figures suggested by *Goskomstat* for adjustments in the 1988 national income balances. Thus in essence they were a sort of income compensation to the Central Asian republics for their previous year's losses on turnover tax and subsidies.

The other big source of distortions in prices and a channel of value added redistribution is profits, which accounted for almost one third of the Union State budget revenues. We don't have sufficient statistics on these but even isolated indices give same impression of the significance of this factor. For example, according to the data assessed by the Vice-President of the Uzbek Academy of Sciences, I. Iskandarov, since the republic suffered from a "colonial relationship with the Soviet Union," "cotton is sold for a mere fifth of its real worth, 90 percent is exported to the center and the profit stays in the center."[20] This simple example indicates the size of price distortions and the large resultant profit transfer, which has a negative influence on all parameters of economic and social life in the area. Despite all of these distortions in distribution and the lack of reliable statistics one thing is obvious: there is a strong division of labor among republics accompanied by overspecialization and monopoly.

The Role of Integration

The Soviet administrative-command mechanism created a more internally integrated economy than the European Economic Community and to a certain extent even than the U.S. economy if one is to compare it with inter-state economic relations. In domestic prices, inter-republican trade (excluding "non-productive") services in the USSR reached 21 percent of GDP in 1988; that was 1.5 times more than EEC trade in goods and services among its members, which was only 14 percent of GDP.[21] However while the trade of member countries in the European Community with the rest of the world was almost the same as internal trade, the Soviet republics' exports abroad amounted to barely one fourth of the value of the trade among them.[22] In 1988 the ratio of inter-republican trade to net material product (value added) in all republics, except for Russia, was higher than the all-Union index (29.3 percent) (see Table A.1).

Central Asians, characterized by a high degree of product specialization and dependence on trade with other republics, had the following percentage: Turkmenistan—50.7 percent, Kirgizia—50.2 percent, Uzbekistan—43.2 percent, Tajikistan—41.8 percent. Kazakhstan with more balanced production was somewhat less dependent on other neighboring republics and close to the All-Union ratio—31 percent, and to a certain extent in this respect could be compared with Russia (18 percent) and the Ukraine (39 percent). Belorussia coupled with smaller republics in the Baltic, Transcaucasus and Moldavia had the highest ratio. In this respect we may note that while a few EEC countries, such as the Netherlands, reach similarly high ratios, intra-EEC trade indices of the larger members were 25–50 percent less.[23]

Looking at foreign exports relative to value added we see a reverse picture. Russia had the highest share—8.6 percent. Among the Central Asian republics only Uzbekistan, with 7.4 percent, was close to the all-Union index of 7.5 percent, sharing the second place with Estonia. As for other republics, Tajikistan had 6.9 percent, Turkmenistan—4.2 percent, Kazakhstan—3.0 percent and Kirgizia—1.2 percent. On the all-Union scale, Central Asia's involvement in export abroad was somewhat higher than that of Transcaucasia and less than the western republics (the exception is Uzbekistan). The statistics show that the Soviet republics participated much more in intra-Union trade and much less with the rest of the world than do members of EEC. The same is true of Central Asians, with the provision that Uzbekistan was more fully involved in export abroad than other republics, while Kazakhstan was less dependent on intra-Union trade.

The role of inter-republican trade under the existing mechanism of commodity and finance transfers in the economic development of the republics can be assessed also by an analysis of the share of exports in the value of production and of imports in consumption. The 1988 data, published by *Goskomstat* (see Table A.9, columns 5 and 6), show the following:

1. Inter-republican trade played a substantial role both in production (11 percent—28 percent) and in consumption (14 percent—29 percent).
2. The economies of small republics were much more vulnerable to shocks in mutual trade than were those of the larger republics. The share of exports in production and imports in consumption, for example, varies from 24–28 percent and 27–29 percent in the Baltics, 26–28 percent in Transcaucasus, and 27–28 percent in Moldavia, to 11 and 14 percent in Russia, and 16 and 18 percent in the Ukraine. The same is true within regions. In the case of Central Asia Kazakhstan had respective indices (12 and 20 percent), Uzbekistan (18 and 24 percent), Kirgizia (21 and 28 percent), Tajikistan (21 and 29 percent), Turkmenistan (22 and 25 percent).

3. The role of domestic intra-union trade in the economy of each republic was much higher than the influence of foreign trade in the Soviet republics' production and consumption: in 1988, exports in the gross value of total output for the USSR were 30 percent, and imports 64 percent.
4. The Economic Background of Interdependence. The calculations of Soviet economists (Table A.9, columns 1 and 2) revealed that in integration and trade in general, in the USSR the share of trade among republics between 1966 and 1988 was almost the same as that of market economies. It showed that bureaucratic integration failed to provide progressive types of specialization and cooperation based on new technologies and that the rapid increase in the exchange of unfinished goods in comparison to the general growth of trade was a direct function of the growth of production commodity and specialized enterprises, with old-fashioned equipment and technology.
5. Slight changes in the shares of export and import in the economies of different republics are best explained through changes in price structures. In this respect the terms of intra-Union trade became more unfavorable for almost all Central Asian republics. For example, the share of exports in the total value of production decreased between 1966 and 1988: in Uzbekistan from 23.5 down to 18 percent, Kazakhstan 14.6 to 12 percent, Kirgizia 23.6 to 21 percent, Tajikistan 26.8 to 21 percent (for Turkmenistan the 1966 data are not available). The trend of prices was inversely proportional to the size of export shipments which grew for some goods like cotton even faster than production. As for the slight decline of import share in the consumption of the Central Asian republics (in Kazakhstan by 0.5, Tajikistan—0.7, Kirgizia—1.5 and Uzbekistan—3.8 percent) this was connected to government attempts to introduce import substitution production.

The inconsistent macroeconomic measures of the center along with unilateral steps by the republics—various forms of export restrictions, political frictions, "war of laws," food and consumer goods wars—caused shocks in all republics. By spring 1991 both the center and the majority of the republics had come to the conclusion that the integration and interdependence of the Soviet republics required coordinated action. Unilateralism, protectionism by any republic, as well as Union inflexibility towards the need for real decentralization of economic power created stronger shocks in the 1990s for the Soviet republics than had the 1973 OPEC oil price increase for importing countries. Philip Hanson of Birmingham University has calculated that the once-off effects of a switch to dollars would reduce the Baltic States' GNPs by 10 percent in the first year alone.[24] The president of Kazakhstan, N. Nazarbaev, when speaking in favor of closer union within CIS in the fall of 1992, argued that 85 percent of the fall in production in the country was connected to the disruption of ties with other republics and former Comecon countries.[25]

Conclusions

The Central Asian republics, richly endowed with mineral and human resources, were unable to overcome their social and economic backwardness in the course of more than 70 years of Soviet rule. Indeed the gap between them and other more developed republics grew during that time. The main reason for their backwardness was that an overcentralized administrative command system forced the Central Asians, first, to remain raw and agricultural material producers with a monoculture of cotton and minimal manufacturing production, and second, to maintain an orientation towards major industrialization, cooperation and state management in agriculture with giant plants and farms, expensive irrigation, and an non-efficient public sector, trade and services. Thirdly, of all republics, the Central Asian ones received the smallest allocations and investment, and thus had the lowest level of fixed assets and productive stock capital (excluding Kazakhstan). Finally, government policy impeded in all possible ways the naturally growing private sector and enterprise, with the strong commitment of Central Asians to private ownership. The situation was aggravated by a demographic explosion and environmental problems. The result was social backwardness with the lowest Soviet income per capita, labor earnings, and quality of life in the Soviet Union.

Distributional and redistributional mechanisms agravated the situation through non-equivalent exchange because of huge disparities in prices of raw materials and manufactured goods, distorted turnover taxes and subsidies, and transfer of profits. At the same time, administrative-command integration created undue interdependence among Soviet republics and weak ties between them and the outside world. Quantitatively, their interconnections are much higher than in any other economic community.

Under administrative-command integration all republics became losers. The Central Asian republics, though "long-term recipients" lost more through the price and finance system than they gained through state grants. The Baltics lost more through profit transfers than they gained from the import of cheap oil or the export of manufactured goods comparatively expensive in the Soviet market. Russia was also a loser, because cheap distorted domestic prices for fuels which had a good hard currency market were not compensated by gains in turnover taxes and subsidies. The only winner then was the administrative command system with its huge non-productive expenditures on defense, bureaucratic apparatus, etc. But it too eventually became unable to organize efficient production and an acceptable level of welfare for its people. The crisis of the overcentralized totalitarian system and the failure of *perestroika* reforms created the impression that a quick dissolution of the Union was the best way out for the people of the republics.

Post-Soviet developments have confirmed that it is impossible to achieve real independence overnight, and it is especially unrealistic in the economic field because of the interdependence of the republics and the lack of infrastructures to reorient them towards countries outside CIS. A transition to a market economy and integration into the world economy is inevitable for any independent country pursuing economic reforms; however it requires time. Meanwhile for Central Asians it is important to avoid civil war (especially the Afghanistan type started in Tajikistan), and not to go to extremes either through full disruption of economic ties with the former Soviet republics or through attempts to restore an all-Union type relationship. Dismantling the overcentralized system through a gradual transition to an economic community with a completely different relationship among independent states could be facilitated by active and comprehensive cooperation with highly industrialized neighboring countries and an independent political and economic strategy.

Notes

1. For a discussion of the Soviet economic system as it affected the constituent national republics see Gertrude E. Schroeder, "Nationalities and the Soviet Economy," in M. Beissinger and L. Hajda, eds., *The Nationalities Factor in Soviet Politics and Society,* Boulder, Westview, 1990, pp. 43–71.

2. Directorate-General for Economic and Financial Affairs, Commission of the European Communities, 1990, "Stabilization, liberalization and devolution: Assessment of the Economic Situation and Reform Process in the Soviet Union." *European Economy,* No. 45, December.

3. *The Economist,* July 13, 1991, p.23, August 11, 1990.

4. *Pravda vostoka,* April 6, 1991.

5. *Vestnik statistiki,* 1990, No. 3, p. 36.

6. *The Economist,* October 21, 1990, and July 13, 1991, p. 23.

7. It is a pity that this distinction is not made in the *Economist* on the issues indicated in note 5. These data are given in the table and graph entitled "Trade Balance of Republics with the Rest of the Soviet Union" and "Mother Russia." This distinction is also omitted from the capable analysis by Misha V. Belkindas and Matthew J. Sagers in *Soviet Geography,* volume XXXI, November 1990, p. 650, table 12, entitled "USSR: Interrepublican Trade, 1988," even though its source, *Vestnik statistiki,* no. 3, 1990, p. 49, deals with all export and import of the Soviet republics, including their foreign exchange. This is an important fact, because the better part of the above-mentioned gain is connected with distorted foreign import prices. As was stressed in *Vestnik statistiki* no. 3, p. 37, in 1988 Soviet foreign import was higher than foreign export in world prices by 2 bln rubles, and in domestic prices by 50 bln rubles, in which the contribution of Russia was 33.59 bln rubles (page 36). So at least half of the losses of Russian republics were due to foreign import prices.

8. *Pravda,* December 5, 1990.

9. As mentioned in the article by Belkindas and Sagers, for some republics, which produce only a few products in the aggregated group, these coefficients can lead to major distortions. "For example, Lithuanian exports of calculators would be converted to world market prices at the coefficient for machine-building as a whole or perhaps for all electronic equipment" (p. 650–651).

10. *Vestnik statistiki,* 1990, No. 3, p. 38 (new data which permit adjustments in turnover tax subsidy). There were some data on purchases by migrants, which are difficult to figure out, because of the absence of an exact source of information and the possible increase of wholesale prices in Soviet industry.

11. "Standard Fiscal Issues" (draft paper), December 1990, *World Bank Report on USSR,* Vol. 1, p. 45.

12. Ibid., p. 34.

13. Z. Salokhitdinov, "Otsenka effektivnosti kapital'nykh ulozheniĭ v usloviakh otkrytoĭ ekonomiki" *Ekonomika i zhizn',* 1985, No. 10, p. 17.

14. Donna Bahry, *Outside Moscow,* Columbia University Press, New York, 1987, p. 55.

15. "Structural Fiscal Policy," p. 77.

16. Ibid., p. 77.

17. For data on 1989, including only grants to the Central Asian republics from the Union budget see *European Economy,* No. 45, December 1990, Table A.11. Statistics for 1970–1988 from M. Belkindas and M. Sagers, 1990.

18. See James W. Gillula, *The Economic Interdependence of Soviet Republics,* Joint Economic Committee, U.S. Congress, *Soviet Economy in a Time of Change,* Vol. 1, Washington, DC: U.S. Government Printing Office, 1979, pp. 618–655.

19. M. Belkindas and M. Sagers, 1990, p. 641.

20. *The Christian Sciences Monitor,* March 29, 1991.

21. *IMF World Bank Report,* 1991, Vol. 1, p. 193.

22. Ibid.

23. *European Economy,* December, No. 45, p. 75.

24. *The Economist,* July 13–19, 1991, p. 23.

25. RL/RFE Report No. 42, October 1992.

Appendix to Chapter 10

TABLE A.1 USSR: Republican Trade[1] in Relation to Value added, 1988

	Exports			Trade Balance		
	Inter-republican	Abroad	Total	Inter-republican	Abroad	Total
			(As percent of GDP)[2]			
USSR	21.1	5.4	26.5	—	-5.8	-5.8
			(As percent of NMP)			
USSR	29.3	7.5	36.8	—	-8.0	-8.0
RSFSR	18.0	8.6	26.6	0.1	-8.7	-8.6
Ukraine	39.1	6.7	45.8	3.5	-6.4	-2.9
Belorussia	69.6	6.5	76.1	15.5	-7.5	7.9
Estonia	66.5	7.4	73.9	-8.2	-10.2	-18.4
Latvia	64.1	5.7	69.8	-1.7	-8.2	-9.9
Lithuania	60.9	5.9	66.9	-9.1	-8.1	-17.2
Moldavia	62.1	3.4	65.5	-2.4	-10.8	-13.2
Georgia	53.7	3.9	57.6	2.8	-8.6	-5.8
Armenia	63.7	1.4	65.1	-5.8	-13.4	-19.2
Azerbaidzhan	58.7	3.7	62.3	19.2	-9.1	10.2
Kazakhstan	30.9	3.0	33.8	-19.9	-7.1	-27.0
Turkmenistan	50.7	4.2	54.9	-2.0	-3.9	-6.0
Uzbekistan	43.2	7.4	50.5	-8.0	-0.8	-8.9
Tadzhikistan	50.7	6.9	48.7	-20.8	-2.8	-23.7
Kirgizia	50.2	1.2	51.4	-8.7	-14.3	-23.1

Source: *Osnovnye pokazateli* (1990), pp. 4, 34-39, 43, 44; *Narkhoz 1989* (1990), p. 634. IMF...Report, 1991, Volume I, p. 225.

1. Trade figures exclude "non-productive" services.
2. GDP figures are not available on a republican basis.

TABLE A.2 USSR: Interrepublican and Foreign Trade Balances by Republic, 1987 (in billions of rubles)

	At Domestic Prices[1]			At World Market Prices[2]		
	Inter-republican	Abroad	Total	Inter-republican	Abroad	Total
USSR	—	-50.4	-50.4	—	7.7	7.7
RSFSR	3.6	-32.4	-28.8	28.5	12.8	41.3
Ukraine	1.6	-7.7	-6.2	-3.9	-1.5	-5.4
Belorussia	3.1	-2.0	1.2	-2.2	-0.2	-2.5
Estonia	-0.2	-0.4	-0.7	-1.1	-0.2	-1.4
Latvia	-0.3	-0.6	-0.9	-1.4	-0.3	-1.7
Lithuania	-0.4	-0.7	-1.1	-3.3	-0.2	-3.5
Moldavia	0.6	-0.9	-0.3	-1.5	-0.4	-1.9
Georgia	0.6	-0.9	-0.3	-1.5	-0.2	-1.8
Armenia	0.6	-0.7	-0.1	-0.3	-0.3	-0.5
Azerbaidzhan	2.0	-0.8	1.2	0.2	-0.3	—
Kazakhstan	-5.4	-2.1	-7.5	-6.6	-1.1	-7.7
Turkmenistan	-0.3	-0.2	-0.5	—	-0.1	-0.1
Uzbekistan	-3.9	-0.1	-4.0	-4.5	0.1	-4.4
Tadzhikistan	-1.1	-0.1	-1.2	-1.4	0.1	-1.3
Kirgizia	-0.5	-0.7	-1.2	-1.0	-0.4	-1.4

1. *Osnovnye pokazateli* (1990), p. 41.
2. *Ekonomika i zhizn'*, No. 10, 1990.

TABLE A.3 USSR: Adjustments in Trade and National Income Balances of the Republics, 1988[1]

		Adjustments					
	Unadjusted Balance (1)	Turnover Tax (2)	Consumer Subsidies (3)	Total (4) (2)+(3)	Adjusted Balance (5)=[(1)+(2)+(3)]	NMP_{pr}-NMP_{used} Unadjusted National Income Balance (6)	Adjusted National Income Balance (7) (4)+(6)
		(*In billions of rubles*)					
USSR	-50.4	—	—	—	-50.4	8.565	8.565
RSFSR	-33.3	-3.4	-5.1	-8.5	-41.8	9.505	1.005
Ukraine	-2.9	-1.2	1.6	0.4	-2.5	5.170	5.170
Belorussia	2.1	-1.1	1.7	-0.6	2.7	4.142	3.542
Lithuania	-1.5	-0.4	0.8	0.4	-1.1	-0.912	-0.512
Latvia	-0.7	-0.2	0.4	0.2	-0.5	-0.478	-0.278
Estonia	-0.7	-0.1	0.2	0.1	-0.6	-0.528	-0.428
Moldavia	-1.0	0.9	0.3	1.2	0.2	-0.418	-0.218
Georgia	-0.6	0.6	-0.3	0.3	-0.3	0.238	0.568

Azerbaidzhan	1.1	1.8	-0.4	1.4	2.5	1.672	3.072
Armenia	-1.1	0.2	-0.3	-0.1	-1.2	0.695	0.525
Kazakhstan	-7.3	0.2	1.0	1.2	-6.1	-5.597	-4.397
Uzbekistan	-1.8	1.5	—	1.5	-0.3	-3.100	-1.600
Kirgizia	-1.1	0.3	0.1	0.4	-0.7	-0.998	-0.598
Tadzhikistan	-1.1	0.4	-0.1	0.3	-0.8	-0.680	-0.380
Turkmenistan	-0.3	0.5	0.1	0.6	0.3	-0.146	0.454
			(*As percent of NMP*)				
USSR	-8.0	—	—	—	-8.0	—	—
RSFSR	-8.6	-0.9	-1.3	-2.2	-10.8	2.5	0.3
Ukraine	-2.9	-1.2	1.6	0.4	-2.5	5.0	5.4
Belorussia	7.9	-4.2	6.5	2.3	10.2	15.8	18.1
Lithuania	-17.2	-4.5	9.0	4.5	-12.5	-9.3	-4.8
Latvia	-9.9	-2.8	5.7	2.9	-7.0	-6.4	-3.5
Estonia	-18.4	-2.5	4.9	2.4	1.60	-11.4	-9.0
Moldavia	-13.2	11.7	3.9	15.6	5.4	5.1	10.5
Georgia	-5.8	5.9	-2.9	3.0	-2.8	12.3	5.3
Azerbaidzhan	10.2	16.5	-3.7	12.8	24.0	15.3	28.1

TABLE A.3 (continued)

		Adjustments					
	Unadjusted Balance (1)	Turnover Tax (2)	Consumer Subsidies (3)	Total (4) (2)+(3)	Adjusted Balance (5)=[(1)+(2)+(3)]	NMP_{pr}-NMP_{used} Unadjusted National Income Balance (6)	Adjusted National Income Balance (7) (4)+(6)
Armenia	-19.2	3.5	-5.2	-1.7	-20.9	12.0	-10.3
Kazakhstan	-27.0	0.7	3.7	4.4	-22.6	-17.2	-12.8
Uzbekistan	-8.9	7.2	0.0	7.2	-1.7	-13.0	-5.8
Kirgizia	-23.1	6.0	2.0	8.0	-15.1	-16.6	-8.6
Tadzhikistan	-23.7	8.4	-2.1	6.3	-17.4	-12.0	-5.7
Turkmenistan	-6.0	10.6	2.1	12.7	6.7	-3.0	9.7

Source: *Vestnik statistiki*, Nos. 3 and 4, 1990; columns 4,5,7 calculated by B. Islamov.

Explanation of columns:

(1) Net trade balance in existing domestic prices.

(2) Change in trade balance if turnover tax were reallocated in proportion to labor expenditures incurred in production.

(3) Change in trade balance if consumer subsidies were charged in consuming republic.

(4) Change in trade balance adjusted (turnover tax + subsidies).

(6) Balance of national income produced and used.

(7) + as a share NMP produced; - as a share of NMP used.

1. Combined trade balance with other republics and in foreign trade.

TABLE A.4 USSR: Turnover Tax Revenue, 1989

	In Billions of Rubles	As Percent of Total	As Percent of Net Output[1]
Total	111.1	100.0	-
Heavy industry	36.5	32.9	-
Metallurgy	0.6	0.5	2.5
Petroleum products	12.0	10.8	60.9
Chemical and petrochemical	4.3	3.8	24.6
Chemical industry	2.0	1.8	-
Petrochemicals	2.3	2.1	-
Electric power	2.4	2.1	25.9
Machine building	6.6	6.0	7.0
Forestry industry	0.4	0.3	2.4
Building materials	1.3	1.2	11.3
Other[2]	9.0	8.1	-
Light industry	19.8	17.9	68.4
Textiles	9.3	8.4	-
Footwear	1.9	1.7	-
Knitwear	5.4	4.9	-
Other	3.2	2.9	-
Food and beverages industry	52.0	46.8	227.9
Fats and oils	1.6	1.4	-
Confectionary	1.7	1.6	-
Alcoholic beverages	41.9	37.7	-
Beer	1.8	1.6	-
Spirits	31.0	27.9	-
Wine	9.1	8.2	-
Tobacco products	1.8	1.6	-
Grain products	1.9	1.7	-
Other	3.1	2.8	-
Other industry	3.4	3.0	-
Refunds	(0.6)	(0.5)	-

Source: U.S.S.R. Ministry of Finance, Goskomstat, and IMF staff estimates, as it is given in "Structural Fiscal Issues," December 20, 1990, Table 6.

1. In wholesale prices of enterprises, excluding turnover tax.
2. Includes Main Directorate for Diamonds and Gold.

TABLE A.5 USSR: Interrepublican Trade Balances by Sector by Republic, 1988

	Res.	RSFSR	Ukrain.	Belor.	Eston.	Latv.	Lith.
Total	—	260	3,624	4,050	-332	-118	-808
Industry	-882	3,833	1,966	4,079	-299	-274	-837
Electric power	-104	-36	2	-110	101	-59	73
Oil & gas	-1,347	5,868	-3,574	-644	-256	-483	-741
Coal & other fuel	81	255	-41	-60	11	-3	-23
Ferrous metals	-1,087	-996	3,757	-1,131	-133	-297	-340
Non-ferrous metals	12	1,459	-983	-337	-80	-123	-172
Chemicals	-748	2,064	-895	275	-139	4	-408
Machine-building	1,842	6,266	2,632	2,958	-462	-300	-404
Wood & Paper	304	3,381	-1,167	72	47	-6	26
Building materials	161	401	385	-8	-10	-15	-18
Light industry	1,335	-5,168	-2,299	2,351	292	296	615
Food-processing	-1,494	-10,537	4,318	658	343	677	620
Other industry	163	877	-171	55	-14	34	-66
Agriculture	181	-3,617	1,432	52	-28	-14	29
Other material sphere	702	45	226	-81	-6	170	—

Source: Vestnik Statistiki, No. 3, 1990, IMF...Report, 1991, Volume I, p. 228

1. Residual calculated as sum of republican balances.

Mold.	Geor.	Armen.	Azerb.	Kazakh.	Turk.	Uzbek.	Tadzh.	Kirg.
-186	290	-335	2,099	-5,349	-97	-1,667	-997	-435
-388	246	-243	1,912	-6,691	-211	-2,517	-983	-476
-2	-51	22	7	-145	50	-11	7	48
-514	-375	-437	544	-455	650	-349	-279	-303
-136	-12	-17	-7	159	-7	-23	-7	-10
-259	-148	-252	-192	-148	-104	-541	-124	-179
-157	-60	-29	2	241	-4	104	110	41
-392	-194	53	133	-496	-50	-163	-226	-314
-679	-623	-106	-153	-3,870	-881	-1,949	-576	-10
-118	-164	-98	-134	-747	-103	-483	-100	-103
-37	-99	-26	-58	-142	-33	-105	-24	-52
347	381	621	871	-138	721	1,786	479	180
1,557	1,621	-10	912	-745	-339	-649	-178	258
3	-29	36	-15	-205	-113	-133	-65	-33
219	63	-95	182	1,356	109	469	-22	43
-18	-20	3	5	-14	5	381	7	-2

TABLE A.6 Foreign Trade Balances by Sector by Republic, 1988 (in millions of domestic rubles)

	USSR	RSFSR	Ukrain.	Belor.	Eston.	Latv.	Lith.
Total	-50,431	-33,588	-6,551	-1,977	-416	-578	-722
Industry	-41,812	-28,054	-5,549	-1,382	-281	-463	-520
Electric power	742	101	525	21	-10	—	—
Oil & gas	9,746	8,664	357	338	2	—	178
Coal & other fuel	925	424	573	-12	-7	-24	-35
Ferrous metals	308	-1,005	1,407	-49	-13	2	-22
Non-ferrous metals	552	344	-120	-50	—	—	-5
Chemicals	-3,787	-2,649	-538	-79	-61	-53	-59
Machine-building	-18,724	-14,981	-1,996	-375	-114	25	-220
Wood & Paper	845	1,712	-395	-55	16	14	5
Building materials	-634	-410	-63	-19	-6	1	-2
Light industry	-19,047	-12,422	-3,417	-759	-110	-245	-247
Food-processing	-12,199	-7,418	-1,768	-402	24	-175	-108
Other industry	-539	-415	-114	59	-1	-9	-5
Agriculture	-8,382	-5,291	-1,023	-546	-124	-136	-202
Other material sphere	-236	-243	22	-48	-11	21	—

Source: *Vestnik Statisiki*, No.3, 1990; IMF...Report, 1991, Vol. I, p. 229.

Mold.	Geor.	Armen.	Azerb.	Kazakh.	Turk.	Uzbek.	Tadzh.	Kirg.
-837	-882	-775	-990	-1,906	-187	-174	-136	-714
-724	-754	-671	-800	-1,706	-177	9	-78	-663
94	11	—	—	—	—	—	—	—
—	62	—	142	13	—	-10	—	—
-1	—	—	—	6	—	—	—	—
1	34	-5	-89	99	-8	-23	-12	-8
-22	2	—	13	292	—	-10	92	16
-98	-31	-50	-72	-51	-7	4	-23	-20
-154	-62	-54	-147	-548	-21	-41	-6	-31
-38	-27	-31	-42	-166	-26	-87	-21	-15
-13	-22	-20	-14	-27	-4	-25	-7	-4
-406	-326	-237	-324	-890	11	584	-1	-258
-86	-387	-267	-260	-414	-119	-379	-97	-343
-1	-8	-7	-7	-20	-3	-5	-2	-1
-114	-132	-102	-196	-201	-20	-185	-59	-52
1	4	-2	6	1	10	2	—	—

TABLE A.7 Budgetary Grants to Selected Union Republics in the Union Budget
(million rubles)

	1975			1985			1989		
	State budget expenditure	Grants from the Union	Grants as % of budget	State budget expenditure	Grants from the Union	Grants as % of budget	State budget expenditure	Grants from the Union	Grants as % of budget
Uzbekistan			5.2	7,780	406	5.2	10,029	1,961	19.6
Kazakhstan	6,515	231		10,982	479	4.4	14,254	2,698	18.9
Kirghizia				1,944	150	7.7	2,692	511	19.0
Tadjikistan							2,375	322	13.6
Turkeminstan	773	74	9.5	1,420	169	11.9	1,934	403	20.8
Total[1]	95,971	305	0.3	172,179	1,204	0.7	229,143	5,895	2.6

Source: USSR Ministry of Finance, Commission of the European Communities, European Economy, No. 45, December 1990, p. 150.
1. Total State budgets of all Union republics.

TABLE A.8 Union Grants to Central Asian Republics in the 1990 Budget: Detailed Breakdown (million rubles)

	Uzbekistan	Kazakhstan	Kirghizia	Tadjikistan	Turkmenistan	Total
Total Grants	3,122.2	3,792.8	555.4	405.8	705.1	8,561.3
1. Income compensation for regional differences, total	1,712.2	200.0	165.4	125.8	425.1	2,628.5
2. Subsidies on sugar prices			110.0			110.0
3. Development of social infrastructure	1410.0	715.0	280.0	280.0	280.0	2,965.0
4. Compensation for work under difficult environmental conditions		670				670
5. Subsidies on agricultural prices		2,207.8				2,207.8

Source: USSR Ministry of Finance, as it is given in Directorate-General for Economic and Financial Affairs, Commission of the European Communities, European Economy, No. 45, December 1990, p. 150

TABLE A.9 Export and Import Shares of Goods Produced and Consumed, Selected Years (percent)

	1966		1987		1988	
	Share of exports in value of production	Share of imports in value	Share of exports in value of production	Share of imports in value	Share of exports in value of production	Share of imports in value
RSFSR	8.0	8.8	N/A	N/A	11.0	14.0
Ukraine	14.8	13.5	N/A	N/A	16.0	18.0
Belorussia	N/A	N/A	29.7	28.0	27.0	26.0
Uzbekistan	23.5	27.8	18.8	27.1	18.0	24.0
Kazakhstan	14.6	20.5	13.1	24.3	12.0	20.0
Georgia	23.4	26.9	25.1	26.4	26.0	27.0
Azerbaijan	25.4	25.5	26.9	22.1	26.0	22.0
Lithuania	21.5	21.0	26.3	31.3	24.0	27.0
Moldavia	24.1	21.0	30.1	31.7	28.0	27.0
Latvia	28.1	26.3	26.4	31.5	24.0	27.0
Kirghizia	23.6	29.5	19.3	29.4	21.0	28.0
Tadzhikistan	26.8	29.7	22.1	33.7	21.0	29.0
Armenia	29.3	31.4	28.4	29.1	28.0	29.0
Turkmenia	N/A	N/A	23.5	28.4	22.0	25.0
Estonia	24.1	24.4	27.1	33.6	25.0	29.0

N/A — not available.

Sources: Columns 1 and 2: Granberg, 1975, p. 227; Gillula, 1979, p. 640; Columns 3 and 4: Granberg, 1990, p. 95; Columns 5 and 6: *Vestnik Statistiki*, No. 3, 1990, p. 36. It is given in M. Belkindas and M. Sagers, 1990, p. 652.

About the Book and Editor

Since the demise of Soviet power, the newly independent republics are redefining their identities and their relations with the world at large. In Central Asia, which lies at the crossroads of several cultures, the emerging trends are complex and ambiguous.

In this volume leading experts explore factors that have driven the region's historical development and that continue to define it today: Overlapping Islamic, Russian, and steppe cultures and their impact on attempts to delimit national borders and to create independent states; the legacy of Soviet and earlier imperial rule in economic and social relations; and the competition between Uzbek, Tajik, and other group identities.

The authors make few predictions, but their original and thought-provoking analyses offer readers new insight into those aspects of Central Asia's past that may shape its future.

Beatrice F. Manz is associate professor of history at Tufts University specializing in the history of Iran and Central Asia in the medieval and modern period. She is the author of *The Rise and Rule of Tamerlane* and numerous articles in scholarly journals. Her major interests lie in the strucure of nomad society, nomad-sedentary relations, and the political dynamics of plural society.

About the Contributors

Edward Allworth (A.M. University of Chicago, Ph.D. Columbia University), emeritus professor of Turko Soviet studies and special lecturer, Columbia University. He is head of the Central Asian Circle; member, Executive Committee, Harriman Institute, Columbia University; and Editor of the Central Asia Book Series, Duke University Press. He specializes in cultural/intellectual and literary history and languages of Central Asia, and in nationality problems of the USSR and of ex-Soviet Union states. Professor Allworth's recent publications include *Tatars of the Crimea . . .* (ed.), 1988; *Central Asia, 120 Years of Russian Rule* (ed.), rev. ed. 1989; *The Modern Uzbeks . . .* (1990); "The Arguments of Abdalrauf Fitrat, The Bukharan," *Central and Inner Asian Studies* No. 5 (1991), pp. 1–21; and "Literary Tone and Ethnic Identity in Central Asian Short Prose before 1986," *Central Asian Monitor* Nos. 5 and 6 (1992), pp. 29–35, 29–36.

Reef Altoma is a Ph.D. student in political science at Harvard University, currently researching questions of national identity formation in independent Kazakhstan and other Central Asian republics. She has lived and worked in Kazakhstan for several months.

Muriel Atkin is associate professor of history at the George Washington University. She is the author of *The Subtlest Battle: Islam in Soviet Tajikistan, Russia and Iran, 1780–1828* and numerous articles on Tajikistan and on Soviet Iranian relations.

Donald S. Carlisle earned his A.B. from Brown University in 1958 and his Ph.D. from Harvard University in 1962. He is professor of political science at Boston College, where he is also associate director of its Center for Russia, East Europe, and Asia. Since 1968 Professor Carlisle has been an Associate Fellow of the Russian Research Center at Harvard University. For several years he has served as a United Nations' consultant on Central Asia. Professor Carlisle is the author of studies of Soviet and Russian domestic and foreign policy and has published many works on Central Asia. He traveled to Uzbekistan for the first time in 1963 and has made numerous visits since then, including two trips in 1993.

Bakhtior A. Islamov is a leading researcher at the Institute of Economics of Uzbek SSR Academy of Sciences. His work has focused on the problem of transition from command to market economy and the integration of Uzbekistan into the world economy. He also worked as chief of the foreign relations department for the Uzbek SSR Academy of Sciences from 1988–1990. Concurrently, from 1989–1990, he was a scientific consultant for the Industrial Association for Foreign Cooperation. From 1983–1987 he served as chief of the information department for the Ministry of Foreign Affairs in Tashkent. Dr. Islamov was awarded his Ph.D. in economics from the institute of Economics of World Socialist Systems in Moscow in 1981 and received his Certificate of

Training in International Economic Relations at the Diplomatic Academy in Moscow in 1988. He is the author of many articles in Soviet and Central Asian journals.

A. M. Khazanov, FBA, is professor of anthropology at the University of Wisconsin–Madison. Formerly a senior scholar at the Academy of Sciences of the USSR and then a professor at the Hebrew University of Jerusalem, he has published more than 150 articles and other publications, including nine books. His present research interests include historical and cultural anthropology, pastoral nomadism, ethnicity and nationalism, modernization and social/cultural change, and the former Soviet Union.

Edward J. Lazzerini is professor of Russian and Inner Asian history at the University of New Orleans, having earned his Ph.D. from the University of Washington in 1973. He specializes in the history of the Turkic peoples, particularly the Tatars of the Volga region and Crimea, and has published extensively on their cultural and intellectual evolution since the eighteenth century and their problems of adaptation to Russian/Soviet hegemony. He is presently completing a study of Ismail Bey Gasprinskii, the nineteenth-century Tatar reformer.

Morris Rossabi (Ph.D. Columbia University) is professor of history at the City University of New York and is adjunct professor at Columbia University. Born in Egypt, his books include *China and Inner Asia* (1975), *Khubilai Khan: His Life and Times* (1988), and *Voyager from Xanadu* (1992). He is currently working on the catalog for the first show of Mongol art to be exhibited in the United States.

Maria Eva Subtelny is associate professor and chair of the Department of Middle East and Islamic Studies at the University of Toronto. She received her Ph.D. in near eastern languages and civilization from Harvard University in 1979 and is the author of numerous articles on the history and culture of medieval Iran and Central Asia in *Studia Iranica, Central Asiatic Journal, Journal of Turkish Studies, Journal of the American Oriental Society, Iranian Studies, Zeitschrift der Deutschen Morgenländischen Gesellschaft,* and others. Most recently, she is co-editor (with Lisa Golombek) of *Timurid Art and Culture: Iran and Central Asia in the Fifteenth Century* (1992). Of interest to readers of this volume may be her article "The Cult of Holy Places: Religious Practices Among Soviet Muslims" in *Middle East Journal,* 43, 4 (1989), pp. 593–604.

John O. Voll is Professor of history at the University of New Hampshire. He is author of *Islam: Continuity and Change in the Modern World* (2nd ed., 1994) and a past president of the Middle East Studies Association.

Index

Printed in the United States
206514BV00002B/176/A

9 780813 336381